studies in jazz

Institute of Jazz Studies
Rutgers—The State University of New Jersey
General Editors: Dan Morgenstern and Edward Berger

1. BENNY CARTER: A Life in American Music, *by Morroe Berger, Edward Berger, and James Patrick, 1982*
2. ART TATUM: A Guide to His Recorded Music, *by Arnold Laubich and Ray Spencer, 1982*
3. ERROLL GARNER: The Most Happy Piano, *by James M. Doran, 1995*
4. JAMES P. JOHNSON: A Case of Mistaken Identity, *by Scott E. Brown;* Discography 1917–1950, *by Robert Hilbert, 1986*
5. PEE WEE ERWIN: This Horn for Hire, *as told to Warren W. Vaché, Sr., 1987*
6. BENNY GOODMAN: Listen to His Legacy, *by D. Russell Connor, 1988*
7. ELLINGTONIA: The Recorded Music of Duke Ellington and His Sidemen, *by W. E. Timner, 1988; 4th ed., 1996*
8. THE GLENN MILLER ARMY AIR FORCE BAND: Sustineo Alas / I Sustain the Wings, *by Edward F. Polic;* Foreword *by George T. Simon, 1989*
9. SWING LEGACY, *by Chip Deffaa, 1989*
10. REMINISCING IN TEMPO: The Life and Times of a Jazz Hustler, *by Teddy Reig, with Edward Berger, 1990*
11. IN THE MAINSTREAM: 18 Portraits in Jazz, *by Chip Deffaa, 1992*
12. BUDDY DeFRANCO: A Biographical Portrait and Discography, *by John Kuehn and Arne Astrup, 1993*
13. PEE WEE SPEAKS: A Discography of Pee Wee Russell, *by Robert Hilbert, with David Niven, 1992*
14. SYLVESTER AHOLA: The Gloucester Gabriel, *by Dick Hill, 1993*
15. THE POLICE CARD DISCORD, *by Maxwell T. Cohen, 1993*
16. TRADITIONALISTS AND REVIVALISTS IN JAZZ, *by Chip Deffaa, 1993*
17. BASSICALLY SPEAKING: An Oral History of George Duvivier, *by Edward Berger;* Music Analysis *by David Chevan, 1993*
18. TRAM: The Frank Trumbauer Story, *by Philip R. Evans and Larry F. Kiner, with William Trumbauer, 1994*
19. TOMMY DORSEY: On the Side, *by Robert L. Stockdale, 1995*
20. JOHN COLTRANE: A Discography and Musical Biography, *by Yasuhiro Fujioka, with Lewis Porter and Yoh-ichi Hamada, 1995*

21. RED HEAD: A Chronological Survey of "Red" Nichols and His Five Pennies, *by Stephen M. Stroff, 1996*

22. THE RED NICHOLS STORY: After Intermission 1942–1965, *by Philip R. Evans, Stanley Hester, Stephen Hester, and Linda Evans, 1997*

23. BENNY GOODMAN: Wrappin' It Up, *by D. Russell Connor, 1996*

24. CHARLIE PARKER AND THEMATIC IMPROVISATION, *by Henry Martin, 1996*

25. BACK BEATS AND RIM SHOTS: The Johnny Blowers Story, *by Warren W. Vaché, 1997*

26. DUKE ELLINGTON: A Listener's Guide, *by Eddie Lambert, 1998*

27. SERGE CHALOFF: A Musical Biography and Discography, *by Vladimir Simosko, 1998*

28. HOT JAZZ: From Harlem to Storyville, *by David Griffiths, 1998*

29. ARTIE SHAW: A Musical Biography and Discography, *by Vladimir Simosko, 1998*

30. JIMMY DORSEY: A Study in Contrasts, *by Robert L. Stockdale, 1998*

31. STRIDE!: Fats, Jimmy, Lion, Lamb and All the Other Ticklers, *by John L. Fell and Terkild Vinding, 1998*

32. GIANT STRIDES: The Legacy of Dick Wellstood, *by Edward N. Meyer, 1998*

Serge Chaloff

A Musical Biography and Discography

Vladimir Simosko

Studies in Jazz, No. 27

The Scarecrow Press, Inc.
Lanham, Maryland, & London
and
Institute of Jazz Studies
Rutgers–The State University of New Jersey
1998

SCARECROW PRESS, INC.

Published in the United States of America
by Scarecrow Press, Inc.
4720 Boston Way
Lanham, Maryland 20706

4 Pleydell Gardens, Folkestone
Kent CT20 2DN, England

British Library Cataloguing in Publication Information Available

Library of Congress Cataloging-in-Publication Data

Simosko, Vladimir.
    Serge Chaloff : a musical biography and discography / Vladimir
Simosko.
        p.   cm. — (Studies in jazz ; no. 27)
    Includes bibliographical references and index.
    ISBN 0-8108-3396-4 (alk. paper)
    1. Chaloff, Serge, 1923–1957.   2. Chaloff, Serge, 1923–1957—
Discography.   3. Saxophonists—United States—Biography.
I. Title.   II. Series.
ML419.C47S56   1998
788.7'165'092
[B]—DC21   98-15920
                                                                          CIP
                                                                          MN

◎ ™ The paper used in this publication meets the minimum
requirements of American National Standard for Information
Sciences—Permanence of Paper for Printed Library Materials, ANSI
Z39.48–1984. Manufactured in the United States of America.

Contents

Editor's Foreword (Dan Morgenstern)   vii

Introduction   1
Early Years   5
A New Conception   21
First Solos   25
With the Second Herd   35
Chaloff and the Second Herd   49
Jam Sessions with Alan Eager   53
All-Star Sessions and Leader   55
Hiatus   67
Late Recordings   75
The Legacy   97
List of Sources   99
Additional Readings   101

Introduction to the Discography   103
Solo Index to the Discography   105
The Discography   109

Second Herd Tune Index   153

Appendix: Leo Parker Discography   165

Name Index   179

Subject Index   185

About the Author   187

Editor's Foreword

It gives me special pleasure to add the name of Vladimir Simosko once again to the list of *Studies in Jazz* authors. The publication of this excellent work reestablishes, after a hiatus of more than a quarter century, the connection between Simosko and the Institute of Jazz Studies.

The institute's massive collection had arrived at Rutgers University's Newark campus and only been given sporadic attention until Simosko was appointed the institute's first curator in 1968—a position for which his combined skills as a professional librarian and a practicing jazz musician made him uniquely qualified.

Simosko served the institute well until 1971, when he moved to Princeton University, but his connection with jazz scholarship was by no means finished. In 1974 the Smithsonian Institution Press published his (and Barry Tepperman's) highly praised *Eric Dolphy: A Musical Biography and Discography*, the standard work on that important modern jazzman, a revised edition of which was brought out by Da Capo Press in 1996.

In 1993, Simosko also contributed detailed and most informative notes to Mosaic Records' *The Complete Serge Chaloff Sessions*—a sneak preview, so to speak, of the far more extensive work to hand. This, one fervently hopes, will spark a much overdue rediscovery of the musical legacy of a great and sadly neglected artist, whose short and ultimately tragic life is illuminated here with a wealth of new information and sympathetic insight.

Dan Morgenstern
Series Editor

Introduction

Serge Chaloff is most widely remembered (when he is remembered at all) as the flamboyant baritone saxophone star with Woody Herman's Second Herd whose problems with drugs extended to erratic personal behavior. Nevertheless, there were many brilliant sessions featuring his work before and after his stint with Herman, the best of them led by Chaloff himself.

Unfortunately, ill health cut short a career that had already fallen into obscurity by the time of his death in 1957. Chaloff had provided the usual ingredients for fulfilling the stereotypical "legendary tragic hero" role that has been romantically assigned to several prominent jazzmen whose lives traced similar patterns across North American culture in the twentieth century. This was the syndrome: "Creative genius, frustrated by society, debauches to extremes and dies young," a syndrome that was brought to the public's awareness by Bix Beiderbecke and then carried to extremes, with racist overtones, by Charlie Parker. However, as with many others also fitting that mold (some of whom didn't even debauch), Chaloff remained relatively obscure. His work has been recognized, treasured, and collected primarily by knowledgeable jazz lovers.

It is an unfortunate trend in public taste that, when major jazz artists with problems achieve legendary stature out of respect for their artistic achievements (or even popular stature due to becoming a fad), more attention is paid to their problems and/or debaucheries than to their artistic legacy. For example, Hollywood, it has come to be assumed, will distort to unrecognizability any career the cinema sets out to depict. Thus, the movies allegedly based on the lives of the major jazz artists Charlie Parker and Billie Holiday seem to be more about the problems of drug addicts who happen incidentally to be musicians, if the movie's perspective is to be taken at surface value, than about them. *The Fabulous Dorseys* (in which Chaloff appeared, as he was a sideman with Jimmy Dorsey at the time) was allegedly a screen biography of Tommy and Jimmy Dorsey. Perhaps because the Dorseys were alive, plus perhaps the relative acceptability of alcohol as a drug of choice, little attention was paid to any debaucheries in their circle. Nevertheless, one would have thought from the movie that their career was primarily a springboard for the romance of the fictional couple at the center of the film's development, and that the personal problems surrounding the brothers' legendary squabbling was the essence of their activity.

Fortunately, in books about musicians it is possible to concentrate

1

more appropriately on the musical aspects of their careers and invade their personal lives only as necessary. Of course some attention must be paid to Chaloff's drug problems as they affected his career, as well as certain other relevant aspects of his personal life, but the focus in this study is on his music.

In 1993, Mosaic Records issued the complete studio recordings of Serge Chaloff as a leader in a boxed set of four compact discs (MD4–147, also available as five LPs on Mosaic MQ5–147), for which I wrote the liner notes, titled *The Complete Serge Chaloff Sessions.* This set provided the most essential work of this master musician, much of it long unavailable except as rare collector's items. At almost the same time, a CD was issued by Cool & Blue (C&BCD102) titled *Serge Chaloff Memorial.* This CD contained the master takes of all 1940s studio record sessions at which Chaloff was featured as soloist, whether as leader or sideman (except for the Woody Herman material, represented only by a broadcast recording of "We the People Bop"), plus the three tracks recorded at the Christmas 1949 All-Stars concert (see discography). About a year later, a CD of rare private and broadcast recordings that had been virtually unknown prior to their distribution, including material live from clubs where Chaloff was performing with his own groups, was issued by Uptown Records (UPCD27.38) under the title *Serge Chaloff: Boston 1950.* It should be clear that by the mid-1990s, Serge Chaloff's work had begun to emerge from obscurity and unavailability to a level of recognition not enjoyed since his peak.

Contemporary interest in reexamining the available legacy of many of jazz's great artists from throughout the art form's many peak periods demonstrates that the music and artists of the more vital years of jazz history are not only not being totally forgotten, but are being recognized (at least by the knowledgeable) on a deeper level. This recognition probably even surpasses the level of appreciation these artists received at the time of their creative vitality. It is gratifying to observe the renewed interest in the life and legacy of Serge Chaloff in this context.

Although blurbs in biographical encyclopedias fill in some details concerning his life, as do liner notes to some of his albums, the focus of interest for Chaloff, as with all musicians, remains the recorded legacy. Scanning the discography reveals the outline of his career rather well. Unfortunately, as a sideman in the big bands led by Tommy Reynolds, Shep Fields, Ina Ray Hutton, Boyd Raeburn, Georgie Auld, Jimmy Dorsey, and others, he was given no opportunity to solo on records, and those parts of the list are useful to the Chaloff scholar only to document his stay with these units and lend insight into his working environment and repertoire. As Chaloff emerged from being a sideman in the so-called Big Band Era, he evolved artistically into one of the more important and popular soloists and stylists of the then avant-garde "bebop" approach. While this history alone would be enough to make him an interesting figure, the significance of Chaloff as an artist is in his continued evolution and growth, both in scope and depth.

Most artists in any medium tend to develop a style, perhaps grow within or beyond it for a while, and then either crystallize into immutability or sell out into commercial adaptions. Only a very few provide that most interesting of artistic phenomena: the continued evolution and growth of the artist into further artistic breakthroughs and discoveries. Most of those who did do this, unfortunately, seemed to burn out and either die young, or, in rare cases such as Artie Shaw, quit at a peak while still showing evidence of potential growth.

Serge Chaloff was clearly one of the artists who continued to exhibit dynamic creative growth until dying tragically young. It should be noted that even those artists most frequently named as achieving legendary status in the "creative genius dies young" category generally had reached the point of either crystallization or selling out first. Many enlightened observers feel that despair over having reached this stage may even account for those artists' excessive debaucheries at that point, at least to some extent. In Chaloff's case, however, the heroin dependency stopped while the development continued.

Despite the almost breathtaking revitalization of his career and music in his later years, as revealed by his recorded legacy, there is evidence that much of what Chaloff actually accomplished is masked because it was undocumented. Much of what he could have achieved is therefore barely hinted at. While this study will help to bring much of this into focus, it is the recorded legacy of music featuring his solo work that reveals his abilities and depth; that legacy remains to be studied and enjoyed.

Chaloff himself cited his own record debut for Leonard Feather's *Encyclopedia of Jazz* as the September 21, 1946, Dial session on the forms filled out for Feather by the musicians themselves (Serge Chaloff file). The only earlier recordings featuring Chaloff's solos issued prior to the 1990s are the privately recorded jam session performances Jerry Newman released on collector's label LPs in the 1950s, from January 24, 1946. Chaloff was still twenty-two years old at sessions, but already was revealing himself to be a mature soloist with a strong conception and an articulate, swinging style. His other work in the 1940s that reveals his brilliance as a soloist is limited to two sessions in 1947 (one under Red Rodney's leadership and the other under his own name, which fortunately survive with alternate takes available for study); two sessions in 1949 under his own name, adding only five further performances on which he solos; his work with Woody Herman from late 1947 to late 1949, which offered a few studio sessions and many broadcasts featuring his occasional short solos; and such rare private recordings and broadcast material as his solo on Jimmy Dorsey's "Perdido" (September 25, 1946), his duets with Rollins Griffith from late 1946, and the Christmas 1949 All-Stars concert. In the early 1950s, there were the Metronome All-Stars sessions, his solos on two titles with Count Basie, and some broadcasts (some of which were issued on the Uptown CD) before the hiatus from studio recordings from early 1951 to early 1954, during which no private tapes or broadcasts have emerged. The recordings he made (primarily under his own name) from his return to recording in 1954 to his last known recorded session in early 1957 reveal the extent and profundity of his growth as an artist. To a certain extent, this renaissance can be seen as a reflection of the directions and growth of jazz styles in that period, but the content of Serge's soloing revealingly demonstrates his own depth as a growing artist. As with too many artists of worth, it is about quality, not quantity.

Early Years

Serge Chaloff was born in Boston, Massachusetts, on November 24, 1923. Both of his parents were distinguished musicians and educators. His father, Julius L. Chaloff (1892–1979), was of Russian descent. A pianist and composer, he graduated from the New England Conservatory of Music in 1910. At the time of Serge's birth, he was playing piano with the Boston Symphony. He recorded for the Ampico label in the 1920s, and later opened his own music school, the Chaloff School of Music, located for many years on Newbury Street in Boston.

Serge's mother, Margaret Stedman Chaloff (1896–1977), was of English descent. Julius was her piano teacher at the New England Conservatory; they married in 1919. Known as Madame Chaloff, she went on to teach at the New England Conservatory, Brandeis, Boston University, and the Berklee School of Music. Her students included Leonard Bernstein, George Shearing, Alan Hovhaness, Toshiko Akiyoshi, Dick Twardzik, Steve Kuhn, Herbie Hancock, Chick Corea, Keith Jarrett, and Mulgrew Miller. She is often respectfully referred to in interviews with former students. Mulgrew Miller, for example, once said:

> I went to Boston and studied with Madame Chaloff, who was Serge Chaloff's mother. It was a unique experience. She was a very spiritual and mystical woman and she had this very involved technique. (Miller 1993)

Serge's older brother, Richard Stedman Chaloff (b. 1920), did not pursue music. Instead, he founded Stedman Ltd. in Brookline, Massachusetts, in 1946. This company designs and custom-builds high-end audio and video installations. Commissions have included, for example, wiring the Kennedy and Vanderbilt mansions and grounds for sound.

In a 1985 interview with Richard Chaloff, Lewis Porter and Norman Saks asked for more background on the family. Richard responded with some fascinating details:

> Stedman was my mother's maiden name. It has a background of coming from England. The Stedman Chapel. There was a Captain Giles Stedman from Salem. She came from the Dodges and the Whites (among the early Pilgrim settlers), that came over on the *Mayflower*. So my mother was very proud of her background and unfortunately, when she married my dad, who was Russian–Jewish, they dropped her out of the Blue Book. In those days of the 1920s, you did not intermix. There were no marriages out of the faith, so to speak.
> My mother played the church organ out in Gary, Indiana. Her mother was very religious, Protestant, and my mother as a teenager, a young girl,

5

learned to play the church organ at her own church. And then later, the silent movies came in, and they needed an organist to play the old Wurlitzers. She was very talented. She had absolute pitch. She was very beautiful, a very pretty woman, a petite figure, under five feet, close to five feet.

But her friends insisted she go to Hollywood and in those days the dream of a young girl was to be in pictures, and she couldn't make up her mind whether to go into movies.

A Borros Morros, he was a director, he wanted mother to come out during the silents, this was before 1918. She went out there and took tests and they were beautiful. I had the films, but they were stolen. Silents, 35mm professional, you know, real movies. But she got homesick for music and someone told her about the New England Conservatory of Music when she was in Hollywood. So she came all the way from Hollywood to Boston, without knowing a soul here, and signed up at the New England Conservatory of Music, asked for the best teacher.

My dad had just won, in 1919, a competition that students came to from all over to compete in, and he won it as the best pianist. So, she was very proud in having him for a teacher and she married him. My mother became the giant in technique and she passed my dad. My dad, really, my dad was a fine teacher, but mother I believe was the genius of the family.

My dad was teaching at the conservatory. The RCA Victor people wanted him to go onto the Red Seal, the old shellac 78 rpm 12-inchers, one-sided, you know, that was the old days. And then the Ampico people bought him out. He must have made over two dozen Ampico rolls. Tushinski, the president of Sony Superscope, was a collector of my dad's piano rolls, and he put a whole hour on WCRB radio and he rated my dad in the day of Rachmaninoff and Levine, my dad's technique. He's closer to a Rubinstein. Closer. My dad did not care for jazz ever. He didn't believe in it. He was for the Beethoven, Bach eras. He was born over here, but he went to Europe to study. He studied with an Ignace Friedman, from Germany, and he did a lot of composition with Ignace Friedman, not just piano technique. It was the Romantic music, he wrote like Rachmaninoff.

My dad played the organ in the house. My dad had a very early model of the Everett Orgatron. It was an electric organ before the Hammond, and as babies the two of us [Serge and Richard] had bedrooms on the second floor and we used to hear our dad play this Everett Orgatron. He'd come home at 12:00 at night from the conservatory and sit down and play some toccatas and fugues. I can still whistle every note and my brother, I remember, put the pillow over his ears, but I enjoyed the organ. (Chaloff 1985)

Richard provided many vivid stories and descriptions of the brothers' childhood and family life. Attractive and photogenic, the boys were even models in some advertisements, but Richard's stories reveal them to have been normal, mischievous children within a relatively ordinary family lifestyle despite their parents' status:

We'd play pranks just to get a rise out of people. Of course we were punished but the laughs were worth it. Serge was younger and maybe more intimidated at first, so he'd sometimes squeal on me if cross-examined by our parents about some prank, and being the older, I'd get the brunt of the punishments.

When I was ten years old my dad bought me a 1930 *Radio Magazine* showing how to construct a one-tube radio. I decided to build the radio into my bed pillow complete with headphones, batteries, etc. so I could listen to all the late night radio broadcasts of Ted Weems, Isham Jones, etc. Mother would look in almost every evening and find me apparently sleeping with the pillow wrapped around my head. When I wouldn't loan my radio-pillow to Serge more than one night a week, he informed our parents of my secret, and they confiscated my pillow! That disturbed me greatly and I plotted a diabolical revenge.

Serge loved Goobers Chocolate Coated Raisins and always had a box or two on his bedside table that he could eat in the dark if he woke up at night. Behind our garage, I had a rabbit hutch full of rabbits. One afternoon I emptied several of his Goober raisin boxes and filled them with the similar-looking rabbit droppings, and replaced the boxes on his night table. That night about 1:00 a.m. I woke to the sounds of my brother coughing, spitting, and screaming that he had been poisoned. Mother and Dad ran down the hall to Serge's bedroom. My father apparently tasted the brown residue; I heard HIM violently spitting, and seconds later hollering, "DICK! COME HERE IMMEDIATELY! I WANT TO TALK TO YOU!" Well, I ran up to the third floor attic eaves and hid until morning, after the situation had calmed down.

Even later in life, Serge could never pass a candy counter with Goober Chocolate Raisins without saying "Ugh!" This actually happened at a Hollywood candy store counter when Serge was with Jimmy Dorsey's band making the movie *The Fabulous Dorseys* in September 1946. I was present with Ralph Burns and Serge when Serge went to purchase some cigarettes, and when he caught sight of some boxes of Goobers, he still said "Ugh!"

Well, I got it for that one, too, but Serge never told on me again! But after that, when Dad would get after me, Serge would really love it.

True story: when my father was a teenager, while living in Dorchester, Massachusetts, a neighboring house had a defective gas heater that caused a tremendous gas explosion one early morning that blew out the entire side of the house adjacent to my father's bedroom. He was so shaken up by this tremendous explosion that in his later life he would never go into a basement with the gas heater operating.

When my brother and I were kids, my father was recording for the Ampico Company in New York and made friends with a world-famous announcer, Olin Downes, who was the announcer for the New York Philharmonic Orchestra concerts that were broadcast every Sunday afternoon during this era. One day Olin Downes phoned my father and suggested that they go fishing together on Cape Cod. He was planning to drive from New York to Newton, Massachusetts, one Saturday morning and pick my father up at 5:00 a.m. and then continue to Cape Cod.

According to my father there was absolutely no way that he could get up at 5:00 a.m. as he was a "night owl" and spent most of his life teaching until 11:00 or 12:00 at night and then was able to get up only at about 9:00 or 10:00 a.m. to continue teaching the next day. The problem was how to get him up because he was a very sound sleeper and in no way could my mother or an alarm clock wake him. My brother and I devised a fiendish plan in which we would set off several giant 6-inch firecrackers in a metal ash can and then inform him that his gas heater had blown up!

On the date of the fishing engagement, my brother and I went into the basement about quarter to five in the morning, lit the firecrackers with long stems, put the ash can cover on, and then dashed upstairs to our bedrooms. In a matter of 15–16 seconds a tremendous explosion took place that blew open the basement door to the hall, flooding the whole house with gunpowder smoke. Serge decided that I should be the one to knock on my father's bedroom door and inform him that the gas heater had blown up, which I did. My father ran down the stairs and out into the street screaming, "Call the Fire Department, my beautiful house is burning up!" As he approached the front door of the house he sniffed gunpowder and immediately thought of me. The next sound we heard was my father screaming, "Dick, I want to see you right now!"

My brother ran for his bedroom and looked out the front window as my father started chasing me around two large 30-foot spruce trees in the front lawn. He was running around each tree chasing me waving a leather belt and screaming, "Wait till I catch you!" Being very trim and fast on my feet, I ran around the trees several times and then decided to speed up and run BEHIND him. As he ran around the trees after me, with me right behind him, one of our neighbors across the street, who happened to be George Wein's grandmother, heard the commotion and lifted up her window and yelled out in a heavy Yiddish accent, "Dickie! Why are you chasing your father?" That defused the situation and everybody had a good laugh, especially my brother Serge!

I guess we gave Dad a hard time. Like, on weekends when the weather was good, the family would go for picnic outings, but Dad would often be tired from work and would hide in the bathroom soaking in a hot tub while we waited and Mother would yell at him through the door. Serge and I knew how to get at the plumbing inside the wall and open the tub drain so the water would drain out. Dad would storm out annoyed at losing the bath water and yelling "Margaret, call the plumber!" but it would get us on our way. (Chaloff 1993–95)

In personal discussions concerning Serge, Richard noted Serge had always seemed interested in jazz and girls:

My brother at a very early age loved jazz. He liked all kinds of jazz at the beginning. He'd duck off to any jazz concert there was, he'd beg my mother to let him go; even though he was 10, 12, 13 years old, he wanted to go. And for some reason, he strayed away from the classics. There's a lot of funny stories on my brother. When he was a young fellow, he was interested in girls a lot sooner than I was, though he was younger. I was building radio stations at the age of 13, and my brother was interested in music and young ladies.

I can remember one winter when we were teenagers. We'd had a really big snowfall. I was maybe 15, 16, so Serge would have been 12 or 13. I was up in my bedroom working on my ham radio set, I used to talk to people like Barry Goldwater, who was a kid into ham radios then too. I looked out the back window and there was Serge building an igloo. I didn't think too much of it and next time I looked there it was, finished, and Serge was taking in a sled stacked with pop and chips and snacks. Next thing, he's escorting in a young lady, a neighbor girl about our age somewhere, and they disappear inside and I see Serge push a block of snow into the opening from inside, sealing them in. Well, I was just into my radio, you know, but I kept glancing out, and eventually, a long time later, here they come out of the igloo, slightly disarrayed but both of them smiling blissfully. I was intrigued and asked him about it later, but all he did was smile. (Chaloff 1993–95)

Serge's parents provided him with a thorough grounding on piano between the ages of six and twelve, the age at which he began playing the baritone saxophone. He also took clarinet lessons with Manuel Valerio of the Boston Symphony, but his baritone work was self-taught. "Who could teach me?" Serge was quoted as saying in an article by Leonard Feather (Simon 1971, 348). "I couldn't chase [Harry] Carney all around the country." Feather went on to write,

The baritone and Serge's burgeoning jazz ambitions were a sore spot with Chaloff pere, and Serge has vague recollections of being chased around the attic in the course of numerous attempts to reform him. Chased but not chastened, he listened to records featuring Carney and Jack Washington, Basie's perennial baritone man. (Feather 1950)

Richard Chaloff described Serge's earliest musical activities as follows:

How did my brother get started in music? When he was a very young teenager, he went to Newton Junior High School and he joined the band. I think they gave him a trumpet and I think he played trumpet for a while, he took trumpet lessons at Newton.

He heard music at home from the day he was born. He didn't like the trumpet and straight music where you just counted the beats. He was not that kind of conformist. Then my mother bought him a clarinet and he took clarinet lessons.

So, he wanted to go into jazz, and my dad, of course, was, well, you thought he was from the age of Brahms and Beethoven. He wore a shoestring tie and the old musician's hat and he lived the part and acted the part, I guess. He felt that the organ should only have Bach played on it. Anything else was sacrilegious. And when he had a big concert grand in

the living room, that only the classics should be played on it. And here my
brother was blowing the clarinet upstairs, playing all kinds of . . . he started
with some Dixieland type of music and later on he went modern, quite
modern in his time.

My mother went along with him. She felt pushing him into the classics
was not the solution. My father offered to teach him, go to the conservatory and go into the classics. My father almost begged him, but he said,
"No, Dad, all jazz." And that was it. So he stuck to his guns and Mother
went along with it. (Chaloff 1985)

Richard recalled that the stress between their father and Serge's blossoming jazz orientation resulted in Serge considering "the old man"
as "pretty square." Richard then related the following story in private
discussions:

One winter we were driving down an icy hill near our home. Dad was
driving, and Serge and I were in the back seat. The car went slightly out
of control due to the slipperiness and he ran a stop sign. Wouldn't you
know, right there was a cop who pulled us over. Dad was dressed as usual
in his old-fashioned, clergyman-like style, and when this big Irish police-
man looked in and saw him dressed like that, he assumed he was a priest,
and with a flourish of "Excuse me, Father, but you should be more care-
ful," let him off. The funny part was Dad was going along with it, saying,
"Thank you, and bless you, my son." Here's this strict, conservative Jewish man impersonating a priest! Serge was sitting there shaking with
laughter. He just couldn't believe it, and kept saying, "I didn't think Dad
had it in him." (Chaloff 1993–95)

While on the subject, Richard expanded on his family's religious orientation:

Actually, Dad wasn't particularly religious. Serge and I were brought up
in Mother's faith, Presbyterian. Even Dad converted to Christianity eventually, after getting miffed at the rabbi from his synagogue, who was pres-
suring him for money. (Chaloff 1993–95)

Thus, Serge Chaloff was not Jewish, as has often been assumed. Ac-
cording to Jewish tradition, one is born Jewish only if one's mother was
Jewish at that time; the father's background is considered irrelevant.
Otherwise, one is not Jewish unless one formally converts.

In the 1985 interview, Richard continued with his discussion of
Serge's early musical studies:

Then after he went with the clarinet, he switched to the tenor sax and it
clicked a little with him, in fact it sounded pretty good. Of course if you
could play the clarinet you could switch over. Then he went to the baritone

and he really loved that instrument. He could play that like the tenor sax. He could get it right up there. The only time you knew it was a baritone was when he took it down low. He played it high.

He was very amazing. He had a finger dexterity, I used to watch him, you couldn't believe the speed that he had. He was precise, he was a perfectionist. He would be up in his bedroom as a teenager. He would be up by the hour to one, two, three in the morning and I'm trying to sleep and I'd hear him go over a phrase or piece and he did it until it was perfect. He would try his own. He would experiment. Many of the tricks he did on some of the pieces he did on these tapes and records are ones that he developed as a youngster, and then he put them in later.

He was a perfectionist. I mean he'd play the phrase over and over until he got it just right, you know. He used to drive me . . . I used to put the pillow over my head, we had battles. I used to hear him, he'd play a lot by himself. He'd just be in the bedroom with the sax. I could see the improvement in technique. He expanded almost every week, every month. You could feel his technique and ability growing, you could almost see him blossoming, I would say, and he listened to the tapes and records from his very beginning to where he was at the end, and anyone can see he really came a long way.

I had the record player in my bedroom and he used to listen to Coleman Hawkins quite a bit. "Body and Soul," that, I think, was one of his favorites. "I've Got the World on a String," he liked that one very, very much, and "The Sunny Side of the Street." Whatever he heard, he was influenced by it, if it was good. (Chaloff 1985)

Most sources, including Chaloff's own data on the form he filled out for Leonard Feather's *Encyclopedia of Jazz* (Serge Chaloff file), state that Chaloff's first professional experience began late in 1939, when, at the age of sixteen, Chaloff allegedly joined Tommy Reynolds' big band on tenor sax shortly after the band was formed. However, testimony from Serge's brother, Richard, indicated that even earlier, while Serge was still living at home attending high school, he was causing his family much suspenseful anxiety by running off with his saxophone to sit in at Ort's Grille, a nightclub at 25 Essex Street that featured jazz. There he quickly became one of the paid performers. As Richard Chaloff recalled it:

There was a place in Boston called Ort's down in the "combat zone" of Boston, I believe down on Essex Street, and there was a fellow by the name of Izzy Ort, who used to write newspaper articles that he had to pay for. He wrote them as a musical column or a jazz column, but they were an advertisement with "Come to Izzy Ort's" at the bottom. So he used to advertise that he was looking for young talent and he was looking for a band that would play down there, because the sailors, you know, during that era, would come off the ships, they were really rough fellows, they weren't like today. They were really rough and ready. They had fights down there, barroom brawls like you see in the movies. And my brother went down there, he wasn't past fourteen years old, he didn't have a permit to work, but he was pretty tall and went down to see Izzy Ort, the story goes, and played for him and Izzy liked the sax, he liked the big band sound in those days, and he hired my brother to work nights.

We sorta took that as a joke, really. We weren't serious about it because Ort's was too rough a place to go anywhere. He didn't have much of a future except being hit with a bottle. I mean, the place was raided. It was in the papers all the time. My mother used to pray on Sundays that he'd make it outa there. My mother went to church and my father went to the temple. They prayed differently. But I know that Mother prayed that Serge would make it outa there each week. But they paid him very well, and he came home very proud by the fact that he was getting top money at the Grille, as much as what many of the other men were getting. But it wasn't the money; he liked playing in it. He didn't care where he played.

My brother sat in with bandsmen that were in their thirties and forties. Some of the men were a bit on the old side, and here he was fourteen, fifteen years old and he played right along with them, and he did so well they kept him, they let him play every time that he came down.

From there, he met a man by the name of Billy Beaupre, and he was a fellow that, believe it or not, played the calliope. Well, I never heard of a band with a calliope, but he had one. It was up in the Hampshires and he played at some very swanky resort near the White Mountains, and he asked my brother to come with him. I believe my brother got the job through an agent, some Duke Davis, who was an old-time agent in Boston. He handled my brother, of all things, at his age. Duke was a good friend of my brother's. He realized that Serge had something about him that was a little different than the average musician and I think Duke was one of the first ones to befriend him, and he got him involved with this Billy Beaupre.

We went up to hear Serge play up there in one of the hotels, and Billy just played the calliope as a joke I think. But the band played straight to dance to and all that. [Serge] got tired of the calliope, couldn't stand it, he told me later. (Chaloff 1985)

Of course Serge did join Tommy Reynolds' band a bit later. When asked about the story of Serge's joining Reynolds' band shortly after its inception, which would have been late 1939 and Serge just turning sixteen, Richard said, "That's about right." (Chaloff 1993–95) Serge was probably with the band well into 1942, as he can be seen on-screen in a "soundie" movie short made by Reynolds' band on February 3 and 4, 1942, playing tenor sax in the section with a baritone on a stand beside him. Oddly, in appearance, Serge seemed to resemble a young Bix Beiderbecke.

Reynolds had emerged on the Boston scene in late 1939 with a working arrangement with Boston promoter Si Shribman similar to the one that had given Artie Shaw and Glenn Miller their starts. Shribman booked the band to play at the Roseland State ballroom two nights weekly, broadcasting with a CBS radio hookup, and touring around Shribman's chain of New England nightspots for one-nighters in between. The band was billed as "The Band of Tomorrow"; but despite this forward-looking implication, Reynolds, a clarinetist, modeled himself and his band after Artie Shaw, who was making headlines that season for walking out on the band business:

> The band is fashioned after Shaw's, and Reynolds himself, who plays clarinet, looks and acts much like Artie. While this aping doubtless will bring early attention and give the band a start, local critics feel that Tommy will have to adopt a style more individual if he expects to reach the top-brackets. (Tommy Reynolds Build-up 1939)

Chaloff began playing tenor sax with Reynolds' band, but went back to baritone as soon as possible. He stated that he had made several record dates with Reynolds during his year or so with the band (Feather 1950), although he does not appear in personnel listings in the various discographies. Evidently, Serge occasionally got a tenor sax solo "live." In George T. Simon's entry on Tommy Reynolds in *The Big Bands*, he quoted Barry Ulanov's having described Chaloff as "a tenor man with a good tone and unremarkable ideas" at that time. Tommy Reynolds' band was described as "one of the loudest," with contagious raw enthusiasm (Simon 1967, 478). However, none of the Tommy Reynolds material that has surfaced from the period Serge was with the band featured Chaloff soloing (see discography).

Although Chaloff noted himself as being with the orchestra of Dick "Stinky" Rogers during 1941–42 (Serge Chaloff file), he was cited by Feather (1950) as being with Dick Rogers' band for only "a couple of weeks" after leaving Reynolds' band. Consequently, he was probably not present for the only Dick Rogers record date indicated in standard discographies. If nothing else, this session would probably be representative of their repertoire, but since Chaloff did not solo on any of his early records, the question of his presence becomes purely academic. Dick "Stinky" Rogers was a "kooky" singer with Will Osborne's popular dance orchestra and inherited the band when Osborne gave it up to go to Hollywood early in 1941 (Will Osborne 1941). In *The Big Bands,* Dick Rogers was described as a good singer with an attractive personality, who kept the band "in fine musical shape, thanks to fine arrangements by Jerry Bittick." (Simon 1967, 510)

Chaloff reported spending 1943 with the Shep Fields all-sax band (Serge Chaloff file). This was more probably a mid-1942 to mid-1943 stay, as closer examination of Serge's documented activity reveals. Although this band made records for Bluebird, 1943 was the year of the recording ban, when few bands recorded except for small independent labels, and the major labels were prevented from recording anything but singers with vocal group accompaniment. However, broadcast recordings have been issued on collectors' labels covering the period when Chaloff was with the band. Again, since he did not solo, these recordings are of interest primarily in documenting his musical environment and its repertoire.

The Shep Fields band in question formed in the spring of 1941. A writeup in *Metronome* reported:

> Shep Fields is making the jump from two reeds to thirty five with startling results. . . . There's no brass. Instead: ten saxes! The scoring's a new conception. For the most part it's high reeds against low reeds, just as most bands have brass against saxes. . . .
>
> Then, too, tonal coloring is at a maximum. Starting from the bottom, there's one bass sax, one baritone, six tenors, four altos, three bass clarinets, ten clarinets, one alto flute, eight flutes, and one piccolo. Judge, for yourself, what's likely to happen. (Shep Fields 1941)

The band also had the conventional rhythm section of piano, guitar, bass, and drums, plus vocalists. Simon noted in *The Big Bands*:

> It turned out to be one of the most musical dance bands of all time. The varied reeds produced wonderful tone colors, via some fine arrangements, first by Glenn Osser and Lew Harris, and later by Freddy Noble, who became Shep's musical director. . . . In a February 1942 review I commended the band for its great blend and lack of obtrusiveness, while still projecting all the excitement of a band with brass sections. . . . The big difference, though, was the amazingly rich ensemble sounds the all-reed band achieved when all nine horns played similar lines. . . . To play the satisfying but difficult book, Fields loaded his group with top-notch musicians. (Simon 1967, 200)

Gunther Schuller, in his book *The Swing Era*, also praised the band, noting:

> The unusual and original instrumentation with its great potential for a wide range of tone colors was used in such a versatile and effective way. . . . The group's ensemble playing—much of it without vibrato—was quite extraordinary in terms of balance, blend, and impeccable intonation. (Schuller 1990, 766–67)

Chaloff obviously would have been faced with an interesting and very demanding book requiring considerable doubling. While Chaloff left the band to go with Ina Ray Hutton sometime in 1943, Fields continued with this approach until 1947, with varying personnel over the years.

On January 28, 1943, Serge was visiting his family in Newton, Massachusetts, after having been on the road. Richard Chaloff made an acetate home recording featuring Serge and his mother playing piano four-hands on some untitled boogie-woogie and "Honeysuckle Rose," plus engaging in some verbal banter. Madame Chaloff can be heard saying it had been a long time since she'd had both her sons home together, and mentioned the date. Serge then performed "Body and Soul" twice on piano, according to Richard. The first performance is Tatumesque and slightly stiff, but the second "take" is far more impressionistic and fluent, performed with wit and feeling. Without Richard's testimony, it would be tempting to attribute the first version to Madame Chaloff, as Richard had stated that she admired jazz and could play very much like Art Tatum.

However, these are not the earliest private recordings featuring Chaloff known to exist. An undated acetate recording was made by Richard Chaloff in Serge's bedroom, of Serge performing an unaccompanied tenor sax version of "Body and Soul," obviously heavily reflecting Coleman Hawkins. Afterwards, Serge says, "What did you think of that tone? Stinks, doesn't it?" Richard said he thought this recording had been made "several years earlier" than the piano acetates, possibly in 1939–40 (Chaloff 1993–95). Concerning these acetates, Richard Chaloff noted,

> I used a Presto acetate cutter, in the WW II days. I was using a Presto cutter with my own amplifiers and I used to sit there with a paint brush, brushing away the cuttings. Of course, if you didn't, you'd hear a "tick" every time a cutting got under the stylus. My brother didn't like hearing noises on the recording, he'd say, "Brush it away." I used to sit there brushing away, you know. (Chaloff 1985)

In 1943–44, Serge was with Ina Ray Hutton's band. Ina Ray Hutton, often billed as "The Blonde Bombshell of Rhythm," led an all-female band since 1934. Occasionally, after 1939, she would appear as a brunette, or with an all-male band, toning down her glamour image, and continued into the television era. Although a good singer, Ina Ray had her younger half-sister June Hutton (who later replaced Jo Stafford with The Pied Pipers vocal group) singing with her band for a while, and also used a Polish-Chinese female vocal group, the Kim Loo Sisters, who were featured with the 1943–44 band. Stuart Foster was the male singer with this band, prior to his stint with Tommy Dorsey.

During this interval, Ina Ray's band was appearing regularly on the radio playing the "Coca Cola Spotlite Bands" shows for the Armed Forces Radio Service from assorted camps and bases. Existing broadcast transcriptions from the period Serge was probably with the band include dates played at Fort Monroe, Virginia; Fort Knox, Kentucky; the Naval Air Station in Miami, Florida; the Naval Air Station at Quonsett Point, Rhode Island; and the Army air base at Spence Field, Georgia, among other locations (see discography). The band is revealed to be crisp and swinging. Their broadcast repertoire primarily featured vocals by Ina Ray, Stuart Foster, or the two together, plus a few with the Kim Loo Sisters, but some pieces were jazz arrangements that sound up-to-date for the time. Throughout this material there are several good jazz solos apiece by Joe Megro (tenor sax), Roger Ellick (trumpet), Hal Schaefer (piano), and especially Jack Purcell (guitar).

Ina Ray and the band also appeared in a full-length feature movie, *Ever Since Venus*, for Columbia Pictures. Curiously, on his *Encyclopedia of Jazz* form (Serge Chaloff file), Serge reported this film as *One Touch of Venus*, a more famous and popular movie made a few years later, but of course not featuring Ina Ray Hutton's band or including Chaloff.

The movie *Ever Since Venus* was essentially a silly comedy with short feature spots for Ina Ray and her band scattered throughout. Directed by Arthur Dreifuss, with credits for Musical Director as Mario Silva and orchestrations by Lyle Murphy, the band had a string section added for the film. Aside from unidentified incidental music behind the action or conversation, featured numbers include "The Wedding of the Boogie and the Samba" early in the film, "Glamour for Sale" (both as a feature number and later as part of a "Beauty Through the Ages" medley), and "Miss 1944," as well as an unidentified jazz piece in which the sax section can be seen standing and playing a four-bar unison break. Of course the musical features are primarily to show off Ina Ray, usually with the band visible behind her as she sings or dances her numbers. In this film, Chaloff can be seen performing in the band during several of their feature numbers, playing bass clarinet as well as baritone sax. Unfortunately, neither on any of the broadcasts mentioned above nor in this movie was Serge featured as a soloist, and none of the arrangements heard could be identified as his work (see discography).

In 1995, Pat Cooper, youngest of the Kim Loo Sisters, now living on Long Island with her husband, Sid Cooper (the former Tommy Dorsey alto saxophonist who is still active in the studios), reminisced about the Kim Loo Sisters and being with Ina Ray while Serge was in the band. Originally a quartet, the Eurasian beauties (their father was a Chinese waiter, their mother a Polish seamstress) were from Minneapolis, Minnesota, and had been good friends with the Andrews Sisters there while growing up, having dinner at each other's homes. Pat related:

The Kim Loo Sisters started in Louie's Chinese Revue in Minneapolis when I was four years old. Mother went along when we went on the road, and we had tutors, a chauffeur, we were really looked after. In 1939–40 we were in George White's Scandals, but we were too sheltered for any scandals. Eventually, our manager then, Charlie Yates, who also managed Ina Ray, got us together and Ina Ray liked the contrast between her blondeness and our exotic appearance, and hired us. We were with the band for at least a year, maybe a year and a half, and I'm certain Serge was already in the band when we started. This was 1943, and the first half of 1944, until Ina Ray broke up the band and married [trumpeter] Randy Brooks and moved to California. By then the Kim Loo Sisters were a trio, as Genevive [the third sister] married a Chinese student in 1942 and moved to China. This Chinese student eventually became General Lee Jung Jen in China, but their marriage didn't last.

Serge was always a gentleman to us, very nice, but he was already a bit wild. As I say, we were sheltered and protected, and didn't have a lot to do with the men in the band except when we were on the stand, but I remember Serge as very nice. He would occasionally get a solo with the band, I recall, and did do some arranging, mostly jazz instrumentals. I remember he once did an arrangement for us to sing, and there were wild chords, and some unusual voicings. I usually sang melody lead, and this was very modern. We even questioned him about the ending, as it had some difficult intervals, but it worked. I wish I could remember what the tune was!

We weren't in the band's movie, *Ever Since Venus*, because at the time we were working in another movie, *Miss Bobby Socks*. After Ina Ray broke up the band, the Kim Loo Sisters toured Europe and then we returned to get married. Margaret married trumpeter Dan Kenyon, Alice married guitarist Jack Purcell, and I married Stuart Foster, who by then was with Tommy Dorsey. But we still perform together. All four sisters reunited for a nostalgia tour on a cruise ship just this summer, and I found these pictures that show us with Serge in the band when we were looking for background memorabilia for the tour. That brought a lot of it into focus. (Cooper 1995)

In the Feather interview, Chaloff stated that he was with Ina Ray Hutton for a year, "around 1943. She had some good men, and some of us worked together later with Boyd [Raeburn] and Woody—Stan Fishelson and Ollie Wilson." (Feather 1950)

Richard Chaloff had vivid recollections of Serge's stint with Ina Ray:

I remember she was a classy gal with a beautiful figure and she always faced the orchestra, so you only saw one side of Ina Ray. When she conducted, everything wiggled and for a while she was a minor sensation. She always wore slinky dresses and as a youngster I used to sit there with amazement, you know. I really didn't know much about everything but she was attractive from the point of view I could see her at. (Chaloff 1985)

A later student of Serge's, Steve Adamson, who was interviewed at length concerning his relationship with Serge, recalled:

He did talk about playing with Ina Ray Hutton, and I would remember this big smile on his face and his eyebrows would be jumping up and down. She was one hell of a knockout. She was a good-looking lady, sexy as hell and Serge was attracted to her. (Adamson 1991)

Largely overlooked by discographers, the recording career of Ina Ray's bands is sketchy, and this band, at least during Serge's stay, seems not to have made any commercial recording dates. Of course, this was the period of the recording ban. Even their movie, *Ever Since Venus*, is difficult to track down, and most of their Spotlite Band material apparently remains unissued. Only a few tracks from spring 1944 were issued, surfacing on collectors' label LPs (see discography). The AFRS broadcast from Spence Field, Georgia, on June 5, 1944, issued on the Sunbeam label, revealed the band in good form. Ina Ray's singing and the Kim Loo Sisters' singing in the manner of the Boswell Sisters, Andrews Sisters, and King Sisters sound very good.

A review of the band by Leonard Feather in the March 1944 *Metronome* while the band was at the Strand Theatre in New York provided more details:

Considering that it has no pretentions to being strictly a jazz outfit, this Hutton band gets a lot of good music into its stage show. Ina Ray herself adds the virtues of a stunning appearance and a pleasant voice. . . . Later in the show she does a duet with Stuart Foster. . . .
    The band has some convincing swing arrangements, mostly by John Benson Brooks. It also boasts several remarkable soloists: Jack Purcell on guitar . . . Hal Schaefer, an exciting pianist . . . Joe Megro, whose tenor came through nicely in the opening flag waver . . . and Roger Ellick, a good trumpet. (Feather 1944)

Actually, Pat Cooper recalled that many arrangements were also being done for Ina Ray's band by George Paxton, who would sometimes fill in with the sax section, by Fred Norman, as well as several by Serge. This band would probably offer much music of interest if it were better documented.

According to George T. Simon, Ina Ray Hutton was

a much better leader than she is given credit for . . . she knows what she wants to hear, she's very astute, she follows an act wonderfully and she has a great conception of time. She worked awfully hard, too hard, in fact, so that during a theatre tour in Texas in 1944 she collapsed and the doctors told her she'd have to quit or else. So she quit, the band broke up. (Simon 1971, 348)

According to Richard Chaloff, Serge had become disillusioned with Ina Ray's band by the time it folded. Although he had tried his own arranging skills for the band during this period, Richard said, "To him it was just straight, you know, nothing really dramatic, nothing really avant-gard." (Chaloff 1985).

A New Conception

Precise dating of Ina Ray Hutton's collapse and the band's demise is vague, but some discographies show Stan Fishelson, Ollie Wilson, Joe Megro, and Serge with Boyd Raeburn's band as early as their July 9, 1944, AFRS "One Night Stand" broadcast from the Roosevelt Hotel in Washington, D.C. (although much of the information about Raeburn's personnel and activity is vague and contradictory). The discography attempts to sort out the available information, but is subject to revision pending better data. In any case, again Serge was not offered any solo space on any reviewed performances by Raeburn's band.

It was while he was with Raeburn that Serge was exposed to and joined the modernists developing the new "bop" style at that time. As Serge put it, "I heard Bird" (Feather 1950), and he also found himself working with musicians like Benny Harris, Earl Swope, Oscar Pettiford, occasionally Dizzy Gillespie, and other pioneers of the new style. According to Feather's article, "he became one of the earliest bop enthusiasts, and finally began to develop enough of a style to enable him to take solos."

The Raeburn band was one of the first big bands to perform in the new style with arrangements by Dizzy Gillespie, George Handy, and Ed Finkel, among others, providing some of the most advanced charts to be heard on surviving recordings by any band of its day. While the Raeburn band has always been recognized among musicians and jazz scholars as one of the best, most advanced, and most interesting big bands of the mid-1940s, it did not have a large public following and only made a handful of commercial record dates. Fortunately, interest among collectors led to a number of collectors' label issues of broadcasts and transcription recordings, as well as reissues of their few commercially recorded discs. Again, however, since Serge was not a featured soloist, the major point of interest for the Chaloff scholar is the documentation of his working environment and career movement. Evidently, Serge was with Raeburn from roughly early July 1944 through March 1945, except for an interval when Raeburn disbanded in the fall. Documented gigs for the Raeburn band in that interval include:

June 30–July 6, 1944	West End Casino, Long Branch, New Jersey
July 9–14, 1944	Roosevelt Hotel, Washington, D.C.
July 16–19, 1944	West End Casino, Long Branch, New Jersey

July 20–27, 1944	Hunt's Inn, Wildwood, New Jersey
August 19–24, 1944	Dayton, Ohio
August 25–31, 1944	Detroit, Michigan
September 1–7, 1944	Palace Theatre, Cleveland, Ohio
September 8–14, 1944	Oriental, Chicago, Illinois
September 16–17, 1944	Topper Club, Cincinnati, Ohio
September 19–25, 1944	Tune Town, St. Louis, Missouri
October–early December	(disbanded)
December 13, 1944	Roosevelt, New Orleans, Louisiana
December 15–31, 1944	St. Louis, Missouri
January 19–25, 1945	Apollo Theater, New York City
February 23–24, 1945	Topper, Cincinnati, Ohio
March 2–15, 1945	Sherman, Chicago, Illinois
March 22–?, 1945	New Yorker, New York City

On January 9, 1945, Serge participated in a record date under bassist Oscar Pettiford's name, featuring vocalist "Rubberlegs" Williams and such major figures as Dizzy Gillespie, Vic Dickenson, and Don Byas, but again Serge was not given the opportunity to solo. There were also, of course, many airchecks, transcription recordings, and studio record dates Serge participated in with Raeburn's band throughout that period, but again without any solo spots for Serge (see discography for details).

Richard Chaloff recalled Charlie Parker's impact on Serge:

> He "palled" with him in New York. Anytime he had the chance, he would pal with him. He would sit in with him at night; these fellows would be playing their dates in New York, and after the dates were over, the musicians would drift together and they would all find each other, wherever the greats were, and they would all pal and play all night. My brother used to say how he was up till 4, 5, 6 in the morning with the Bird, or what have you. Dizzy, you know. They would all get together. All the beboppers all found each other out. (Chaloff 1985)

Concerning his conceptual development in the new idiom during this period, Serge was quoted by Feather as stating,

> It was in the Georgie Auld band, just after that, that I was most influenced, especially by Al Cohn, and Georgie himself—he plays every style well. We made some fine records for Musicraft. No, I still didn't have any solos. (Feather 1950)

Discographies show Serge present in Auld's big band over a span of more than a year, from May 1945 through June 1946, overlapping part of his stay with Jimmy Dorsey's band. Despite being named *Metronome*'s Band of the Year in 1945, the Georgie Auld big band was not working steadily in 1946. The band reconvened for occasional record dates while members worked elsewhere. Auld had emerged from Bunny Berigan's 1937–38 big band to join Artie Shaw's 1938–39 band just as it peaked as the most popular band in North America. He became a star in this setting while still a teenager and went on to work with Benny Goodman and return to Shaw's 1941–42 orchestra before forming his own band.

Engagements for the Georgie Auld band during Serge's stay have been traced as follows:

April 20–26, 1945	Paradise, Detroit, Michigan
May 4–10, 1945	Apollo Theatre, New York City
May 25–31, 1945	Royal, Baltimore, Maryland
July 17–August 22, 1945	Trianon Ballroom, Los Angeles, California
September 1945	(various one-nighters)
October 5–11, 1945	Paradise, Detroit, Michigan
mid-October–mid-November	(various one-nighters)
November 22–?, 1945	Howard Theater, Washington, D.C.
December 1945	(various one-nighters)
December 31, 1945	Symphony Hall, Boston, Massachusetts
January 2–17, 1946	Latin Quarter, Detroit, Michigan
January 18–24, 1946	Fan's, Philadelphia, Pennsylvania

Trombonist Mert Goodspeed, who worked and recorded with Serge later, recalled meeting Serge at the New Year's Eve concert at Symphony Hall in Boston:

I was on the stand with him. December 31, 1945, in Boston Symphony Hall, the same stand with him. I recall he did solo with Georgie's band, but . . . it was only the one time I saw him with Georgie Auld, was that New Year's Eve. Of course Georgie took most of the saxophone solos himself, and did not necessarily feature baritone solos. (Goodspeed 1991)

The band was also reported to have played a concert at the Philharmonic Auditorium in Los Angeles on July 30, 1945, during their engagement at the Trianon. Between September 1945 and January 1946, *Down Beat* reported the band had played 92 one-nighters, interrupted by just a couple of theater dates as indicated. It was during this road tour, according to the best information, that Serge developed his heroin habit. Auld broke up the exhausted band at the end of January 1946, and Serge immediately went with Jimmy Dorsey.

The declining popularity of big bands after the war caused the demise of many excellent bands. By 1947 Auld was leading a sextet which included Serge, following Serge's touring with Dorsey. Meanwhile, some significant events documented Serge's emergence as a soloist.

First Solos

Despite the existence of the 1943 private recordings on which Serge can be heard playing piano, both solo and four-hands with his mother, plus the even earlier recording of an unaccompanied tenor sax solo version of "Body and Soul" (exhibiting a slavish Coleman Hawkins influence), the earliest documentation of his baritone sax solo work to have surfaced to date were the private recordings made at a jam session in the apartment of Jerry Newman in 1946.

Newman had already made a series of private recordings at Monroe's Uptown House and Minton's Playhouse during the early 1940s which documented some of the earliest work of the emerging bop stylists in jam session settings. Regulars among the joys of these recordings were Thelonious Monk, Dizzy Gillespie, Ken Kersey, Kenny Clarke, and Charlie Christian stretching out in long uninhibited solos.

On January 24, 1946, at 2 a.m. on the night before the Auld band closed at Fan's in Philadelphia, Newman held the session that featured Serge's earliest solo work to be issued to date. The group included Serge along with Sonny Berman and Marky Markowitz (trumpets), Earl Swope (trombone), Al Cohn (tenor sax), Ralph Burns (piano), and Don Lamond (drums). The intended bassist, Chubby Jackson, failed to show, and no other bass player was present. Don Lamond was also hampered by not having a full kit on the session, but the music nevertheless has a freewheeling power and interest, despite the low fidelity. Four extended pieces were recorded, including a version of "Woodchopper's Holiday" that ran more than ten minutes long, a composition that Chaloff, Berman, and Burns would record again later that year for Dial Records with a different group.

For releasing this material on his Esoteric label in 1954, Newman brought in bassist Eddie Safranski to overdub appropriate bass lines and Lamond with a full kit to augment his drum part. Consequently the result is an engineered product rather than the more usual (for the time) unaltered product of the musicians' efforts. In the discography, the original Esoteric release titles, which Newman made up for the issue, are followed by the retitling of these pieces for the Onyx LP reissue. The session has also been reissued on CD by Cool & Blue.

It is notable that Serge should be in company with several then-current and future members of Woody Herman's band. While several of the musicians' solos tended to ramble, Serge was in good form, soloing with conviction on all four titles. His work shows stronger conception and maturity than one would imagine a pioneering twenty-two-year-old might have to offer at his first recorded jam session.

Serge was already with Jimmy Dorsey for their February 6, 1946, recording session for Decca. There were three commercially oriented vocal features for singer Dee Parker, and an instrumental version of "Perdido" which, being held to the three-minute 78 rpm record format, did not include the extended Chaloff solo heard on the broadcast version from the following September that has been issued on collectors' label albums. It has not been possible to review other surviving broadcast versions of "Perdido" to check for Chaloff solos.

Actually, Jimmy Dorsey's recordings issued on Decca were originally recorded for World Transcriptions, and most of that material was then released on Decca records, causing some confusion for discographers. This section of the discography was carefully checked by Rick Pauloski and Erik Raben, but some confusion still remains.

Although Jimmy Dorsey was a highly respected, influential, and dynamic hot soloist in jazz from the early 1920s, by the time he was making records under his own name in the late 1930s his band was predominantly commercially oriented, heavily featuring singers and novelty tunes. This was still the case while Serge was with the band. Good jazz performances occasionally emerged, however, especially from broadcasts.

The band went on tour soon after their February 6 record date. Documented engagements included:

February 11–13, 1946	Plymouth, Worcester, Massachusetts
February 14–17, 1946	Metropolitan, Providence, Rhode Island
March 3–12, 1946	Terrace, Newark, New Jersey
March 14–20, 1946	Adams, Newark, New Jersey
March 28–April 3, 1946	RKO, Boston, Massachusetts
April 4–13, 1946	Terrace Room, Newark, New Jersey

At the end of April, Serge was in Georgie Auld's sax section for another big band record date. Despite being named *Metronome*'s Band of the Year for 1945, Auld could not find work regularly and had disbanded in January 1946, reconvening for record dates and using whatever former sidemen were available, even though they may have been working for other leaders. Another session in mid-June turned out to be Serge's last record date with Georgie Auld, although he was part of Auld's small groups for much of 1947. It is worth noting that for both of these final big-band sessions, Auld hired Sarah Vaughan for his female vocalist.

No engagements for the Jimmy Dorsey band were traced for the interval between mid-April and the band's booking at Edgewater Beach, San Francisco for July 3–6, 1946. However, aircheks by the band, allegedly from New York and dated "June 1946," have been reported by discographers. Presumably, the band was either on tour or on vacation much of that spring.

In July 1946, Tommy and Jimmy Dorsey, in partnership with Harry James, purchased the Casino Gardens Ballroom in Ocean Park, California, on the edge of Santa Monica. For the entire month of August, the Jimmy Dorsey band was reportedly in residence at the Casino Gardens, presumably making the indicated broadcasts from that location.

During September 1946, both Tommy and Jimmy Dorsey and their bands were involved in making the film *The Fabulous Dorseys* (in which Serge can be glimpsed in Jimmy Dorsey's band during a brief sequence during which they play their theme song, "Contrasts," and back Helen O'Connell and Bob Eberly on "Green Eyes"). They were also performing from their Casino Gardens Ballroom. Jimmy's band was cited as appearing at the Casino Gardens from September 11 through 25.

Richard Chaloff recalled this period well:

> I had a convertible, a '39 Plymouth convertible, that I drove all the way out [to Hollywood] because my brother invited me to come out and meet all the people out there, and Borros Morros was still alive, the director who had befriended my mother during the silents. And I went out to meet Borros, he was working over at 20th Century Fox. They had set up some sets with Tommy and Jimmy playing together, the "life of the Dorseys." My brother was there and I had a chance to meet all of the people. They [the Dorseys] used to call me the "healthy Serge." I was always the big fat fellow. I was always 200, 250 pounds and my brother was always very slim. So they used to say, "Here comes the healthy one" because I'd show up, listen to them. I enjoyed it. I wish I had done more of it, but you never know what's going to happen in anyone's future, and I thought he [Serge] would go on and on, and I never realized his life would be so short. (Chaloff 1985)

Elaborating on Serge's physical description in private discussions, Richard stated:

> Serge was about 5'9" or 5'10" tall, and maintained a fairly stable weight of about 165 lbs. most of his life after he matured. Given his lifestyle, that's pretty amazing. He was usually in pretty good shape; he loved golf—he was very good—so he got fresh air and exercise that way. (Chaloff 1993–95)

Serge was in California with Jimmy Dorsey's band working on the movie and playing the Casino Gardens when the first studio record session offering him solo space was recorded by Ross Russell for Russell's Dial Records label in Los Angeles on September 21, 1946. At the Dial session, Serge again found himself in company with musicians associated with Woody Herman. The material has been issued under various leadership credit, including as the "Sonny Berman/Bill Harris Big 8" and "The Woodchoppers" (despite Herman's absence, due to the number of musicians then also part of Herman's small group of that name out of his so-called First Herd). The basic group was an octet consisting of Sonny Berman (trumpet), Bill Harris (trombone), Flip Phillips (tenor sax), Serge Chaloff (baritone sax), Ralph Burns (piano), Chuck Wayne (guitar), Artie Bernstein (bass), and Don Lamond (drums). Two takes each were issued of the three up-tempo pieces featuring Serge's powerful baritone solos: "Woodchopper's Holiday" and "Curbstone Scuffle" were with the octet, and variations on "Cherokee" (usually issued as "Blue Serge") were performed by Serge and the rhythm section only. There was also one take of the lovely ballad "Moon Burns" (also known as "Nocturne") by the octet, which included a short, sensitive Chaloff solo, and two takes of a number played by just Bill Harris and the rhythm section also recorded at that session. Retitling and strange reissuing made the session difficult to sort out until the complete Spotlite issue of the session appeared in the 1970s, as the various takes appeared on reissues on several labels, often retitled and without indicating which take was used.

Serge, missing the dating a bit, cited his debut recording for the *Encyclopedia of Jazz* (Serge Chaloff file) as, "1945—Dial Record—(Blue Serge—Dialogue)," which in fact was the earliest material to be released crediting Serge as leader (on some issues). This of course referred to the up-tempo version of "Cherokee" performed by just Serge and the rhythm section. Serge began improvising on the melody before it was more than hinted at, hence the retitling. One take fit the standard three-minute 78 rpm record format, and was issued with the title "The Mad Monk." Serge's solo was dynamic and interesting, followed by exchanges of eight-bar phrases, then four-bar phrases, with Burns' piano. The other take was double length, unusual for the time. Serge's long opening solo represented one of the highlights of his early features. He was followed on this take by a good guitar solo by Chuck Wayne. The second half of this performance, beginning with a longer piano solo from Ralph Burns, continued with exchanges between Serge and Burns, as with the earlier, shorter take. This half was originally issued as "Dialogue," and the full version, on LP issues, as "Blue Serge."

On these and the other performances from this session on which Serge also played memorable solos, the one flaw was the bass work. The veteran bassist Artie Bernstein, widely respected and prominent since the early 1930s, was either out of sorts or unable to adapt to the new style, and he played stiffly and uninterestingly throughout, almost destroying the pulse of the music on occasion. In Feather's interview (1950), Serge stated, "The bass player not only played in two, he played bad notes in two!" Feather went on to say of Chaloff:

. . . the recording gave a vivid idea of the extent to which he had absorbed Bird's modern conception, and adapted it to baritone. . . . By this time Serge's style was fully developed. He could get around on the horn at any tempo, played changes with incredible agility both of mind and of fingers, and generally was equipped to astonish anyone who thought the baritone was too cumbersome to be worth developing to this point.

Although Serge was not featured on any of the commercial records he made with Jimmy Dorsey's big band, at least one aircheck—the version of "Perdido" broadcast on September 25, 1946, from the Casino Gardens—his long opening solo revealed his style well. This is obviously the best documentation of his work with Dorsey.

Shortly after, the band left the Casino Gardens to go on tour again. On September 27, 1946, the Dorsey band moved to the Plantation in Dallas, closing on October 8. They were at the Plantation in Houston from October 10 through 19, then moved into the Chase Hotel in St. Louis, Missouri, from October 25 through November 7. The last known engagement for Chaloff with Dorsey was at the Meadowbrook Ballroom in Cedar Grove, New Jersey, from November 19 through December 9, 1946.

Evidently Serge got some time at home between the Chase Hotel and Meadowbrook Ballroom engagements, or he made a trip home during the Meadowbrook gig, or else the date of the private recordings of him duetting with pianist Rollins Griffith, which were recorded at the Chaloff home by Richard Chaloff, was off by a few weeks. Griffith, who became a prominent educator, was later recognized as the first black school superintendent in the Boston area. He attended the New England Conservatory of Music and eventually held two Master's degrees, but did not pursue a musical career, although in the late 1940s he performed in Boston nightclubs and recordings exist of his accompanying Charlie Parker at a gig at the Hi-Hat. These four titles with Serge, allegedly recorded in November 1946, possibly after a music lesson with Madame Chaloff, were released on an Uptown CD in 1994 (see discography). Both men acquit themselves well, although this was obviously an informal jam session.

The Herbie Fields big band record dates on December 11–12, 1946, again offered Serge no solo space. This was apparently just a studio pickup date, and not a working unit. Shortly afterwards, Serge rejoined Georgie Auld, this time in a sextet format.

On January 16, 1947, Serge was participating in a jam session which included trumpeter Sonny Berman, with whom he went off to have a heroin fix. The unevenness of the drugs caused Berman to inadvertently overdose, and he died, officially, of a heart attack. Richard Chaloff discussed this incident briefly, while mentioning Serge's problems with drugs, in a 1993 conversation:

I remember Serge coming home right after that, that night. He was white as a sheet. His friend Sonny Berman had died literally right in his arms from an overdose. Serge was really shaken. (Chaloff 1993–95)

Richard commented on Serge's efforts to kick the habit:

You know, this drug business is terrible. It is a sickness that once it grabs you and you go too far, you know, you can say you can kick it but you can't. When you start to ache all over, and start to sweat, and the DT's come and everything goes, the whole place goes with you. You need it so bad that you'll do anything, according to him. In fact, he used to cry when he came back. He said, "Dick, help me get through it." I took him to a private hospital out in West Roxbury, a private hospital. We took him in one Saturday night. He went right through the window. Saturday night they lost him. They looked for him, the windows were open, all we saw was the pillows puffed up in the bed. (Chaloff 1985)

Richard continued in private conversation,

He tried several times to kick it. He'd come home and ask for help, then jump out and go running off to find a fix. Once I chased him across the yard and tackled him to hold him back. But you couldn't stop him when he went after it. (Chaloff 1993–95)

Georgie Auld began the year 1947 with a sextet that included Red Rodney (trumpet), Serge Chaloff (baritone sax), George Wallington (piano), Curley Russell (bass), and Tiny Kahn (drums). Auld played soprano and alto sax as well as the tenor sax with which he is usually identified; he even sang on occasion, providing the group with a varied palette of tonalities.

On January 29, 1947, four members of this group participated in a record date under Red Rodney's leadership for Keynote, with Allan Eager's Lester Young-styled tenor replacing Auld, Al Haig instead of Wallington on piano, and Chubby Jackson replacing Russell on bass. They did four tunes: "All God's Children Got Rhythm," "Elevation," "Fine and Dandy," and "The Goof and I," with alternate takes of all but "Elevation" also eventually becoming available in the Japanese *Complete Keynote Collection* boxed set on the Nippon Records label. Chaloff soloed well on all seven performances, as did Eager, and the group sparkled with energy. The two standards were up-tempo, with "Fine and Dandy" taken at breakneck speed. Rodney occasionally seemed to depend on bop cliches, a minor problem not as noticeable on Al Cohn's "The Goof and I" (to which Serge would return) and Gerry Mulligan's "Elevation."

Later that winter, Town Hall in New York City held a Saturday midnight concert headlined "Great Names in Modern Jazz: Harris, Rodney,

Chaloff, Lambert, Stewart, Ventura, Tristano, Leighton, Cole, Thomas and Marie Bryant" promoted by Harry Lim of Keynote Records. It is of interest that already in early 1947 it seemed sufficient to advertise such an event using only the last names of these figures. Dave Lambert, Buddy Stewart, and Marie Bryant were vocalists; Lennie Tristano and Bernie Leighton, pianists; Joe Thomas and Red Rodney, trumpet stars; Bill Harris a trombonist; Charlie Ventura a multireed player; and Cozy Cole a drummer. Unfortunately the *Down Beat* review devotes more space to discussing the audience and the way the concert was run, rather than who played what with whom. The reviewer noted:

> At no time did any group know in front what tunes it was going to play; throughout 80 percent of the evening bass men were fumbling for changes on unfamiliar tunes. . . .
> The crowd and musicians both showed considerable bewilderment at the entire proceedings. Despite this, Serge Chaloff, playing baritone with the Rodney beboppers, came out with more of his extraordinarily facile jazz.

Around this same time, Savoy Records, like Keynote an independent label devoted to providing recordings of less commercial jazz and documenting the new music, provided Serge with his first record date as leader on March 5, 1947. This time the working group of the Georgie Auld Sextet was intact except for trombonist Earl Swope replacing Auld, and the band sounds even tighter and more inspired than on Rodney's Keynote session. Three of the titles were Serge's compositions: "Pumpernickel," "Serge's Urge," and "A Bar a Second." Drummer Tiny Kahn contributed "Gabardine and Serge." All four titles had fairly uptempo, typical late-1940s bebop lines. With all titles from this session, the originally issued take consistently seemed to be conceptually tighter, with a slight extra confidence. Mosaic Records was assured by the company leasing the masters that only the two takes of each performance as issued by Savoy existed, but additional takes of three of the numbers later turned up (see discography).

"Pumpernickel" was a thirty-two-bar AABA-form composition. It opened with an eight-bar introduction from George Wallington on piano, followed by the ensemble playing the head. Serge was in good form for two full choruses before Red Rodney and Earl Swope split a chorus, Swope taking over on the bridge for the last half. The ensemble then closed with the first half of the head. The earlier, so far unissued two takes included ensemble riffing behind the second chorus of Serge's solo. Although this sounded effective, it was dispensed with in the two released takes. A "take 3" was a false start of only a few seconds' duration.

Tiny Kahn's "Gabardine and Serge" was a twelve-bar blues tune, again opening with an eight-bar piano introduction, followed by an ensemble reading of the head through twice. Swope and Rodney then each took two choruses, and Chaloff four choruses, before a one-chorus ensemble reading of the head took it out. The first take was a breakdown, although most of the performance was completed.

"Serge's Urge" was taken fast. It opened immediately with the ensemble stating a sixteen-bar line with slight alterations the second time through. Chaloff soloed first with two full thirty-two-bar choruses, followed by a chorus from Rodney and sixteen bars each from Swope and Wallington. The ensemble then took it out with the sixteen bars of the second half of the head. The "take 1" acetate has been lost.

"A Bar a Second" was another twelve-bar blues composition, with a hint of its tempo in the title. It opened with an unaccompanied four-bar cadenza from Serge. After the ensemble played the head twice, Serge took three choruses. Three of the four takes then featured two choruses each from Rodney and Swope before the final twelve bars from the ensemble. In the last take, Swope had an extra chorus in his solo spot. The first take began abruptly midway through Serge's solo on circulating dubs.

According to Mark Gardner, who wrote the liner notes to the two-LP anthology album *The Brothers and Other Mothers* (Savoy SJL 2210), which devoted one side of an LP to reissuing all four titles and an alternate take of each, "The leader was in exceptional form, playing with commendable agility and inspiration" (Herman and Troup 1990, 81). This record date was unquestionably the highlight of Serge's pre-Second Herd recordings, both in the quality of the music and in the number of takes of each title available for comparison, not to mention the three original compositions by Serge adding insight into this dimension of his musical persona.

Auld took his group into New York on March 14, 1947, for a two-week gig. According to Feather (1950), Serge caused a sensation while appearing with Auld at the 3 Deuces, a 52nd Street club with a jazz-oriented clientele. Boris Rose issued material on one of his collectors' labels from an aircheck of their opening night, which he personally dubbed off the air, thus providing the only documentation of this Georgie Auld group to have surfaced. Rose noted the irony of Serge's being unaccountably absent from the group on that evening, at least for the broadcast.

By then, Serge was acquiring enough of a reputation to be featured in a "Battle of the Baritone Sax" with Leo Parker at one of promoter Johnny Jackson's "Blue Monday Jazz Concerts" at Small's Paradise, a Harlem nightclub at 7th Avenue and 135th Street, on Monday, April 14, 1947. Parker was billed as "baritone sax now with Illinois Jacquet's band" and Chaloff as "baritone sax with Georgie Auld's band." The rest of the group was listed as Miles Davis (trumpet), Steve Pullman (trombone), Hal Singer (tenor sax), Earnie [sic] Washington (piano), Jimmy Butts (bass), and Art Blakey (drums). As if this were not enough, the ad also noted:

> Extra Added Attraction: ROBERT HARVELL and His Trio—
> He Sings Like King Cole

Unfortunately, neither a review nor any private or aircheck recordings have surfaced from this event. Leo Parker (1925–62) was the only serious challenger to the claim that Serge was the first prominent bop soloist to emerge on baritone sax, and ironically his career pattern and lifestyle paralleled Serge's to a degree. Both worked as sidemen in prominent big bands that were defining the bop style as it emerged, but without getting solo space on record. Both began recording impressive solos, both as sidemen and under their own names, by 1946–47, attracting much attention and respect. Sadly, both also developed heroin habits contributing to their dropping out of sight during much of the 1950s, and died in their thirties while making promising comebacks (see appendix).

Auld continued to tour with the sextet, moving on to The Continental in Milwaukee, Wisconsin, from mid-April into May, and the Jumptown in Chicago from June 3 into July. That month, Auld expanded the sextet to a nonet, adding a trombone and two additional saxophonists. The August 13, 1947, *Down Beat* contained an article about the expansion, saying:

> It's a ballad heavy, sweeter band for Georgie Auld, according to the tenor man's rehearsal plans. At press time, Georgie was talking about the prettier things of life to Red Rodney, trumpet; Gene Roland, trombone; Gene Zanoni, alto and flute; Al Young, tenor; Serge Chaloff, baritone; Tiny Kahn, drums; Jimmy Johnston, bass; and Harvey Leonard, piano.
>
> The nucleus of what Auld terms his "hotel band" is the jazz sextet he recently had on tour. If the customers want it, Georgie intends to use the inner unit for bop sessions.
>
> The band, using almost as many arrangers as side men, will count most heavily on Gerry Mulligan for paper work, with Tadd Dameron contributing specials and George Handy some production numbers. Johnny Richards has written the band's new theme. (Auld Sets 1947)

This band actually opened at the Troubador in New York, just down 52nd Street from the 3 Deuces, in late July. An excellent photo of this group on the bandstand appeared in the book *Black Beauty, White Heat.*

According to the Feather article, they were still playing at the Troubador in September 1947, when Serge got a call to join Woody Herman's new band on the West Coast. Of course, Serge was happy to be joining a band that contained so many musicians he admired and with whom he had been associated.

With the Second Herd

Serge Chaloff spent a little over two years with Woody Herman's Second Herd, from the beginning of rehearsals in September 1947 to the band's last one-nighter on December 4, 1949. Treichel listed the Second Herd personnel as it went into rehearsal in September 1947 as follows:

> Woody Herman(cl,as,v), Stan Fishelson, Bernie Glow, Irv "Marky" Markowitz, Shorty Rogers, Ernie Royal(tp), Earl Swope, Ollie Wilson(tb), Bob Swift(btb), Sam Marowitz(as), Herbie Steward(as,ts), Stan Getz, Zoot Sims(ts), Serge Chaloff(bar), Fred Otis(p), Gene Sargent(g), Walt Yoder(b), Don Lamond(d), Jerri Ney(v,p,vbs). (Treichel 1978, 4)

The band's first public performance was a one-nighter on October 16, 1947, at the Municipal Auditorium in San Bernadino, California. One-nighters in San Diego and Long Beach followed on the next two nights before the band's first recording session for Columbia in Los Angeles on October 19. This record date produced two "novelty" vocals by Herman and no solo features for Chaloff aside from a brief break on the offensive "I Told Ya I Love Ya (Now Get Out)," one of the least "politically correct" sets of lyrics the Second Herd would record.

More one-nighters followed, including Bakersville on the 22nd and Watsonville on the 23rd. On October 28, the band performed at the Edgewater Beach Ballroom in San Francisco, and the following night at The Havana in Oakland, across the bay. Treichel noted:

> The Herd's engagements in the Bay area produced its first review in the national trade press, written by Ralph Gleason in *Down Beat*. Gleason compared the new Herd unfavorably with the current Kenton outfit, which was the popular jazz big band of the day, and, inevitably, with the First Herd.
>
> Considering that the band had only been playing publicly for two weeks, Gleason's criticisms did not have to be taken too seriously. The problem of comparison, however, was not one which was going to disappear, at least not until the new Herd produced a body of identifiably new music. . . . It was here that the inspired contributions of Chaloff, Royal, and Lamond made the difference.
>
> More ominous for the future than Gleason's comments was his report that the crowds were not turning out for Herman like they used to. Bad reviews one can overcome if they don't become a habit, but the shortage of paying customers is a terminal condition. Just at this time *Billboard* in a story headlined "Band Biz One-Niter Blues," was reporting that the major big bands were now obliged to take cuts in pay for one-nighters. . . . Herman's price was not reported, but it was probably in the $1,000–$1,200

range. Out of that princely sum had to come the band's costs, i.e., pay for eighteen musicians, travel expenses, agents' fee, all of which presumably had gone up. Higher costs and lower pay—not an encouraging prospect. One sees clearly the financial advantage of having a band full of unknowns, as Woody did. (Treichel 1978, 4–5)

In early November the band played Reno, Nevada, and toured the northwestern states. Their first extended engagement was at the Coconut Grove in Salt Lake City, from November 17 through December 7. They then opened at the Tune Town Ballroom in St. Louis, Missouri, on December 9, closing on the 17th. Despite earlier discographers' citing an early December aircheck by the band, Treichel noted this listing was spurious. (1978, 5)

More one-nighters followed, in Chicago on the 18th and at George Devine's Million Dollar Ballroom in Milwaukee, Wisconsin, on the 19th. Treichel reported that Ted Hallock authored a rave review for *Down Beat*, including photos from the Milwaukee gig; Royal, Chaloff, and Lamond were singled out as outstanding.

On December 22, the band was back in Los Angeles for another Columbia recording session. The infamous 1948 recording ban was scheduled to go into effect on December 31, and the Second Herd was in the studios on five separate occasions in the time remaining as Columbia tried to stockpile material for future releases.

On the 22nd, they recorded four titles, two of them again with vocals by Herman. These were the sluggish "Cherokee Canyon" (not released until later, on a 10″ LP), and "I've Got News for You" (another characteristic Herman novelty vocal). The instrumentals were the bombastic "Sabre Dance" (what would later be termed a Third Stream type of arrangement by Ralph Burns of Aram Khachaturian's famous composition) and a swinging jazz item, "Keen and Peachy" (based on the chords of "Fine and Dandy" and affording Serge his first real solo opportunity on record with the Second Herd).

The December 24 session produced another of the band's classic jazz performances in "The Goof and I" (the Al Cohn item on which Serge had already recorded memorable solos at the Red Rodney Keynote date the preceding January, and which again afforded him noteworthy solo space). The other number recorded that day was another of Woody's ballad vocal features, "Lazy Lullaby" (again not released at the time and only appearing later on LP). Treichel (1978, 8) noted that on this and other ballads, the sax section could be heard doubling clarinets, with Chaloff on bass clarinet, for ensemble textures.

December 27, 1947, produced the band's classic "Four Brothers" record which served to define their identity and has remained one of the enduring items in big band repertoires ever since. Based on the chords of "Jeepers Creepers," it was another swinging jazz chart arranged by Jimmy Giuffre (who would join the Second Herd a few months later) and again included a noteworthy Chaloff solo. Its session mate was the famed "Summer Sequence pt. 4" with its composer/arranger Ralph Burns replacing Otis on piano. (The First Herd had recorded parts 1–3, and Burns extended the composition with this fourth movement.) As Treichel (1978, 9) noted, the voicing near the end of "Summer Sequence pt. 4" and Stan Getz's tenor solo both prefigured the famed version of "Early Autumn" recorded a year later.

The December 30 session was devoted to vocals by Woody and Mary Ann McCall, with Serge featured only for a short break on one of the novelty vocals by Herman, the offensive "My Pal Gonzales." The silly "Baby I Need You" remains unissued, but several broadcast versions indicate that's just as well. "Take a Little Time to Smile" from the 31st also remains unissued, and no other versions have surfaced by which to judge its likely quality. Discographies have indicated there were other tracks alleged to have been recorded by the Second Herd on that session, but they were spurious attributions, actually being by Les Brown and his Orchestra.

Despite Mary Ann McCall being with the band for their Columbia record date on December 30, the Second Herd began 1948 with singer Terry Swope along on their touring schedule. Jimmy Raney also replaced Gene Sargeant on guitar. On January 1, 1948, the band opened at the Edgewater Beach Ballroom in San Francisco, closing on the 4th. In mid-January the band went to Salt Lake City, where Al Cohn replaced Herb Steward in the sax section. According to Treichel (1978, 13), it was not until this phase that the "four brothers" sound in the sax section (three tenors and baritone) became fully established as a characteristic of the band's music. Steward had doubled on alto for conventional scoring and played tenor for the charts utilizing that lineup, but with Cohn's replacing him, the four brothers sax section became the Second Herd's trademark. Since the Columbia record of "Four Brothers" was issued after Cohn had joined and he was visible soloing with the band in their first film short made February 2, 1948, the usual perception of the four brothers band has been that the original tenor team was Al, Zoot, and Stan. This is particularly ironic as Al Cohn never made a record date with the band due to the recording ban. Of course, he is wonderfully in evidence on many broadcasts.

The film short made on February 2, 1948, was for Universal-International. It was titled *Woody Herman and His Orchestra* and directed by Will Cowan. For this film, the vocal group The Modernaires was also featured for two numbers with the band, as well as the dance team of Don & Beverly for another two performances. Of course, in stage shows, the big bands all backed other acts, including dance teams, much as this film short documents. Nevertheless, viewing this film short, it is astounding to contemplate the high-powered talent of the Second Herd reduced to the trivia of backing such acts, especially considering their material. Don & Beverly were a sort of weak imitation of Fred Astaire and Ginger Rogers, while the Modernaires, despite the presence of Paula Kelly (who was a very good singer), presented painfully silly pop material. Adding to the triviality of this document, the Second Herd's only band features were the bombastic "Sabre Dance," a version of "Caledonia" (Woody's rather silly novelty vocal hit with the First Herd), and finally (and at last) a shortened version of one of their better jazz numbers, "Northwest Passage," unfortunately with drastically reduced solo opportunities. Serge was only featured for a four-bar break in the latter title, in contrast to the extended solos of broadcast versions of this piece. One astute observer commented sadly, "If they had to do this sort of thing a lot, it's no wonder so many of the guys in the band were junkies."

On February 3, 1948, the Second Herd opened at the Hollywood Palladium in Los Angeles. Billed as "the dining, dancing and entertainment capital of the West," the Palladium was a major band location with a radio wire. The band was booked in for six weeks.

Treichel (1978, 14) noted the value of the airchecks made by the band from this location as providing "a glimpse of the band on the job, in many cases playing material which it never recorded." He cited three categories of material preserved on the band's airchecks that were of special interest:

- Second Herd renditions of tunes identified with the First Herd.
- Versions of jazz originals that were never recorded by the band in the studios.
- "The numerous excellent vocals of Mary Ann McCall."

In addition, of course, there were renditions of tunes that the Second Herd *did* record in the studios. These performances provided fresh interpretations, with the extra edge of excitement that live performances usually generate. However, all of the known broadcasts of the Second Herd from the Hollywood Palladium originated as Armed Forces Radio Service "One Night Stand" shows. Treichel (1978, 18) warned that the Armed Forces Radio Service would sometimes dub recordings of performances by the band from earlier transcriptions onto later broadcasts, so that the discography may include repeated performances in a few cases. Where this practice could be identified, the information has been noted in the discography.

The Second Herd left the Hollywood Palladium on March 15 to tour. They also left bassist Walt Yoder, who was replaced by Harry Babasin.

The band's next extended location engagement was in the Century Room of the Hotel Commodore in New York City for a month. Again, they had a radio wire and again the surviving dubs were from AFRS "One Night Stand" shows. *Down Beat* heralded "Woody Herman returned to Gotham in a blaze of glory." Several photos of the band from that location have been published, and some eventually appeared on collectors' edition LP issues of broadcast material by the band, as well as in books on jazz.

Closing at the Century Room on May 17, the band opened on the 20th for a month at New York's Capitol Theatre, where Ralph Burns replaced Fred Otis on piano. The usual theater show routine had the band playing four shows daily and five shows on Saturdays. The movie was *The Bride Goes Wild* and the band shared the bill with comedian Jean Carroll, bird-call specialist Fred Lowrey, dance routines from Hal Leroy, and a special cowboy number by Dorothy Rae. A reviewer for *Billboard* noted that for "Sabre Dance" the band waved cardboard knives at the beginning of the number and concluded with the knives buried in each others' backs. Apparently, the band's theater shows were on the same level of sophistication as their February video.

The band closed at the Capitol Theatre on June 17. Their next location engagement was a week at the Click Club in Philadelphia, from June 28 through July 4. Another "One Night Stand" broadcast documented their stay there, but the AFRS tagged onto the show two numbers that had originated from the May 12 broadcast at the Century Room.

The band was on tour for July, including a mid-month engagement at the Eastwood Gardens in Detroit. In this period, Chubby Jackson replaced Harry Babasin on bass. Treichel (1978, 23) credits Jackson with being the catalyst for orienting the band more completely towards bop. Trombonist Bill Harris also joined the Second Herd at this point.

From July 28 through August 7, 1948, the Second Herd was in the Asbury Park, New Jersey Convention Hall, then moved into the Steel Pier in Atlantic City from August 8 through 14. Their opening night at the Steel Pier was documented by another AFRS "One Night Stand" broadcast. A Harrisburg radio station provided another broadcast on August 26, from Hershey Park Ballroom in Hershey, Pennsylvania. During this broadcast, Herman was interviewed and stated that he would be returning to California the next day for six days, before opening in Youngstown, Ohio, for a three-day engagement. However, when they opened at the Palace Theatre in Youngstown on September 2 it was for a run of three weeks. By then, Terry Gibbs had joined the group on vibes. Gibbs had been a member of Chubby Jackson's group when it toured Sweden the year before and had then been with Buddy Rich.

Closing on the 22nd, the band next moved into the Orpheum Theatre in Omaha, Nebraska, for a week, opening September 24 and closing on the 30th. Around this time Ralph Burns left the band and was replaced by Lou Levy.

After the Second Herd played at the Riverside Theatre in Milwaukee, Wisconsin, October 7–13, they continued touring, including a one-nighter in Buffalo, New York, on the 20th. The band opened at the Royal Roost in New York City for another extended engagement, beginning October 24, 1948. The Royal Roost was "no ordinary jazz joint," as Treichel put it:

> If you had walked down Broadway in 1948 on the block between 47th and 48th Streets, you would have come upon a restaurant specializing in chicken and named, with more imagination than many of today's eateries, the "Royal Roost." . . . The chicken was supposed to be pretty good, but that was not the important story about the place. If you went into the Roost in the late night hours, they might sell you some chicken if the kitchen was open and you tramped on them hard enough. But in the dark night time hours this innocuous poultry parlor became the mecca of modern jazz. Virtually every big name in bebop came to play there and had been in before the Herd. In September Miles Davis and his "cool" nonet, sharing the bill with Charlie Parker, could be heard and they were followed by Dizzy's powerhouse [sic]. Tadd Dameron had the house band with people like Fats Navarro, Allan Eager, and Kenny Clarke. The *house* band. This was no place for trivial sounds. (1978, 24–25)

Treichel also listed the band's personnel for the opening:

> Woody Herman(cl,as,v), Stan Fishelson, Bernie Glow, Marky Markowitz, Shorty Rogers, Ernie Royal(tp), Bill Harris, Earl Swope, Ollie Wilson(tb), Bob Swift(btb), Sam Marowitz(as), Al Cohn, Stan Getz, Zoot Sims(ts), Serge Chaloff(bar), Terry Gibbs(vbs), Lou Levy(p), Chubby Jackson(b), Don Lamond(d), Mary Ann McCall(v).

Shortly after their opening, Red Rodney replaced Markowitz on trumpet. Treichel also noted:

> The band's month-long stay at the Roost was both a turning point and a high point . . . the stronger bop influence, exemplified by Chubby and the men whom he had gotten into the band and the tunes which he brought in, was fully evident during the Roost engagement. (1978, 24)

The Second Herd was broadcasting on WMCA in New York with "Symphony Sid" Torin as announcer. There were also a few CBS broadcasts preserved from this period, bringing the total number of preserved airchecks from the Roost to nearly a dozen. Some nights there were two broadcasts, with the Second Herd making a token appearance on one show along with the Tadd Dameron group, and being exclusively featured throughout the other.

The band closed at the Royal Roost on November 24, 1948, and worked its way across the country again, opening at the Empire Room in Los Angeles on December 7. It was reported that the band would be broadcasting from the Empire Room six nights per week, but all that has surfaced from December 1948 has been a handful of AFRS "Just Jazz" programs. According to Treichel (1978, 29), the AFRS would dub the Empire Room broadcasts and rebroadcast them later along with material from other artists. One of these shows included the only known recording of the Second Herd performing Bud Powell's composition "Tempus Fugit" (which included a fine Chaloff solo).

At the end of December, the Second Herd celebrated the end of the 1948 recording ban by making a series of records for Capitol in Los Angeles. Chaloff had solos on "That's Right" (a reworking of "Boomsie," a Chubby Jackson tune the Second Herd had been performing), George Wallington's "Lemon Drop," and "Keeper of the Flame" (based on the chord structure of "I Found a New Baby"). They began 1949 with a New Year's double-broadcast from the Empire Room, carried live by CBS. The band closed at the Empire Room on January 3 and went on tour again, leaving behind Chubby Jackson, who had gotten married in Los Angeles and decided to stay. Jackson was temporarily replaced by bassist Jimmy Stutz before Oscar Pettiford joined the band.

Treichel reported that during early January the Second Herd became stranded by a blizzard in Salt Lake City, Utah, where Dizzy Gillespie's band was supposed to be playing at the Coconut Grove. However, Gillespie's band was stranded by the blizzard in Denver, so the Second Herd played the gig with Dizzy joining the band, playing in the section and soloing. (1978, 33)

From January 10 through 23, 1949, the Second Herd was at the Blue Note in Chicago. *Down Beat* reported "hordes of musicians and tradespeople" were at the Blue Note opening, and that the Second Herd put them "in a daze" (Treichel 1978, 33). The band then went on tour again:

January 27–30, 1949	Paramount Theatre, Toledo, Ohio
January 31–February 5	Music Bowl, Chicago, Illinois
February 6–12	Showboat, Milwaukee, Wisconsin
February 13	Mandel Hall, University of Chicago, Chicago, Illinois
February 14	Champaign Junior High School, Champaign, Illinois
February 15	University of Iowa, Iowa City, Iowa
February 16	Iowa State University Student Union, Ames, Iowa

February 17	Notre Dame, South Bend, Indiana
February 18	Kalamazoo, Michigan
February 20	Carnegie Hall, New York City
February 22	Syria Mosque, Pittsburgh, Pennsylvania
February 24	Uline Arena, Washington, D.C.
February 25	Town Hall, Philadelphia, Pennsylvania
February 26	Eddie Condon TV Show, New York City
February 27	Symphony Hall, Boston, Massachusetts
March 3–9	Hippodrome, Baltimore, Maryland
March 10–16	Click Club, Philadelphia, Pennsylvania
March 17–23	Adams Theatre, Newark, New Jersey
March 25–27	State Theatre, Hartford, Connecticut
March 31–April 6	Circle Theatre, Indianapolis, Indiana
April 7–13	National Theatre, Louisville, Kentucky

At around this time, Serge made three studio record dates away from the Second Herd. The first two of these sessions were led by Serge, and produced another five titles ranking among his best recordings from this era. The third and last was a Buddy DeFranco big band session, which contributed no Chaloff solos on the issued performances.

On March 10, 1949, on the same day as the Second Herd's Click Club opening in Philadelphia, Serge had a combo recording date as leader of a contingent of his colleagues from the Second Herd, plus Barbara Carroll on piano and Denzil Best on drums. This session was produced by Leonard Feather for the small, independent Futurama label. The recordings were released on that label for 78 rpm issues. They were later reissued on a 10″ LP on the Mercer label, and eventually on a 12″ LP on Prestige. For this date, Serge contributed only one composition, "Bopscotch," and did not feature himself as consistently as at earlier or later sessions.

"Chickasaw," by Terry Gibbs and Shorty Rogers, was another variation on "Cherokee." The staccato ensemble introduction led into a very fast reading of the AABA line by Serge over ensemble textures, with pianist Barbara Carroll taking the bridge. Chaloff and Gibbs then soloed for a full chorus each, both of them sounding jittery at the fast tempo. A brief ensemble punctuation led into eight bars from Swope's trombone before the last eight bars of the head were restated to take it out.

Serge's "Bopscotch" was another moderately fast thirty-two-bar AABA composition with some interesting twists to the arrangement. Gibbs's vibes led over the ensemble for a brief introduction. The ensemble had the "A" sections of the head with Serge soloing on the bridge. Serge also had the first solo, but after sixteen bars turned it over to Swope for the bridge and last eight bars of the chorus. Rodney then had a sixteen-bar trumpet solo, and Al Cohn's tenor sax finished that chorus. The fourth and final chorus opened with four-bar exchanges between the ensemble and Carroll's piano. Denzil Best was featured for an eight-bar drum solo on the bridge, and the ensemble finished the chorus, slowing down for the ending.

"The Most!" was again a thirty-two-bar AABA composition, this one by Al Cohn. The ensemble and a flurry from Pettiford's bass introduced a smooth, medium tempo ensemble line with Rodney taking the bridge. Cohn's Lester Young–inspired tenor then had a full chorus before the ensemble returned for a half-chorus of four-bar exchanges with Serge, who also took the bridge. The ensemble then took the last eight bars of the chorus to close.

Leonard Feather contributed "Chasin' the Bass," which was a feature for Oscar Pettiford and on which (curiously, as he was the leader) Serge did not solo. As expected from a musician of Pettiford's stature, his work on this blues track was outstanding.

The sound of the group made the date particularly interesting despite the relatively poor recording quality. With four horns and vibes, the arrangements had a lot of color, and the strong bass lines of Pettiford were a great asset. It was evident that Serge had developed conceptually in the two years since his last small group recordings as a leader. He stated in an interview with Nat Hentoff (1951) that "Chickasaw" and "Bopscotch" were his favorites among his early records.

Serge's second date as leader that season occurred in Boston, apparently on April 16, 1949. Serge led a group through two Ralph Burns arrangements for the two sides of a 78 rpm record.

However, Treichel cited the band at the Capitol Theatre in Washington, D.C., April 15–21 (1978, 36). Clearly, Chaloff could not have been in Boston rehearsing and recording at the same time he was playing in a theatre booking in Washington, D.C.; in fact Richard Paulosky has cited the band's stay at the Capitol Theatre as from April 21 through 27. These dates could represent a changed booking, leaving Serge time to get to Boston, rehearse and record, and return to Washington to rejoin the band. Unfortunately, the same logistical difficulty then exists with the Buddy DeFranco studio big band recording session, which has usually been dated as being held on April 23. According to Treichel's dating, the Second Herd was appearing at the Apollo Theatre in New York City April 23–27. Obviously, Serge would have had no problem recording with DeFranco's pickup band on the 23rd and making the Apollo opening in the same city that night. However, Paulosky listed the Apollo engagement as from April 29 through May 5, following the Capitol Theatre run. As the *New York Times* and *New Yorker* magazine failed to list the Apollo appearance during the interval concerned, confirming the exact dates of this engagement has not been possible.

There are still other reasons why the two titles by the Serge Chaloff–Ralph Burns Septet, made up of a pool of Boston musicians including the outstanding Charlie Mariano, have been an enigma. Recorded at Ace Studios for an obscure and short-lived Boston label called Motif, they were usually regarded as being done after Serge left the Second Herd and returned to Boston, presumably due to the well-rehearsed sound of the group and an added depth to Serge's own playing. However, the August 26, 1949, issue of *Down Beat* mentioned the release of these titles in its "Things To Come" column and cited a July 1949 recording date (a time when the Second Herd was in California). Nevertheless, when these previously very hard to find 78 rpm items were reissued on LP by Hep Records in the 1980s, they were dated April 16, 1949.

In any case, these titles turned out to be Serge's finest recordings of the 1940s. Mert Goodspeed (1991), the session's trombonist, noted in discussing this record, "We never saw the music before we arrived. There were no rehearsals. Done in one take. We just ran it down a couple of times, then recorded it."

"King Edward the Flatted Fifth" was a swinging, bouncy twelve-bar blues line, stated once by the ensemble before trombonist Mert Goodspeed took a chorus. After four bars from the ensemble, Goodspeed returned for the remaining eight bars of that chorus. Mariano followed with a thoughtful, Bird-like two choruses. Gait Preddy's trumpet was also featured for two choruses before Serge's two-chorus solo. Ralph Burns then took a two-chorus piano solo with ensemble backing during his second chorus, before the ensemble played the line once more to close the performance.

"Pat," a more intricate composition, provided the highlight among all Serge's early work in his expressive baritone statements. This track, far more than its session-mate, foreshadowed Serge's later work in subtlety and sophistication. A medium tempo thirty-two-bar AABA composition, it opened with an ensemble and piano interplay introduction. Serge then played the "A" sections of the theme over ensemble textures, with the ensemble taking over for the bridge. Serge then had a full-chorus solo, which seemed a clear advance over any of his earlier recordings. The third and final chorus featured the ensemble trading four-bar phrases with the trumpet, then the alto, and finally the piano on the bridge. The final eight bars returned to the dynamic "A" section of the head, with Serge playing a cadenza-like tag ending. Burns's arrangement also seemed particularly imaginative, providing another hint of things to come in Serge's later recordings in terms of style.

Following the Apollo Theatre booking, the Second Herd continued to tour. Personnel changes occurred intermittently, as shown in the discography.

On May 26 there was another Capitol record date, but no solo opportunities for Serge. On the 27th, the band opened at the Howard Theatre in Washington, D.C., for a week, closing on June 2. They were working their way west again, playing the Eastwood Gardens in Detroit during June 10–16 and the Regal Theatre in Chicago June 17–23.

The Second Herd opened at the Rendezvous Ballroom on Balboa Beach, California, on July 1, 1949. Treichel noted:

> During the week . . . the band rested (except for some record dates) and on weekends they regrouped for a series of five engagements at the Rendezvous. The Rendezvous was the site of a remarkable series of broadcasts for Mutual on Saturday afternoons, entitled "Excursions in Modern Music." These sessions were forty-five minutes long and provided an opportunity for the band to present its music to the nation which few bands ever enjoyed. And it made the most of it. . . . The general approach of the show was that the Herd's music was music of substance, to be taken seriously, but it was presented with a light touch and with humor. (1978, 37)

The Second Herd's July schedule was quite crowded despite only performing at the Rendezvous on weekends:

July 1   Rendezvous Ballroom opening
July 2   "Excursions" broadcast from Rendezvous
July 3   Rendezvous Ballroom
July 6   Universal International filming
July 8   Rendezvous Ballroom
July 9   "Excursions" broadcast from Rendezvous
July 10 Rendezvous Ballroom
July 14 Capitol record date
July 15 Rendezvous Ballroom
July 16 "Excursions" broadcast from Rendezvous
July 17 Rendezvous Ballroom
July 20 Capitol record date
July 22 Rendezvous Ballroom
July 23 "Excursions" broadcast from Rendezvous
July 24 Rendezvous Ballroom closing
July 26 Million Dollar Pier, Los Angeles
July 29 Shrine Auditorium concert, Los Angeles
July 30 "Excursions" broadcast from Rendezvous

Also on July 30, following their Saturday afternoon "Excursions" broadcast, the band traveled down the coast to Oceanside, California, for a one-nighter.

The July Universal International film short was no better than the band's first film short from February 1948. Titled *Herman's Herd*, it also featured a tap dancer; several "novelty" vocals by Woody, Mary

Ann McCall, the Mellow-Larks, and an uncredited female; and only one solo from Serge, the one on "Lollypop." However, the "Lollypop" solo was a good spot, with Serge in fine form and well photographed. As these film shorts were usually filmed one day and overdubbed the next for the sound track, the date in the list above (from discographer Ernie Edwards via Treichel) presumably refers to the audio portion. In keeping with the racist policies of the day, the black members of the band were not shown on-screen, although the full band participated in the audio recording.

The Capitol records only included two solo spots from Serge, a short exposure on "You Rascal You" and a fine solo on "Lollypop" (both recorded on July 20).

The "Excursions in Modern Music" broadcasts featured the band extensively, with at least one solo opportunity for Serge on each occasion. These broadcasts included another version of Serge's "Man Don't Be Ridiculous," which unfortunately was cut off before the ending. On the July 30 show, the Second Herd shared the program with Charlie Barnet's band, which took over for August. Their final number joined both bands, in the manner of the "Brotherly Jump" numbers with the Dorseys from three years earlier, for a version of "Ornithology" (unaccountably announced as "How High the Moon" and usually listed as "More Moon"). The entire July 30 broadcast was issued on the Joyce collectors' label in the 1970s.

Another July broadcast, from the Shrine Auditorium concert on the 29th, survived as an AFRS "Just Jazz" show. This was the first of a series of teamings of the Second Herd and the Nat "King" Cole Trio, who shared the billing and broadcast time. Again, there was some merging of the two featured groups for special numbers. The groups were also on the same bill on August 2 for a one-nighter in San Diego.

The band moved up to San Francisco for a one-nighter at the War Memorial Opera House on August 7, sharing the stage with the Nat "King" Cole Trio again. The next night was another one-nighter across the bay in Oakland's Auditorium Theater. On August 10, 1949, the Second Herd and the Nat "King" Cole Trio began a run at the Shrine Auditorium in Los Angeles that lasted until the 28th and resulted in several more AFRS "Just Jazz" broadcasts. After a one-nighter in Portland, Oregon, the band played at Lakeside Park in Denver, Colorado, from August 30 through September 1. Their next long engagement was at the Blue Note in Chicago from September 5 through 18. More one-nighters followed:

September 20	Prom Ballroom, St. Paul, Minnesota
September 21	Terp Ballroom, Austin, Minnesota
September 22	Surf, Clear Lake, Iowa

September 23	Turnpike, Lincoln, Nebraska
September 24	Frog Hop, St. Joseph, Missouri
September 25	Tomba, Sioux City, Iowa
September 26	Legion Pavilion, Breckenridge, Minnesota
September 27	Arkota, Sioux Falls, South Dakota
September 28	Tromar Ballroom, Des Moines, Iowa
September 29	Armar Ballroom, Marion, Iowa
September 30	State College, Normal, Illinois
October 1	White City Park, Herron, Illinois
October 5	Rialto Theatre, Joliet, Illinois
October 6	Palace Theatre, South Bend, Indiana
October 7	Pavilion, Freeport, Michigan
October 8–9	Flint, Michigan

Their next lengthy stay was at the Paramount Theater in New York City, October 18–26. They went into Bop City in New York on the 28th, closing on November 16. During the Bop City engagement, the Second Herd also played Carnegie Hall on November 4, with the following personnel:

Woody Herman(cl,as,v), Ed Badgley, Buddy Childers, Stan Fishelson, Shorty Rogers, Charlie Walp(tp), Bill Harris, Earl Swope, Ollie Wilson(tb), Sam Marowitz(as), Jimmy Giuffre, Don Lanphere, Buddy Savitt(ts), Serge Chaloff(bar), Lou Levy(p), Mert Oliver(b), Shelly Manne(d), Mary Ann McCall(v).

Nat "King" Cole and his trio were also on the program. According to Treichel, the band played an hour of their usual material, no new music. The band reportedly sounded good, and the concert drew well. Unfortunately, it does not seem to have been recorded.

The band continued on the road following their Bop City closing, beginning with a one-nighter on November 18 at either Iowa State University in Ames, Iowa, or the University of Iowa in Iowa City (sources confuse the two, attributing each to the other location). Their next documented date was at Kiel Auditorium in St. Louis, Missouri, on November 27. They also were reported at Oklahoma A&M College in Stillwater, Oklahoma, on November 30 and in Kansas City, Missouri, on December 2. Their final gig before disbanding was at the Municipal Auditorium in Oklahoma City on December 4, 1949.

Woody Herman then took a small group out of the band to Havana, Cuba, for a month's engagement at the Tropicana, but Serge was not part of this group. The Second Herd had passed into history.

Chaloff and the Second Herd

Throughout this period, Serge's drug habit dominated his extramusical life, and his chaotic personal behavior infuriated Herman. The Second Herd was plagued with heroin addicts, but Serge apparently was going through a period of flamboyant excess. There are stories of Serge making connections and distributing drugs to other band members behind a blanket drawn up in the band bus, yet attempting to deny his habit to Herman's face. Richard Chaloff described Serge's explanation of the Second Herd's drug use:

> The trouble was, I think, the way he explained it to me, they went from one top concert—important concert, in those days, and they were extremely dedicated to make a real good showing. They were trying to get onto the *Down Beat* poll, who's the best. There was a competition among the men. They were winning the poll, it was a big thing years ago and every one of those men were on edge to play the best. And they would go two, three, five hundred miles from one gig to the next. And they would arrive shot to blazes, and as my brother said, "We have to play, we have to stand up and do it. And when you're really dragging, you can't even lift up your arms," he said, "some of the men would say, 'Try this.' " You know, a joint, a little marijuana, or this, and the band was trying everything. Woody knew it, he knew he had a sick band. But the men were so marvelous, that even with the heroin problem, they played marvelous too. Of course, they thought they were even better when they were on drugs. But they were so good that even with the drug problem, they played marvelous. (Chaloff 1985)

In some broadcast announcements, Herman seems to be needling Serge when mentioning him, apparently snidely, to the announcer as being among the soloists on an upcoming number, either by referring to him as "our *poll* winner" (emphasis Herman's) or by pronouncing his name the way Sergei Rachmaninoff's was pronounced, as "*Sir Gay* Chaloff" instead of as "Serge" (emphasis Herman's). In fact, Richard Chaloff has noted,

> Given our parents' orientation, it's not surprising that Serge and I were both named after prominent composers, myself after Richard Wagner and Serge after Sergei Rachmaninoff. (Chaloff 1993–95)

In fact, Serge was causing Herman many problems. One story reported that Serge once riddled his hotel room door with bullets (he carried a revolver for a while around this time). When Serge was confronted with the damage report, he indignantly pointed out that he was a jazz poll winner. When he had to pay anyway, he insisted on taking the door with him. Eventually, fearing that Herman was going to fire him, he threw the baritone sax music into a river (he had it memorized anyway), so that Herman would have to keep him at least until the parts were recopied. Herman told a story in his autobiography about being so angry with Serge one evening in a crowded bar, he was left speechless, and in total frustration peed down Serge's leg (Herman and Troup 1990, 81). While this incident may reveal more about Herman's character than Serge's, the fact remains that between the Second Herd's first record date for Columbia in October 1947 and their last broadcast known to collectors in late August 1949, their association produced hundreds of exciting performances preserved from broadcasts and their few record dates for Columbia and Capitol.

The recording ban prevented commercial record dates for most of 1948, but the broadcasts provided ample documentation with the extra excitement present in "live" recordings. The band made fifteen recordings for Columbia in late 1947, some still unissued. Serge only had solo space on five of the titles released:

> "I Told Ya I Love Ya"
> "Keen and Peachy"
> "The Goof and I"
> "Four Brothers"
> "My Pal Gonzales"

The first and last offered only short breaks within Herman's novelty vocals, but the others were three of the band's classic performances. Similarly, of the nineteen titles for Capitol, beginning almost exactly a year after the Columbia sessions ended, Serge was featured on five titles of those released:

> "That's Right"
> "Lemon Drop"
> "Keeper of the Flame"
> "Lollypop"
> "You Rascal You"

"That's Right" and "Keeper of the Flame" were two of the band's classic items, but the others were again novelty vocals. However, these ten titles were less than half of the titles that featured Serge in the band's repertoire preserved from their broadcasts.

While the Chaloff fan is not necessarily a Second Herd collector, attention to his solos on available issues of broadcasts would reveal

Serge improvising with consistent fire and imagination. Additional information may vary this list considerably, but available data indicated Serge's features were the following:

"Apple Honey"	"Man Don't Be Ridiculous"
"Berled in Erl"	"My Fair Lady"
"Boomsie"	"My Pal Gonzales"
"Fan It"	"Non-Alcoholic"
"Four Brothers"	"Northwest Passage"
"Godchild"	"Summer Sequence"
"Half Past Jumping Time"	"Tempus Fugit"
"I Told Ya I Love Ya"	"That's Right"
"Keen and Peachy"	"The Goof and I"
"Keeper of the Flame"	"The Happy Song"
"Lemon Drop"	"We the People Bop"
"Lollypop"	"Wild Root"
"Lullaby in Rhythm"	"You Rascal You"

These twenty-six titles out of 110 from the band's book making up their discography represented a slightly lower percentage of titles featuring Serge in total, compared to the percentages of the commercial records released. Unfortunately, while around 400 performances were listed, it is not known how many may have been repeats (see notes), and there may be other broadcasts not listed that included additional titles. While many pieces were consistently rendered, others exhibited considerable variety in soloist, solo length, etc. Serge's feature number, "Man Don't Be Ridiculous," and some of those that featured him extensively (e.g., "Boomsie") offered another category of appreciation of his work with the Second Herd, relative to the impression given by the short spots in novelty vocals like "My Pal Gonzales" or "I Told Ya I Love Ya" (which only had brief breaks).

Concerning videos featuring the Second Herd, Treichel listed only the two film shorts of February 2, 1948, and July 6, 1949, plus the Eddie Condon TV show which reportedly survived from February 26, 1949.

By this time, Serge had begun winning polls in the music magazines as top baritone saxophonist. As early as 1946 he was coming in third, after the previous unquestioned master, Harry Carney of Duke Ellington's Orchestra, and Ernie Caceres, who had been appearing in a variety of contexts performing in an older style. Being the baritone saxophone star in the very prominent and popular Second Herd was indisputably the catalyst for this tribute, as his other recordings were far more obscure. To this point, his only other records featuring his solo work were the recordings for small jazz labels that had become available, namely, the aforementioned sessions for the Dial, Keynote, Savoy, Futurama, and the even more obscure Motif labels, aside from his work with Herman. Coincident with leaving the disbanded Second Herd and forming his own group, Serge's stature earned him participation in All-Star sessions with other major young musicians in the new style.

Jam Sessions with Alan Eager

Two fragmentary jam sessions including both Serge and Alan Eager were apparently recorded by Milton Green (later known for being Marilyn Monroe's manager for a time), probably around late 1949. It is uncertain whether these sessions occurred before or after the demise of the Second Herd.

"Fine and Dandy" sounds like only Chaloff, Eager, and a drummer (possibly Don Lamond, although Tiny Kahn has also been suggested) were present, but there is a raw energy in both saxophonists' playing that reflects well on both men. The surviving acetate contains about one and a half choruses from Eager, whose solo is in progress as the acetate begins, and then offers four full choruses from Serge in good form. There is then an overlong drum solo, thirty-two bars each from Eager and Chaloff, and the theme closing the performance.

The second jam session with Alan Eager also includes Terry Gibbs (vibes) and unknown piano and bass players. Also recorded by Milton Green, this session is obviously from a different location although probably from around the same period. The musicians play "Cherokee" for about eleven minutes and the performance is complete, if in low fidelity. The mood seems relaxed and solos by Eager, Chaloff, and Gibbs are followed by trading phrases of sixteen-bar, then eight-bar phrases before returning to the unison theme statement.

All-Star Sessions and Leader

Three weeks after the Second Herd disbanded, Serge was part of an all-star concert held at Carnegie Hall on Christmas night, December 25, 1949. Leonard Feather and promoter Monte Kay presented the concert, billed as "Charlie Parker and the Stars of Modern Jazz," and lined up "Symphony Sid" Torin (then at the peak of his popularity as a jazz disc jockey and announcer for countless "live" broadcasts from jazz clubs in New York) as master of ceremonies. Bebop had increased in popularity during the late 1940s to the extent that the jazz magazine poll winners for 1949 were virtually all modernists, many of whom were participating in the concert. Yet another new jazz club with a modern leaning, Birdland (named after Charlie Parker's nickname), had opened on Broadway in midtown Manhattan in mid-December, and many of the all-stars appearing at Carnegie Hall had also appeared at Birdland's opening show. It was a good season for modern jazz as the calendar reached mid-century. However, the overshadowing publicity for Birdland's opening along with the concert being held on Christmas resulted in a poor turnout and little coverage of the concert in the press. Fortunately, it was recorded backstage and transcribed for later use on Leonard Feather's Voice of America radio series, "Jazz Club USA," and eventually issued complete on CD on Jass JCD-16.

It was a good concert. Performers included the Stan Getz–Kai Winding Quintet for two numbers, the Stan Getz Quartet (without Winding) for one tune, Sarah Vaughan with her trio for two numbers, the Lennie Tristano–Lee Konitz Sextet for two numbers, and the Charlie Parker Quintet, which included Red Rodney on trumpet in good form for five or six items (five were preserved and issued, but there is evidence another tune may have been lost). The concert opened with a hot number by the Bud Powell Trio, consisting of Powell (piano), Curley Russell (bass), and Max Roach (drums), who were recording as a trio in that period. They were then joined by Miles Davis (trumpet), Benny Green (trombone), Sonny Stitt (alto sax), and Serge. This all-star group played extended versions of "Move," "Hot House," and "Ornithology." These performances consist of long solos between theme statements, with the added hornmen sounding fairly jittery and fumbling a bit except for Serge, who plays nicely developed solos in his usual style. Unfortunately, the VOA transcription disc for the last title ends during Stitt's solo, but Serge's contribution is intact.

A little more than two weeks later, Serge was on the Metronome All-Stars recording session of January 10, 1950, for Columbia Records. This session featured Serge along with Dizzy Gillespie (trumpet), Kai Winding (trombone), Buddy DeFranco (clarinet), Lee Konitz (alto sax), Stan Getz (tenor sax), Lennie Tristano (piano), Billy Bauer (guitar), Eddie Safranski (bass), and Max Roach (drums). While the series of Metronome All-Star dates typically featured a series of cameo solo spots from all performers within fairly sophisticated arrangements, the quality of the personnel and perhaps the sense of occasion provided for superb performances despite the lack of room for truly personal statements. Both "No Figs" and "Double Date" were outstanding items in the genre. The session was written up in *Metronome* (March 1950), with an often-used photo of Serge in action on page 17, among other photos from the session.

By then Serge's quintet had opened at Birdland. The new club's second triple-bill show featured Lester Young's combo, Erroll Garner's group, and the Serge Chaloff Quintet. Serge's personnel consisted of Earl Swope (trombone), Bud Powell (piano), Joe Shulman (bass), and Don Lamond (drums). Their repertoire included items from the Second Herd book scaled down to quintet charts voiced for baritone sax and trombone, which earned good reviews in both the February 24, 1950, *Down Beat* (Wilson 1950) and the March 1950 *Metronome* (Ulanov 1950). Barry Ulanov wrote in the latter review:

> Serge Chaloff waved his big baritone horn before a small band on the small stage of Birdland last month and inaugurated what will be, at the very least, a very interesting career as a leader.
> Serge's little group was brilliantly cast. . . . The band was best on up-tempo tunes, sometimes swinging with enormous drive and vitality, powered as much by Bud as by Don and Joe, with Serge-ing strength behind and before it, making even such distinctly large-band scores as "Four Brothers" reasonable vehicles for its improvisations. Ballads were as moving or as muddy as Serge's and Earl's moods permitted; at best they were frames for facile melodic variations; at worst they called attention to the curious voicing of the band and its need of ingenious arrangements to justify the mating of baritone, trombone and rhythm.

Unfortunately, the promising start indicated by contemporary comments and reviews did not evolve at that time. At first, Chaloff continued to work fronting his own group in Boston, with varying personnel.

From February 19 to March 5, 1950, Chaloff was at the Hi-Hat, located at the corner of Columbus and Massachusetts Avenue in Boston, with a good local rhythm section. Ads in the *Boston Daily Record* announced "Starting Sunday: Serge Chaloff and the Woody Herman All-Stars," beginning with the Sunday jam session and continuing nightly. Also billed were "Jimmy Tyler and his band" and "the Steve Allison radio broadcast." The group Serge led has been aurally identified as including Nat Pierce (piano), Joe Shulman (bass), and Joe MacDonald (drums). Pierce was prominent for leading a big band around Boston in 1949–51. Shulman had worked with Glenn Miller and Claude Thornhill, recorded with Miles Davis's "Birth of the Cool" band, participated in the Christmas 1949 "Stars of Modern Jazz" Carnegie Hall concert (performing with Lennie Tristano's group), and worked with Serge's quintet at Birdland in January. MacDonald had been working around Boston with Pierce's big band. An acetate recording was made by Serge's brother, Richard, on Wednesday, February 22, 1950, of this group performing "Pennies From Heaven" and an interrupted version of "Gabardine and Serge." Chaloff sounded strong, alert, and happy, displaying prodigious technique and imagination. The rhythm section sounded appropriately attuned to the proceedings, resulting in a refreshing aura to the music. This material was issued on the Uptown CD in 1994 (see discography).

Richard Chaloff (1985) described Serge's situation at that point:

> He was already becoming well known. He was trying to branch out, to have his own band. He always dreamt of having his own group, he always wanted to do that. He tried to make it. But unless you have a tremendous following, a big backing, a financer to pay the payroll, you know. In other words, when you have to pay the payroll at the end of the week, you need a real steady booking to make it work.
>
> He had a problem on the business end of getting the dates close enough together, you know, the areas where he could go to quickly. But he would have one job here, another in Rhode Island, another one in New York. It really wore him out, jumping from one job to the next. It broke him in the end. He had to give up his own band.

By spring, Chaloff was a member of Count Basie's septet, performing with them at the Hi-Hat April 10–22. The big band scene had been deteriorating since the war, and by the end of the 1940s most leaders had given up attempting to sustain a big band in the face of economic impracticability and public apathy. Sentimental vocalists, silly novelty songs, and growing interest in rhythm and blues (which eventually evolved into early rock 'n roll) occupied the buying public and airwaves, while jazz had evolved into a more esoteric underground art form with the development of various approaches to the bop stylists' innovations. Even Count Basie's band, which had been one of the highlights of the swing era and came to represent one of the ultimate examples of how to swing, disbanded. Basie's septet retained the rhythmic feel of his bands, but the interesting personnel on its initial record date indicated a shift of aesthetic and, in being an interracial group, made a social as well as artistic statement. For the occasion, Basie added a tenor saxophonist to the group, increasing it to an octet.

Trumpeter Clark Terry was a holdover from Basie's last big band. Already a veteran of Lionel Hampton's and Charlie Barnet's bands, he went on to join Ellington in 1951. The tenor man brought in for the occasion was Charlie Rouse, who had established himself on record in memorable sessions with Fats Navarro and Tadd Dameron among others and who by the end of the decade had gone on to work as Thelonious Monk's tenor player, a gig that lasted into the 1970s. Buddy DeFranco had emerged as a clarinet star with Tommy Dorsey during the war years, participated in Boyd Raeburn's experiments, and is known as the first clarinetist to establish himself as a stylist in the bop idiom, a position similar to that held by Chaloff among baritone saxophonists. Clearly, the hornmen were an advanced and forward-looking array of unusual talent. Buddy Rich replaced Gus Johnson, Basie's regular drummer at the time. A child prodigy, Rich had enjoyed a prominent position among drummers throughout his career since emerging as a major star with Artie Shaw's 1939 big band. Rich had worked briefly with Basie in 1944 right after Jo Jones and Lester Young were drafted out of Basie's band into the service. These 1944 appearances included two Armed Forces Radio Service broadcasts also featuring his old boss Artie Shaw sitting in with Basie. While Rich was not as modern in conception as the horn players in this 1950 octet, he was always one of the best swing drummers and worked well within Basie's conception.

Unfortunately, their recorded legacy with this personnel consisted only of the one record date for Columbia on May 16, 1950. Chaloff soloed briefly on just two of the titles recorded at this session, "Neal's Deal" and "The Golden Bullet." Alternate takes reveal a consistent conception but notable variations in solos. Nevertheless, the date was more of a souvenir documenting Serge's association with Basie than a representation of the group's potential. Later recordings by Basie's octet in November 1950 used different men, and Chaloff was not present, having been replaced by Rudy Rutherford that summer.

Serge had decided to remain in Boston. Sometime in that period a jam session at Christy's Restaurant in Framingham, Massachusetts, was preserved documenting Serge in an informal setting in company with Howard McGhee and Dick Wetmore (trumpets), Wardell Gray (tenor sax), Nat Pierce (piano), Eli Whitney Cronin (bass), and Joe MacDonald (drums). The private tape of this session has this group performing a long romp on "I Got Rhythm." Obviously, the preservation of such informal jam sessions reveals much about a musician's context and musical spirit, perhaps more than formal record dates can provide, although many musicians feel that the more formal arrangements can provide a better representation of what they want to do musically than a casual jam session context can (assuming the musician concerned has control over what is being recorded in the studios). In any case, such glimpses of Serge in good form and in good company are welcome, if too rare, insights into his musicianship in less formal contexts. Nevertheless, it is unfortunate that a combo including a string section Serge was leading in the late spring and summer of 1950 has not been confirmed as having recorded, as this would give a more profound glimpse of Chaloff's musical orientation at that point than any informal jam session could. Serge discussed this group in a 1951 interview with Nat Hentoff. Chaloff stated that he chose to stay in Boston because he was tired and needed a rest after ten years on the road and because his family was there. Serge also discussed his activities after leaving Basie and his own aspirations as a leader:

> Last year I organized a group—2 violins, 2 violas, a cello, trombone, trumpet, tenor, baritone, and 3 rhythm. We spent 6 weeks rehearsing and I put $600.00 of my own money into special arrangements by Nat Pierce, Sonny Truitt and some of the other first-rate modern writers.
> So we played 2 dates. You know what the booking office said? "Why waste money on special arrangements, special sounds? Get a bunch of stocks and we'll book you." (Hentoff 1951)

Actually, Richard Chaloff noted that the money for the string band arrangements had come from their mother. There have been rumors to the effect that Serge's string group, with whom Sam Rivers played tenor sax, recorded a set for broadcast in a radio station. This material, if the session is genuine, has not surfaced to date. Rivers went on to become one of the central figures of the avant-garde "loft" scene in New York with his Studio Rivbea venue and his many remarkable appearances and recordings in the late 1960s–late 1970s period. He recalled this band in a 1993 telephone discussion as "a very nice group" and expressed regret that there had been no recordings:

> There may have been a radio broadcast when we played opposite Roy Eldridge, at the Hi-Hat, I think it was, but I don't know if it was preserved. Mostly we just rehearsed. There were a lot of standards in the book. Otherwise my association with Serge was mostly jamming, but we jammed together a lot. We'd jam with [pianist] Jaki Byard, [alto saxophonist] Gigi Gryce, [drummer] Al Dawson, Charlie Mariano. . . . Joe Gordon would often be there on trumpet, and Hampton Reese on trombone. (Private discussion 1993)

Other surviving members of this intriguing ensemble recalled acetate recordings being made at rehearsals held in Huntington Hall that season, but no trace of them could be discovered. However, Rick Pauloski has managed to acquire the parts for most of the book for that band, confirming Rivers's statement that there were "a lot of standards" in the band's repertoire. Despite the wide interest in this group's work, it is clear that neither the arrangements nor the compositions were by Serge, so without recordings of his playing solos on this material, the charts are of purely academic interest to the Chaloff scholar.

In the Hentoff (1951) interview, Serge continued by describing the reasons he left the road to settle in Boston:

> Another thing I needed was to get away from the big band scene. For example, playing in a section, you never get a chance to know many tunes thoroughly.
>
> Last summer, I had a relaxed small combo at Hyannis, and I must have learned sometimes as many as 5 or 6 new tunes a day. People would ask me for something and if I didn't know it, I learned it.

The Hyannis gig was probably at the Silver Sea Horse there. Chaloff went on to discuss the advantages of working in a small group:

> Working with small groups again also gave me a chance to reexamine my whole approach to the horn. I'm much more melodic than I used to be. I've gotten away from the meaningless fast passages, the technical fireworks that don't really mean anything.
>
> I've added more color, more flexibility to my work, and like a lot of modern guys, I've gone back, if you could call it that, to swing. I mean, I'm certainly still with all the advances in harmonic and melodic conception, but I realize we have to swing more than we used to. That's why there'll always be a Basie. If a man doesn't swing, then all the technique in the world won't help him play jazz. (Hentoff 1951)

Trombonist Mert Goodspeed, who was active in the Boston area from the late 1940s until late summer 1951, reportedly also played in the string group, although trombonist Sonny Truitt has often been named as the group's trombonist and arranger. Goodspeed (1991) discussed the scene in Boston and something of Serge's activity during 1950–51:

> A whole bunch of us used to live at 454 and 458 Massachusetts Avenue, around the corner from the Hi-Hat. I'm talking about Nat (Pierce); Dave Chapman, alto sax; George Green, tenor and baritone player; Don Stratton, Sonny Truitt, a whole bunch of us. So, Nick Capazutto would be around—trumpet player. Roy Catton, also a trumpet player. But Serge used to hang out with us.
>
> We used to go over to a place called Ort's Grille. Izzy Ort. And there was a house band. They used to play all afternoon, seven days a week, I guess. The house band leader was a guy named Charlie Hooks, black guy, a trumpet player, and people would fall in, sit in, *any* time of the day. I used to go in there and play myself. Nobody gave a damn, there was nobody orchestrating anything. You just came in with a horn. You sat in, that was all. Serge was there at different times. There was a lot of guys that

used to be just hanging out. All of them were in their early twenties, you know.

Goodspeed was part of Nat Pierce's big band, which was active performing and recording around Boston during the late 1940s and early 1950s. When asked if Serge had ever performed with them, Goodspeed (1991) replied,

> No, we were friends with Serge, we used to see him a lot, but he never actually played with the band, on club dates or recordings. We used to hang out, but he never played with the band.

When questioned about Serge's drug habit, Goodspeed continued:

> I wouldn't say he was in pretty rough shape, but we knew when he was bombed! He was still playing quite a bit. Oh yeah! He wasn't having a lot of gigs at that point, but he was active, jamming around.

Freddie Taylor, long active as a promoter and booker on the Boston scene, became associated with Serge's career at this point for a time. As he recalled it, it was probably around the end of January or early February 1950 that he had recorded Chaloff "live" at the Hi-Hat from a front table:

> I recall that very well. I was just getting into the business and can remember booking Serge into the 1950 Winter Carnival at Tufts University, for shortly after that Hi-Hat gig. I can remember sitting at that front table recording the group and watching Serge flirt from the bandstand with this very attractive redhaired girl at another table, who turned out to be Linda Black, whom he later married. That was how they met—eye contact while Serge was on the stand.
> When I booked Serge into the Tufts Winter Carnival, I drove him there, and Linda was along. I think that was their first date. Linda's sister was along too; I dated her very briefly then. Both girls were very young, teenagers, so it was a double-date with sisters, you see.
> Anyway, we came down this long hill, and it was very slippery with ice and new snow. We went into a skid and just missed getting into a very serious accident at the bottom, slithering between big trucks going along the crossroad. That was a close one!
> So, I can remember that whole little sequence that was associated with making that recording and the Tufts gig very well. On that Hi-Hat recording, Sonny Truitt was on trombone, and Jack Lawlor on bass. Joe MacDonald was the drummer. I can't recall the pianist's name, I don't know who he was. Just somebody on the gig. (Private discussion 1993)

In fact, Chaloff researchers have discovered the Tufts Winter Carnival for which Serge had been booked was actually held in 1951. Certainly it is understandable to be off by a year, more than forty years later, in recalling the date of an event. The best guess for the actual date of this set is a Sunday afternoon session (which was when "sitting-in" was permitted) in the early fall of 1950. On the other hand, perhaps Taylor is right, and there is another set of Serge's material out there somewhere. Unfortunately, later evidence indicated Taylor's memory was inaccurate concerning the group's personnel as well. Interviews by Chaloff researchers with musicians from the era listening to the recordings resulted in Sonny Truitt's denial of participation and eventually a nearly certain identification of this band to have consisted of Milt Gold (trombone), Al Vega (piano), Jack Lawlor (bass), and Sonny Taclof (drums). Gold, primarily remembered as a big band trombonist for his work during the 1950s with Claude Thornhill, Stan Kenton and Pete Rugolo, had only been playing professionally about five years at this time. Vega was a Boston pianist and part of the house band at the Hi-Hat along with Jack Lawlor and, briefly, Sonny Taclof (who was later replaced by Jimmy Zitano) during several years in the early 1950s. Lawlor, a left-handed bassist said to resemble actor John Carradine, was active around Boston for many years and later worked with Charlie Mariano and Gerry Mulligan. Taclof, who like Serge performed in Boston's "combat zone" as a teenager, recorded with the Al Vega Trio before leaving the group to work regularly at the Melody Lounge in Lynn.

On these performances Vega sounds discouragingly stiff and inept much of the time. The remainder of the group sounds relatively competent, but not in Serge's league. It may have been Linda's inspiration that had Serge playing with extra fire and imagination, for he clearly outclasses his colleagues in much the same manner as Eric Dolphy's 1961 recordings with European rhythm sections revealed Dolphy having to transcend his earthbound accompaniment in order to soar to his accustomed euphoric heights.

The four tunes Taylor recorded at the Hi-Hat were extended versions of "Gabardine and Serge" (which Chaloff was then using as his theme song), "Pennies From Heaven" (then a standard item in his repertoire), "These Foolish Things," and "Keen and Peachy" for a total timing of about twenty-nine minutes. This material was released on the Uptown CD in 1994 (see discography).

Another gig in that period resulted in Serge being recorded from a broadcast while performing with his quintet at the Celebrity Club at 52 Randall Street in Providence, Rhode Island, on September 3, 1950. The group included Sonny Truitt (trombone), Nat Pierce (piano), George Jones (bass), and Joe MacDonald (drums). Truitt was a multi-instrumentalist who was mainly known as a trombonist, very active around Boston and also a member of Pierce's big band. George Jones was an older musician, active around Boston in the 1930s, who worked with Sabby

Lewis in the early 1940s. This material is presumably from a half-hour broadcast, including a short, amusing interview with Serge. Opening and closing with Serge's theme ("Gabardine and Serge"), the band plays extended performances of "The Goof and I," "Everything Happens to Me," "Pennies from Heaven," and "Four Brothers." Again, although Serge plays marvelously, the band does not adequately provide an appropriate setting for his work. This material was also issued on the Uptown CD in 1994 (see discography).

Serge described his meeting with pianist Dick Twardzik in that period, in a memorial tribute to Twardzik published in *Metronome*:

> My first meeting with Dick Twardzik occurred one night in early September 1950, a night I shall always remember. . . . I had just left the Woody Herman band and was in Boston doing a few singles in the various jazz clubs around town. This particular night I was playing in a club called the "Red Fox" owned by a fellow that once played trombone for the Georgie Auld band in 1945, his name Gus Dixon.
>
> During the evening a very young, studious, good-looking boy came over to me and asked if he could sit in for a couple of numbers. I hated to comply with him, as he was so young looking. It didn't seem possible that a fellow his age could be capable of playing some of the music that was being played. He sat in with us for a set and amazed everyone at the session with his fluent and original ideas. He had a complete new approach to his piano playing and in the way he voiced his chords. Dick was about eighteen years old at the time and we were to spend many enjoyable years together along with a few not so enjoyable ones. Though we both had our rough days we remained very close friends, probably Dick being my closest friend in many years. During the next few years we played together on road trips plus all the local jazz spots and because of this I got to know Dick very well—musically as well as a person. [*sic*]
>
> Musically he had one of the finest discriminating and imaginative minds that I have ever encountered. He progressed so easily and intuitively and absorbed so much of the newer ideas in jazz that he was able to project many original and profound ideas of his own. (Chaloff 1956)

Gus Dixon, who had played with Chaloff in Tommy Reynolds' and Georgie Auld's bands, recalled Serge's gig at the Red Fox Cafe in Lynn very favorably in the liner notes to the 1994 Uptown CD:

> Chaloff could fill a club. In 1950, he played my club . . . on a Monday night. I had placed an ad in the *Boston Daily Record*, and the place was jammed. He was phenomenal. (Uptown CD liner notes 1994)

Certainly among other factors leading Serge to remain in Boston was that he had become very interested in Joann Mary Black, a local model known to all as "Linda" whom Richard Chaloff described as "a very pretty redhead, relatively short for a model." Linda had won a beauty contest the preceding year as "Miss Port of Boston 1949." Richard's wife, Nancy Chaloff, described Linda as vaguely resembling actress Mitzi Gaynor, with a brash and outgoing personality, "very vivacious." Nancy recalled the "whole family" (Dick, Nancy, Serge, Linda, and Margaret) going on a holiday together to a cottage in North Truro near Provincetown on Cape Cod before either couple had married, and having a wonderful time. Presumably, therefore, this would have occurred in the late summer of 1950.

Richard Chaloff recalled Serge's attitude towards women, especially those his mother used to try to get him interested in dating:

> She had a lot of beautiful young ladies that studied piano with her. She really tried. And some of these ladies came from very wealthy homes. My mother was excited: "Listen, you could spend your time writing music, the wife will help you, you'll never have to go out and struggle, you'll never have to work nights and your wife will be beside you."
>
> But all the women, none of them intrigued my brother. He was so dedicated that it took a certain type of woman that would let him do his thing. In other words, he knew it had to be a girl that would let him play all hours of the night, to compose all hours of the night, and really a wife wants a husband in many cases, and these wealthy girls were brought up, I guess, to be pampered, and he realized to take on a wealthy wife—she wants to go out and buy new dresses, and parties, and entertain. He had that insight that it wouldn't work.
>
> We were fairly close as youngsters. Later on, when he started travelling all over the country, we sorta drifted apart, but he always called home every week or so to talk to me, see what I was doing. After the war I started my business in a condemned building in Brookline Village, and my brother used to call and see if the building was still standing, he wanted to see if I was all right (laughter). And then he would call if he was dating. Kay Starr—he was very serious with her for awhile. He was out west and he would call in from her home. She had given him a beautiful watch. He was very proud of it, with all diamonds and his name, "Serge," on the band. She was really in love with him. But for various reasons that I'm not too clear about, they broke up. But he would always call in to say if he had a really good date or whether he's breaking up with someone or where he was going to.
>
> Now, both his wives loved music, and both wives were dedicated in letting him do his thing, and letting him travel and play all night and write all night. They were the best for him. His first wife was Linda Black, and she was a girl that followed the big bands. She was a young lady that loved music, but didn't play anything. She met him by going when the big bands came to town. She would go out to the Totem Pole, or out on Huntington Avenue, there was a ballroom [the Southland] where the big bands came occasionally. Then she used to go down to New York, Radio City Music Hall, stand in line and see the big band people. She followed the big bands

and she followed my brother, this Linda Black. She was a pretty girl. I think she was fascinated by my brother, followed his music. (Chaloff 1993–95)

Serge and Linda married on January 18, 1951. Her name on their marriage certificate was given as Joann Mary Black, age nineteen, and her occupation was listed as "model." (Interestingly, Serge listed his occupation as "teacher.") Both she and Serge gave their address as 278 Newbury Street. This is a brownstone-style house divided into apartments, across the street and a couple of blocks from the site of the Chaloff School of Music in Boston's Back Bay area, not far from the Boston Public Library and its adjacent Copley Square. Now a street lined with boutiques and ethnic restaurants, Newbury Street was similarly bohemian in the early 1950s, but less fashionable, and inhabited by artists, models, musicians, writers, and so forth, according to Richard Chaloff. Their daughter, Linda Jeanne, was born on October 10, 1951. Richard Chaloff recalled in 1993:

> They had a daughter. This girl would probably look like Serge today. When she was a child—I saw her when she was very young, little thing—I think she had my brother's features, build, what have you. (Chaloff 1993–95)

Less than a week after Serge and Joann Mary Black's wedding, he was again in the recording studios for another Metronome All-Stars session, this one for Capitol Records on January 23, 1951. This session, like that of the previous year, was due to Serge again winning the jazz magazine polls as best baritone saxophonist. The other all-stars on the date were Miles Davis (trumpet), Kai Winding (trombone), John La-Porta (clarinet), Lee Konitz (alto sax), Stan Getz (tenor sax), Terry Gibbs (vibes), George Shearing (piano), Billy Bauer (guitar), Eddie Safranski (bass), and Max Roach (drums). This eleven-piece group contained seven of the same musicians as the previous years' ten-piece Metronome All-Stars group. Again, the two sides presented cameo appearances by all present within interesting and sophisticated arrangements. While that earlier Metronome All-Stars session featuring Chaloff had arrangements by Kenton alumnus Pete Rugolo, for the 1951 date Ralph Burns did arrangements showing the influence of Miles Davis's "Birth of the Cool" sound. Both "Early Spring" and "Local 802 Blues" featured Chaloff well, if concisely. Apparently, this was the last studio recording session made by Chaloff prior to his more than three years' hiatus from recording.

Hiatus

Following the January 1951 All-Stars recording, apparently nothing more was recorded in the studios by Chaloff until March 1954, although this remains open to question. Most writing on Chaloff indicates that he fell into obscurity in Boston and was essentially inactive during his apparent hiatus from recording. Actually, he was far from inactive and was not even confining his performing to Boston specifically. In the Hentoff (1951) interview, Chaloff also expressed his chagrin with jazz critics:

> Some New York critic had the nerve to write that because I hadn't been in New York for a long time, I probably wasn't playing well any more. Is that his only criterion for musicianship—playing in New York? Actually I'm playing better now than I ever have.
>
> A lot of other musicians as well as myself are pretty dragged at the state of jazz criticism. From what I read of their work, 99% of the critics don't know what they're writing about. A man spends 10 or 15 years learning his horn, and someone who can't read note one puts him down without knowing what's happening.

He also discussed his feelings about the baritone sax:

> People still ask me why I play the baritone. I took it up, for one thing, because I liked the tone and heard how creatively Harry Carney used it, and also because everybody else was starting on tenor or alto.
>
> People still seem to think it a cumbersome, awkward instrument. It isn't. It's as easy to work with as any horn. In a section, the most interesting parts are for lead alto and baritone. On solo, you can wail with it, play cool, do anything. It's an extremely expressive instrument, but like any other, it takes years of study and practice. (Hentoff 1951)

From March through May of 1951, Serge was appearing regularly as the "relief group" at the Hi-Hat in Boston. Actually, Serge is reported to have played as the house band at the Hi-Hat a total of twenty-five weeks during 1951, but documentation is scanty. Newspaper ads for jazz in the Boston area in that era are rare. In a 1995 interview, Herb Pomeroy was asked how people found out about what was happening in jazz around Boston in those days. He replied that there was a lot of jazz programming on the radio, including "live" broadcasts from various clubs on a regular basis, and that word-of-mouth and posters in the clubs were otherwise all that anyone had felt was necessary.

Drummer Alan Dawson recalled working with Chaloff in this period:

I worked with Serge Chaloff on one occasion for about 10 days. I was actually just more or less subbing for a drummer who he used most of the time—Joe MacDonald . . . at the aforementioned Hi-Hat Club. At the time Serge was really just using a trio, with no bass. There was Nat Pierce and Joe MacDonald and Serge. However, there was a left-handed bass player called Jack Lawlor who came to sit in practically every night but he was not hired on the job! (Gardner 1971)

Dawson also discussed the Boston scene extensively in this interview, but said little else directly concerning Chaloff.

Mert Goodspeed (1991) recalled a prank played on Serge in the summer of 1951:

I don't remember the name of the place, but it's in Yarmouth, on Route 28. I was staying in Harwichport with Don Stratton, who was a trumpet player with Nat's band, I knew him for a number of years, and also Bob Carr, a section trombone player, not a jazz player, with Nat (Pierce). The three of us were hanging around a few days in Harwichport and Serge was playing at this club with Larry Carreno on drums, and Dick Twardzik on piano. So one night we said, "Why don't we bust in on Serge?" So, Don and I got our horns, put them into the car, and went blowing marching right into the club. The owner loved it! It created a little atmosphere. So we played for the rest of the evening. Then the guy hired me. We played for a couple of weeks. Not long. So the trio turned into a quintet, or something like that. Don didn't stay, it was only me.

An intriguing statement appeared in the December 1951 issue of *Metronome* concerning a possible recording session that fall:

Serge Chaloff is playing off and on with a commercial orchestra led by Sal Vasta, a local boy who has pushed many of Boston's singers toward the top with Dick Hyman's smart arrangements. Much of this group's success is coming from the tremendous recording of the band by Elwood Allen of Radax Studios in Belmont . . . producing records which are far superior to many of the major labels. (Coss 1951)

Whether Chaloff recorded with this band or was featured with it could not be determined, as nothing else could be located concerning this material.

There was also an intriguing hint concerning another possible recording session in the December 1951 *Down Beat* article by Nat Hentoff, in which Chaloff mentioned wanting to use trombonist Mert Goodspeed "in the future." In the interview, Serge stated,

I'd also like to start making records again. I have a date coming up, and the last sides I made some months ago were recently issued on Mercer. I usually don't like much of what I do on records, but I think "Bopscotch" and "Chickasaw" on that date came out pretty well.

In discussing his plans with Hentoff, Chaloff also stated:

So now I'd like to get a quintet going, hit Birdland, and then maybe move over the country. Three rhythm, myself, and a trombone. I already have a fine book for that instrumentation. Shorty Rogers wrote it for me when I left Woody. The voicing you can get with trombone and baritone is an exciting sound and a big one.

And I'd like to bring with me an amazingly mature young pianist from here. His name is Dick Twardzik. He's only 21, and he's been working with me at Primo's in Lynn.

During October and November 1951, Serge had an engagement at Primo's in Lynn, Massachusetts. Shortly after his interview with Hentoff, as Chaloff had planned, he took a group including pianist Dick Twardzik on tour, performing at the Preview in Chicago from January 20 through February 17, 1952. The group went on to the Crest Lounge in Detroit, from February 19 through March 3. They next were booked into the Terrace in East St. Louis, from March 11 through 24 (Band listings). The band went on to the Picadilly in Green Bay, Wisconsin, from late March into mid-April, and then to the Log Cabin Inn in Appleton, Wisconsin, until the end of April 1952.

At the Log Cabin Inn, Serge and the group were photographed well in a series of excellent shots by John W. Miner. Many of these photos have since appeared in various publications, including one on the cover of Black Lion BLCD-760923 noted in the discography; several in the Mosaic Records booklet issued with "The Complete Serge Chaloff Sessions" (MD4-147/MQ5-147) in 1993; and another on page 15 of the Mosaic Records Brochure #10 (1993). The members of this group, aside from Chaloff and Twardzik, were bassist Ralph Maisell and drummer Jimmy Weiner.

Following the Log Cabin engagement, Serge was rumored to have joined Elliot Lawrence's big band for a time. However this was apparently incorrect. Certainly the photo allegedly depicting Serge in Lawrence's band, shown in the Mosaic booklet, was really from the same photo session that documented the Georgie Auld Nonet at the Troubador (as shown in the excellent jazz photo history book, *Black Beauty, White Heat*).

Actually, according to Jimmy Weiner, the 1952 touring group went on from the Log Cabin Inn to Chicago again. While there, Serge left the other musicians in order to fly back to Boston. Weiner recalled that Serge's daughter was about six months old at the time, and Serge's mother had sent him the money to return home. Despite this abandonment of his band, Twardzik and Weiner rejoined Serge a little later that spring, with Jack Lawlor now on bass, to play gigs in Schenectady, New York; Bethlehem, Pennsylvania; and Hagerstown, Maryland, among other locations. In an interview quoted in the liner notes to the 1994 Uptown CD, Weiner reported:

> We played a club in Schenectady and Serge got punched out. A guy in the audience was yelling out requests calling Serge "Buster." Serge put down his saxophone and got off the bandstand and went up to the guy and said, "My name's not Buster." Serge was a flamboyant guy who always took people up on their threats. Next thing, Serge is lying on the floor yelling. The trio finished the set without him. He had the imprint of this guy's ring on his forehead for a week. (Uptown CD liner notes 1994)

Weiner mentioned that they had worked in two clubs in Bethlehem, Pennsylvania, but the places were empty due to a steel strike. He also recalled Serge scoring an impressive assortment of drugs and pills while in Hagerstown, and that later, after returning to Boston, Serge had found himself among a gallery of individuals sought by the police on narcotics charges. His car was even impounded. All of this caused Serge to lay low for a while, perhaps explaining why he was out of town for much of 1953. Concerning the vehicle incident, Richard Chaloff (Chaloff 1993–95) recalled:

> Mother bought Serge a beautiful van to travel in when he went out on a long road trip, as reliable transportation was such a problem. But back here in Boston, the police stopped him and stripped the van thoroughly looking for drugs, impounded it. They didn't find anything but that was it for the van, and Mother was out the money.

While in Boston, Serge was active in the Boston suburb of Lynn at two locations: Primo's and the Melody Lounge. Along with the Hi-Hat in Boston, these were the three main venues for modern jazz in the area, according to contemporary articles on the Boston jazz scene. Apparently, the Dixieland revival was blossoming among the Boston nightspots in general, so that more modern musicians were having trouble finding work (Coss 1951).

By early 1953 Chaloff was on the road again, often traveling as a single and working with local rhythm sections, according to Bob McCaffery, then a young pianist working in Minneapolis who spent much of the latter part of 1953 working around the Minneapolis–St. Paul area with Chaloff and becoming good friends with him in that period. McCaffery, who held a master's degree in industrial and labor relations from Cornell and was working as a personnel trainee for Donaldson's (a large department store), had already worked on the road with Charlie

Spivak's big band and in various piano/bass duos in Miami and in Lake George, New York. At the time he met Serge, McCaffery had been sitting in regularly at clubs around Minneapolis and St. Paul with local musicians, including the young trumpeter Don Ellis. McCaffery noted in a 1993 letter:

> A weekly highlight was a Sunday afternoon jam session at a downtown Minneapolis club called the Hoop-De-Doo where "The Three B's" (consisting of tenor saxophonist Bob Crea, pianist Bob Davis, and drummer Bill Blakkestad) were the house band and lots of good players "sat in."
>
> One Sunday in late July or early August while I was sitting-in at the Hoop-De-Doo, Serge Chaloff came into the club. He was scheduled to begin a two-week engagement at Vic's, another local club, later that week. He had arrived in town with only a drummer (Don Sheldon, who was from Rochester, New York, and later worked with Tony Pastor's band) and needed to find a pianist and bass player. Serge didn't play but stayed for several sets. At the end of the session he asked me and a local bass player, Dick Thompson, if we could make the gig at Vic's. We were both flattered and immediately accepted.
>
> We held one rehearsal at the union (AFM local 73) meeting hall before opening at Vic's. Fortunately Serge featured standard tunes (e.g., "All the Things You Are," "Cherokee," "Body and Soul," "Indiana," "Thanks for the Memory") along with assorted blues numbers and "I Got Rhythm" variations, all of which I knew. But some tempos were furious and difficult to sustain. We played "Four Brothers" at a frantic tempo.
>
> For the most part Serge was tolerant when his support was less than superlative. Whenever he expressed unhappiness with either Dick or me, Don Sheldon would assure us that it was just "constructive criticism" and that he really "dug us." Nontheless after the first week Dick and I were replaced by (pianist) Lou Levy and (bassist) Stu Anderson. This was an ego deflator but we managed to rationalize it because our successors were significantly better players.
>
> In spite of the "firing," Serge and I maintained a very cordial relationship during the summer of 1953. (Personal communications 1992–93)

McCaffery also noted Chaloff still had his drug habit and was often strung out:

> He was a contradictory guy. When he was strung out he could be embarrassing, even vicious, but when he was "comfortable" he'd be gracious, funny, and charming.

Their repertoire consisted of blues and standards, with Serge playing many of the same tunes that showed up later on his Storyville and Capitol records. McCaffery recalled:

He'd begin sets playing Woody's theme, "Blue Flame," on piano, then move to his horn. The horn was really beat up: no lacquer, scratches and dents, rubber bands on keys and all, but he was really playing. More like his later records than his earlier work, but not as developed. (Personal communications 1992–93)

Chaloff developed a relationship with a local singer named Dell Scott which McCaffery described as "a love/hate relationship that could have been a model for Elizabeth Taylor and Richard Burton." He described her succinctly as a "hip blonde singer." Apparently Serge was cynical about his relationship with his wife at that point. McCaffery described Chaloff reading a letter from his wife aloud to the band:

It started with local sports news. Then she ended with "By the way," and news about her seeing a lawyer to divorce him. Serge was laughing.

In the 1993 letter, McCaffery continued to discuss Chaloff's Minneapolis adventures:

Following the date at Vic's he remained in Minneapolis, hanging out with the singer, Dell Scott, and sitting in wherever he could. On several occasions he called me in the early evening to accompany him on club-hopping ventures. I can still recall a stoned Serge driving Dell's car erratically as we made the rounds of Minneapolis clubs to sit in for free drinks.

I also remember going with Serge to Bill Blakkestad's house one night to record some tunes. Bill had just bought some kind of tape recorder (it must have been one of the earliest versions) and he wanted to experiment with it. My memory indicates that the playbacks were not in very good fidelity and I have no idea whether the tape survived.

Late in October Serge called and asked if I could make a four-week date with him at "The Flame" in St. Paul. Although I had some concerns about being able to handle a six night per week schedule along with my work at Donaldson's I accepted the offer. Stu Anderson also agreed to rejoin Serge, but by that time Don Sheldon had left town (I think he went with Tony Pastor's band). Serge wanted to use Mel Lifeman, a capable bebop drummer, but the club owner insisted on an older, flashier player named "Chief" McElroy who had a small local following. It was obvious that the owner was nervous about Serge's drawing power because he also encouraged Dell Scott and other local performers to sit in.

In spite of "The Chief's" lumpish playing, the gig went pretty well. Mel Lifeman and (tenor saxophonist) Dave Karr sat in regularly and (trumpeter) Jon Eardley came in when he was passing through town along with another excellent trumpet player named Dick "Buzzy" Mills. Lou Levy was working across the street in a group with (trumpeter) Conte Candoli and we would visit back-and-forth during breaks.

Serge was mostly in a good frame of mind during the four weeks but there were moments when he would "lose it." His relationship with Dell was mercurial. Some of their battles—both verbal and physical—were scary. Once Serge borrowed my wristwatch on the stand to check the length of a set. I forgot to ask for it back until the next night. He then announced that the crystal had been broken during a scuffle with Dell but that they would see that it was repaired. Dell ultimately returned the watch (repaired) about two months later after Serge had left town. My strong suspicion was that it had been hocked to get money for drugs.

During the Flame gig we added a number of tunes to the repertoire including "Easy Street," "You Brought a New Kind of Love to Me," and "All I Do Is Dream of You." All of these appeared on the March 1954 Storyville LP.

There were also some photographs taken of Chaloff in action at this time, including one of Dell Scott singing with Serge backing her and "Chief" McElroy on drums, which appeared in the Mosaic booklet courtesy of McCaffery. In his 1993 letter, McCaffery continued:

After the Flame engagement was over Serge continued to hang out in Minneapolis, staying on and off with Dell and generally scuffling. A couple of times he stayed at my apartment. Finally, just before Christmas, he stopped by admitting to being flat broke. He called his mother and asked her to send money so he could return to Boston. She wouldn't send any money, but said she would arrange for him to pick up tickets at the airport. The next morning I helped get him to the airport and he departed for Boston.

Aside from a letter received a few months later, McCaffery had no further contact with Serge. However, that letter was highly significant in describing Chaloff's musical activities, health, and state of mind in early 1954. Curiously, Serge did not discuss his marital difficulties in this otherwise frankly open letter.

Richard Chaloff (1985) commented briefly on the demise of Serge and Linda's marriage:

They had a very happy marriage until there was the drug scene, and that broke up the marriage. She couldn't stand the drug scene because it was very costly and he used the money to keep his habit going and it broke up his marriage, and then she remarried after the divorce. He admits it was his fault, it wasn't her fault at all.

Sally Nelson, Linda's sister, confirmed this evaluation in a 1995 interview:

I think they had a lot of fun together at first. I'd baby-sit Linda Jeanne while Linda accompanied Serge on out of town gigs and short road trips. But the drug problems were too great. (Personal communications 1995)

After divorcing Serge in 1954 (Norfolk court docket #014541), Linda dropped contact with the family and married a clothing merchant named Marvin Howard Kramer on September 4, 1955. He legally adopted Linda Jeanne, who grew up to marry a mechanic from Sharon, Massachusetts, named William E. Powers in 1971. Linda Jeanne was nineteen at the time of the wedding, the same age as her mother had been when she married Serge. In a 1995 telephone interview, she described her life as "happy" with her husband, two sons (William Jr. and Robert, both in their early twenties) and a dog. She was unaware of Serge's stature in the jazz world, although she knew he was a musician.

Late Recordings

Chaloff's letter to McCaffery, dated March 7, 1954, bore the return address of 120 Riverway, his mother's apartment. Among other things, Serge discussed his current health problems, which included hospitalization for jaundice upon his return to Boston. Concerning his musical activities, Serge wrote:

> Since I left there I've been jobbing around Boston with a rhythm section and myself. I picked up a few college dances, etc., and guess who I've been using on bass? Jack Carter, the fellow you asked me if I knew when I was in Minneapolis. I met him at the Jazz Workshop, a place where all the modern thinking fellows in Boston get together and study or play. It's a very wonderful thing and so far it has been paying off or at least breaking even. I surely would have liked to have a place to go and experiment with my horn when I was a kid. Well, anyway. . . .

He summarized his activities later in the same letter with:

> I was teaching and playing at the Jazz Workshop and different clubs and made six sides for George Wein, the owner of Storyville, called *Jazz at Storyville*. Boots Mussulli, the alto sax player that used to be with Kenton, plus Jack Carter and Buzzy Drootin and a piano player named Ray Santisi.

This record date described in Serge's letter suspiciously resembled the Storyville session usually dated June 9, 1954, with the exception of the personnel. It has not been possible to determine whether the session referred to in Serge's letter was an authentic "lost" session, as no further documentation could be found. George Wein and Ray Santisi both thought this recording session did not take place. Nevertheless, the June 9 date is, in fact, erroneous, as Russ Freeman, the pianist who made the record date, had been in Boston only as part of Chet Baker's group, which was playing there during March 16–29, 1954. Intriguingly, on June 9, Serge was performing at the Boston Arts Festival in the Public Gardens with a group including Charlie Mariano, on the same program with a traditional jazz group featuring Ruby Braff, Vic Dickenson, Buzzy Drootin, and George Wein on piano, among others. At the festival, Wein recorded this group "live" for a Storyville release, LP-311. It could not be determined with absolute certainty whether the Chaloff–Mariano group or the jam session featuring musicians from both groups that closed the concert were also recorded, and if so, whether such tapes still exist. Wein thought that they had not been recorded.

The Chaloff–Mussulli Quintet session represented Serge's return to the jazz world, in critical and public perceptions. Serge wrote all the arrangements. Although he had done some arranging while with Ina Ray Hutton, and did some arranging and composing for his record dates in the 1940s, he did not continue this avenue of expression due to his concentrating on his horn, according to the Feather interview (1950). The point always seems to be made in discussions of these recordings that Serge's mother had also contributed by scoring the ending of "Zdot" (a word that derives from a syllable Serge's daughter, Linda Jeanne, uttered while learning to talk). This entire session was very successful and showed the "new" Serge to advantage.

It was apparent that Serge's style had matured and grown conceptually and expressively. His sidemen were at least adequate; along with Boots Mussulli's fluent alto sax, the group consisted of a rhythm section of Russ Freeman (piano), Jimmy Woode (bass), and Buzzy Drootin (drums). Nevertheless, it was Serge's arrangements, solos, and the overall aura consistently pervading the session which provided its vitality and confirmed the classic status of the recordings. These six performances totalled about twenty-four minutes of music. All pieces except "Easy Street" were up-tempo, swinging, and rather happy-sounding performances. "Easy Street" was a ballad, featuring Serge throughout. Everyone was featured on each of the other pieces except Drootin, who was only featured in four-bar breaks on "Love Is Just Around the Corner." All the tunes were standards except "Zdot," which was Serge's composition. Mussulli's basically "cool" style complemented the feel of the rhythm section, and Serge seemed laid-back and comfortable.

Aside from some gigs and the Storyville record session, as he had written to McCaffery, Serge had also begun teaching at the Jazz Workshop shortly after returning from his Minneapolis adventures and also took on at least one private student in this period. That student, Steve Adamson, offered some vivid details of Serge's life and lifestyle during most of 1954:

This was in the early part of 1954, probably around January or February, I decided I wanted to learn to play the tenor saxophone. At that time in *Down Beat* I read where Serge had either just come back to Boston or was gigging in Boston, and I decided I was going to start at the top. I phoned him. He expressed an interest in teaching me. This is, in retrospect, absolutely incredible. This is 1954, so I was going on eighteen the following summer. We picked a location to meet in Boston. In fact I think it was along the Boston Public Library where we met and just shot the shit. And then he thought, "This kid is enthusiastic and he's a big guy, so I'll do it."

So we worked out an arrangement where Serge would come over to my house. The horn I had was a leaky alto that I borrowed from a classmate. Serge came to my house, I remember the first time, he sat down and looked at this silver leaky alto and he cupped the bell of the horn on his instep, he crossed his legs and cupped the bell; since there was no neckstrap he just had it supported on his instep. And then he went through these cascading chords which a good musician in his lifetime couldn't have put together what he put together in about three minutes of going up and down with that dilapidated instrument, a terrible horn! And he was hitting all these chord changes, sequences and wild fingering, my hair was standing on end and my forehead was breaking into beads of perspiration. I was just in total awe, to use that overworked word.

He then took some tape, some white adhesive tape, and I remember him carefully going around certain valves plugging up leaks, taping pads, and he got the horn in working shape and from there we went on with our lessons.

It was once a week. It lasted for about an hour and those lessons went from late winter, early spring 1954 through the summer. I wanted to play the tenor, and the only thing I had was that leaky alto, and it wasn't mine. Since I wanted a tenor, Serge met me and my father at a downtown Boston music shop, Raeburn's Music, something like that, I don't know. This was just across the Boston Common, downtown. Apparently somebody in the music store was ready for us and Serge kinda engineered the deal. I think Serge might have got 10% of the sale. He was auditioning, playing and showing me horns, probably tooting it but I can't quite remember. I had it in my mind then to get a Conn, and Serge steered me into a Selmer, a Selmer tenor saxophone.

We hit it off personally; we were fond of each other. He was a very likeable guy. Well, he was a heroin addict then. Consequently he got moody. Because of the drugs or because of my terrible playing, he was moody to a certain degree. Sometimes he was impatient with my playing. For him to stay with me was remarkable. He wasn't that tolerant. I had trouble reading and he sometimes would blow his stack when I was trying to do the scale exercises he would write out. Sometimes he would take it and other times he would just, I'm sure, get disgusted with himself having to sit through that and he would blow his stack on occasion. It must have been for the money: it was no more than $5 and my mother would give him a juicy steak. Maybe that's what did it. I remember by the time I was on my second bite, he would have ravaged a steak. He ate with such gusto.

As far as talking about drugs, no. We never mentioned them. He just mentioned the musicians he admired, and first I must tell you, on saxophone, the only two names that ever came out on baritone sax, they weren't Mulligan or Harry Carney, but Jack Washington and Earl Carruthers. He spoke of them in great admiration. Another musician he would mention was Stan Getz. The term he used, just shaking his head, "He has a great ear." He was a little surprised that I wasn't at that time taken by [Charlie] Parker, and the kind of music that he loved so deeply. If there was just one icon in his life, he just referred to him and it was a standard that stood in his mind for excellence and emulation.

Serge laughed readily, he had a deep laugh, a good sense of humor. The laugh came easily from Serge. He was smallish, as far as height, but you got the sense of very muscular without the big proportions. You had this idea of a powerful, powerful man. And when he played, his face would contort. The neck muscles, the veins, the arteries would all come to the surface, so you got this feeling of passion and power just by looking at him. As I recall he wasn't extremely tall, but you got this feeling of power in his body and he handled his body as if he were a powerful man, which he was. He was not as hairy as the average man. His arms, fingers, even facial beard were extremely light, there was just an inkling of a beard on his face. His hair was slicked back, straight back, like a sheen or patent. He had a handsome face, a slightly aquiline nose, very handsome features. I thought of him constantly when I saw Robert De Niro in *New York, New York*—same slicked back hair, same nose, and De Niro even with a tenor looked a lot like Serge. I remember this photo of Chaloff that was very severe looking, just like a hawk, and when I finally met Serge, "Thank God he doesn't look like this menacing predatory animal, like in this picture!" Serge had a gentle, soft face.

He was, a good deal of the time I was with him, preparing for the Boots Mussulli recording. I was with him for a couple of those rehearsals. He used to rehearse at Storyville, right on the main floor. It would be closed down, only a few waiters. There would be no public. It would only be personnel that worked at Storyville puttering around. He was doing rehearsals, doing The Stable. I was once at The Stable for a rehearsal, and I met a couple of times, Peter Littman, a wonderful drummer that's passed away. Dick Twardzik, I met him a couple of times. There was a nice bass player that I met, Jimmy Woode. There was a circle. Herb Pomeroy, he was flitting in and out, he still does. I remember [George] Wein being there, and his disposition. He was kinda cranky.

[Serge] was quite upbeat about the rehearsals; even when he was playing tacky jobs he'd speak of it with enthusiasm. For instance, on Bluehill Avenue, the corner of Bluehill Avenue and Morton Street was a rinky-dink club called at that time the Brown Derby. And I remember he was playing there during that period, and he spoke of it with such pride, but it was just a dump. For that matter, he used to see in dumpy areas Buck Clayton and Pee Wee Russell playing, pretty much near strip joints. So the art we hold in great esteem—the public just ignores them. So they play where they can. It's a problem.

Serge was apparently in so much trouble with his drug addiction . . . oh by the way, the story around in those days of the drug addicts congregating, gathering, exchanging drugs, used to be around the Boston Public Library. Copley Square was their hangout. Serge's focal point for drugs was around Copley Square. But because of the need for drugs at that time, and money . . . I had two horns, a tenor sax which my father bought me, and an alto, the leaky one. Serge would borrow the horns, as he told me for gigs, and I wouldn't see the horn. I would lose track of the horn, Serge, everything, and I would call his mother, and she was just in resignation, saying, "Oh, that again!" He hocked them, and she knew where to go. She would fetch the horns, or horn. I would go to her house, get the horn. I would pick up the horn just from Margaret. Serge wouldn't be around. I was on friendly terms with her. Serge would come give me the lesson, and somewhere along the line borrow a horn or two and we would go through this. I think we went through this two or three times.

Serge at the time lived in the Back Bay. He had an apartment. He shared it with his mother. It was a large one. Not only was he not with his wife. I'd frequently see him when he came over to give me lessons, he would have a young woman, a lady from Boston University, a co-ed, as I recall. I don't know if she was a graduate student or not, but there was some Boston University female connection in his life at that time. Just to fill you in again on his personal life, how he got around. He did not have a car, he used to take the transit, called the "T." Then it was called the "MTA," Mass Transit Authority. He would take the "T" from his house to mine. (Adamson 1991)

In fact, a notebook/diary kept by Margaret Chaloff erratically during this period contained references to Serge's habit of pawning his students' horns for drug money and her having to retrieve the instruments for the students.

Steve Kuhn, who began studying piano with Madame Chaloff and occasionally gigging with Serge as early as 1951 (although in context it is clear his experience with Serge continued until Serge's death), also commented on Serge's problems with his drug habit and his erratic living arrangements. Oddly, he made no mention of either of Serge's wives, although their marriages certainly overlapped Kuhn's relationship with Serge. In an interview published in 1993, he reminisced about Serge and Madame Chaloff. Following some very complimentary comments about Madame Chaloff's teaching and its effect on his work, Kuhn went on to discuss his relationship with Serge:

Serge was like a big brother to me. I was about 13 when I [first] worked with him. He was pretty strung out at the time . . . he came off the road and was living in Boston, sometimes with his mother and sometimes with some girlfriends. He was very abusive to Margaret [his mother] in many ways. He would be taking appliances from her house and pawning them and being physically abusive to her and she just had the patience of a saint. So he stayed around Boston a lot in those last years 'cause he physically couldn't get around.

I worked a fair amount with him and drums. We would work those little joints around Boston, just the trio. For me it was an education. Serge would be screaming and yelling at me if I missed the changes, but I found out I really learned a lot from him. . . . He never approached me as far as the drug situation, never said, "Come on, I want to get you high." It was just musical. Women seemed to be very attracted to him and he was somewhat abusive to them. He had the same kind of personality, in a way, that Stan [Getz] did. . . . It's interesting because there was another brother, Dick, Serge's brother, Margaret's other son, who was very clever with hi-fi and stuff. He was very straight-laced, very together, married and had a couple of kids . . . probably as talented in his area of electronics as Serge was in music, but the personalities were completely different. . . .

But Serge to me was a great education. He was a great ballad player. Yeah, yeah, his ballad playing was unsurpassed even though his intonation was suspect many times. And those were great years in Boston. I used to work at The Stable. When Ray Santisi took time off they used to call me and I'd work with the quintet or sextet with Herb Pomeroy. (Kuhn 1993)

Serge's gigs during 1954 included weekend sessions at the Showboat with his Jazz Workshop students during March. Apparently there were several other concerts by these musicians, including one as far afield as Manchester, New Hampshire, in April. Aside from the Storyville sessions and his appearances at The Stable, as mentioned by Adamson, there was the June 9 Boston Arts Festival concert with Charlie Mariano and Dick Twardzik in the group. Photos from this festival among Margaret Chaloff's effects noted on the back the date and visible personnel. The notes also said that one photo was taken as the group performed "The Goof and I" and another during a final jam session for which Steve Kuhn sat in on piano as the group played "How High the Moon" along with musicians from the traditional group. As noted above, however, George Wein was sure that this material was not recorded, despite his recording the traditional group at this concert.

Boston disc jockey Bob "The Robin" Martin, who was the announcer for regular live broadcasts from Storyville at this time, got involved with Serge during 1954. In the liner notes to the 1994 Uptown CD, he was quoted as stating:

[Serge] walked into the club one day, and I'd always been a fan of his. I met him when he was in the Woody Herman band when he was playing with the Four Brothers and he came in the club and we got chatting. I was doing a show there every afternoon and he got on the air with me talking and we reminisced and it just grew. I was trying to be a friend. I was trying to help the guy. Help him book and keep his records together which was the most difficult part of it. (Personal communication 1995)

A legendary encounter between Serge's sextet and the famed Clifford Brown–Max Roach Quintet with Harold Land and Ritchie Powell, with Serge and Brownie jamming together later with Roach's rhythm section, occurred at the New Storyville in the Copley Square Hotel. The occasion was a Friday afternoon Teenage Jazz Club presentation by George Wein and Father Norman O'Connor. The front line of Clifford Brown and Serge Chaloff with Roach's rhythm section in the final segment was reportedly outstanding.

Teenage Jazz Club member George Barringer, a drummer from Medford, Massachusetts, knew Serge in this period and recalled performing with him along with his friend Dick Wetmore, who had been on the jam session at Christy's playing trumpet and who also played violin and flugelhorn. Evidently Serge roomed with Herb Pomeroy in Charlestown briefly around this time, and Barrington recalled memorable gigs at The Stable and at Danny's Hideaway in Huntington. Bassist Joe di Carlo, who sat in with Serge frequently at the Hi-Hat and also gigged with him at the Silver Bar and the Bradford Hotel Roof in Boston, said in a 1995 discussion, "When Serge would solo, the whole crowd would get quiet. His talent commanded attention instantly."

A long gig at the Brown Derby in Boston lasted from early July to August 20. On August 29, 1954, Serge attended Richard and Nancy's wedding and sat in playing a borrowed tenor sax with Paul Bordeleau's band at their wedding reception at Blinstrub's in South Boston. Family photos from Blinstrub's show Serge in action as well as posing with Richard, Nancy, Margaret, and Julius for a family grouping, among others. Some of these were published in the Mosaic booklet.

The Storyville recording session dated September 3, 1954, produced even more powerful evidence of Serge's development and scope than his earlier Storyville record with Mussulli. The core of this ensemble was a sextet with an instrumentation voicing Serge would favor for the next year, consisting on this occasion of Herb Pomeroy (trumpet), Charlie Mariano (alto sax), Serge on baritone, Dick Twardzik (piano), Ray Olivieri (bass), and Jimmy Zitano (drums). For three titles the group was expanded to a nonet with the addition of Nick Capazutto (trumpet), Gene Di Stachio (trombone), and Varty Haritounian (tenor sax). The masterpiece of this date was Dick Twardzik's intriguing composition "The Fable of Mabel" by the full nine-piece group assembled for the session.

"The Fable of Mabel" was an advanced composition for its time, with changes of tempo and mood involving imaginative solo work by all concerned. It included simultaneous improvisation by Mariano and Haritounian during one segment, and an intriguing piano solo by Twardzik that seemed to anticipate the early Cecil Taylor (who was a student in Boston at the time). Nevertheless, the arrangement was primarily a showcase for Chaloff's imaginative baritone. The episodic character of the composition is discussed in the liner notes by Twardzik, who described his composition as "a satirical jazz legend" introduced by the Serge Chaloff Quartet in 1951–52. The story did not seem to fit the character of the music, although as program music "describing" Mabel's adventures it would be easy to visualize a modern dancer performing the role. The Black Lion compact disc offered alternate takes of most of the numbers from this session, along with two new versions of "The Fable of Mabel" which were remarkably different in mood and interpretation although the form was the same. It is also noteworthy that this composition bore considerable resemblance to works by Charles Mingus, who was also active around Boston then.

The other nonet titles were more conventional. Available in two takes each, Herb Pomeroy's "A Salute to Tiny" (Kahn) and Charlie Mariano's "Eenie Meenie Minor Mode" showcased all soloists well, despite their being fairly brief versions (just over three minutes for the former, and just over three and a half minutes for the latter, the alternate takes being within a couple of seconds of each other). Even "The Fable of Mabel" was relatively short, timing at between 4:15 and 4:28, compared to the two sextet titles recorded at the same session, Mariano's "Slam" at 5:49, and two takes of Al Killian's "Let's Jump" at 6:03 and 6:51. The session was rounded out with a brief (2:06) entirely scored composition by Mariano for just trumpet, alto, and baritone. This was an attractive tone poem called "Sherry." Of course the longer sextet tracks offered more solo space, and it is of interest to compare them with Serge's next date as a leader, the sextet session the following spring.

Over the intervening fall and winter Serge finally kicked his drug habit completely, spending nearly four months in the hospital and writing his autobiography.

On the forms for the *Encyclopedia of Jazz* Serge mentioned his own group appearing at the Melody Lounge during 1954 (Serge Chaloff file). One engagement there was traced as occurring October 19–30. Immediately following this gig, Serge went into a long hospitalization to free himself of his drug habit.

The story of Serge's finally kicking his heroin habit once and for all was published in the *Boston Sunday Herald* of May 1, 1955. The interview/article began:

> Serge Chaloff has nothing to show for $120,000.00 but three black, distended veins inside his left elbow. That, and a wrecked life that he's now reshaping.
>
> That's why the Boston baritone saxophonist—once rated in jazz circles as the country's best—broke his silence. Chaloff has returned from the living death of heroin addiction. And he thinks he owes it to thousands of addicts—including several Boston high school children he knows—to deliver this message: "You can't make the trip alone."
>
> The fool's paradise crashed on top of Chaloff last October 31. He calls it "the blackest Sunday of my life."
>
> In the same apartment where he now lives at 120 Riverway Chaloff that day frantically dialed his friends, begged futilely for money, and listened to each click as receivers were hung up against him as the tick of doom. He had to have four to five shots of heroin each day. And a shot cost $6 to $8.
>
> "I didn't have a cent," he recalls. "I was desperate. I was at the end of the road."

On the walls around the room hung plaques proclaiming him "top baritone sax for" and the years 1947, 1948, 1949, or 1950 finished each phrase. *Metronome* and *Down Beat*, bibles of pop music world [*sic*], had awarded the citations.

"And here I was, four years later, a bum," Chaloff said. "Even my gold-plated saxophone was in hock. But even if I had had it, nobody would have given me work. It was deeper than just being unreliable. Dope had ruined my music, too. My physical wreckage was growing into mental ruin."

Chaloff knew he was beaten. Then three forces that had been working to save him came into play. They were: his mother, Prof. Margaret Chaloff of the Boston University School of Music, who had stayed by him; Dr. S. Irving Copen, a retired dentist who works with the Temple Israel Brotherhood rehabilitation committee; and Bob Martin, a former Boston disc jockey who had known Chaloff several years.

"They talked me into entering a Brookline sanitarium," Chaloff said. "I went in Nov. 1. For two weeks, the sanitarium stepped me down with a non-habit-forming substitute for heroin. It wasn't bad. I thought I was cured.

"Then they talked me into committing myself to the Bridgewater State Hospital. Dr. Copen had warned me that a severe mental depression would follow the loss of physical craving for heroin. I didn't believe it. But I let them take me to Bridgewater."

When he arrived at the state hospital, Chaloff was "shocked" to find himself behind bars. "I thought it was a rest home," he explained. But now he knows those bars rescued him from himself.

"My mother mailed me a copy of Dr. Peale's *The Power of Positive Thinking* when I was in deep despair," he said. "When I got it, I laughed. What the h— do they think I am? I said to myself. Do they think I'm a boob?

"But there was nothing to do but look at those bars or read. So I began reading. I think it's the best book I've ever read. And I began going to services in the hospital.

"I don't want this to sound gushy—I'm not a religious fanatic, or anything like that. But I've got faith now. When drugs left me, there was a cavity that had to be filled. Faith filled it.

"I have to thank the Old Boy Upstairs for pulling me through."

Chaloff got his first shot from another musician in St. Louis in 1945. He was on a tour of 60 one-night stands with sometimes a 500-mile bus ride between engagements. He was 21 at the time, and a veteran of five years on the road.

"I was tense and worn," he explained. "I had talent, but I was trying to keep up with musicians that had talent and 15 to 20 years of experience. I was insecure deep inside. I was worried. This fellow who was trying to be a friend gave me a shot. I began walking on clouds."

Chaloff said he was two years on heroin before "a withdrawal left me in the dumps."

"Like all other addicts, I thought I could quit any time," he said. "I did succeed in quitting sometimes as long as two weeks."

Since leaving Bridgewater Feb. 10, Chaloff has had many opportunities to resume his old habit but refused.

"Runners (dope peddlers) often taunt me that I'll be back," he says. "But I won't.

"Easy to get? Why heroin's as easy to buy as a bag of peanuts. Wherever you go, you're not far from a pusher. Once you're a known addict, the grapevine pushes the word ahead of you. Wherever you tour, you'll find pushers there waiting for you."

Now that he's "clean," the term addicts use for cured, Chaloff has made recordings for Capitol Records which will be released in August. And he's writing a book to help others lick heroin.

"I want to live as an example to other young addicts, an assurance that they can be reclaimed," he says. "But I want to warn them that they must have themselves confined in some institution to beat the habit. You can't do it alone." (Hanley 1955)

Bob "The Robin" Martin also received considerable credit for Chaloff's rehabilitation and "comeback" in a *Metronome* article written by Paul D. Coss:

Bob is associated with one of the great names in jazz in a business partnership. Bob's great confidence in Serge Chaloff and tireless efforts on his behalf have been greatly responsible for the forming of a musician who carries over from his past only his tremendous talent.

With The Robin, I went to see this Serge Chaloff sextet that there is so much excitement about. The other five in the combo are Boots Mussulli on alto, with Herb Pomeroy at trumpet, pianist Ray Santisi, drums by Jimmy Zitano and bassist Everett Evans.

Recently, under Bob's supervision, this group cut 12 sides for the Kenton Presents series. These I have heard and most sincerely believe with Bob Martin that there is no doubt that this group will hit hard as another important jazz ensemble. . . .

DA 693 is the title of a book which is bound to draw much attention to a very healthy and happy Serge Chaloff. Serge is back after four months in the hospital, and has written an autobiography of his life in the music business and what he has done. He hopes that his example will serve to warn other young fellows on the way up.

"Narcotics," says Serge, "is a symbol in a troubled make-up. It's like a man having cancer. It's a sickness."

Literary Serge is a musical Serge again too. He has done a date at Storyville and the Kenton Presents Series. . . . From this corner, we are very glad to have him back. (Coss 1955)

The "Kenton Presents" series sextet album for Capitol Records only offered ten titles of the twelve Coss mentioned being recorded. This LP, titled *Boston Blow-up,* quickly became particularly rare and commanded high prices on the collectors' market for decades. All performances were relatively short, seldom approaching five minutes. Again, there was a short, entirely scored tone poem, "Diane's Melody" by Jaki Byard. The two ballads of the date were both masterpieces. "What's New" and, even more so, "Body and Soul" exhibited even greater emotive intensity and delicacy of phrasing and execution than "Easy Street" from the year before. Both featured Serge throughout, with occasional sparse ensemble textures as backing.

The remaining nine titles (ten performances counting the alternate take of "Herbs") were all similarly structured arrangements. They varied from one another primarily in tempo, which ranged from medium swingers like "Kip" and "Yesterday's Gardenias" to the blisteringly fast "Unison." Most of these arrangements began and ended with ensemble statements, although on "Kip," the brushes-and-piano introduction provided an exception. The three horns always soloed first, sometimes with intermittent ensemble comments, and a piano solo was usually featured before the ensemble endings. Only an occasional drum break near the end varied this pattern. This was also the case with the previously unissued items, the effective "Boomaree Maroja" and the two takes of "Herbs." It is noteworthy to compare the two takes of "Herbs." The slower take had considerably deeper impact and was generally the more effective performance. Curiously, on the three up-tempo numbers recorded on the 4th, Mussulli led the solo order among the horns, with Serge soloing last. On the 5th, Serge invariably led the solo routines with Mussulli soloing last, except on "Bob the Robin" on which Mussulli followed Serge. On all performances, the textures and solos were light and swinging, owing more to the "cool" conception than the aggressive "hard bop" approach which was beginning to dominate in the front line of jazz stylists.

Herb Pomeroy (1995) reminisced about working with Serge in a 1995 interview:

I'd known Serge since about early 1950. I was a freshman at Harvard and would go to the jazz clubs, and Serge was just back in Boston from being on the road with Woody. I'd seen him with Woody in about 1948, but didn't know him then yet. I don't remember a concrete moment when I met Serge, but we were playing together by 1951. I'd left Harvard by then and was studying at the Schillinger School of Music which later became Berkelee. I was a kid working with the big star, and hanging out with Dick Twardzik. Dick and I were very close, and Dick and Serge were *very* close musically, and of course in other ways also, the drugs and everything. Serge didn't let many people close to him personally, but I was as close as any of the Boston musicians with Serge musically, once I proved myself with Serge, and after that we were together a lot. I remember going over to Serge's apartment on Newbury Street with Dick Twardzik. Serge was married to Linda then and they had a little baby daughter.

I was very honored to work with Serge, the strong emotional intensity in his music was so powerful. Take "Body and Soul" from the Capitol album. Standing there next to him in the studio as he played it, we knew this was an important performance, you could feel it, we all felt it. The A & R man missed it somehow; he popped out of the booth and said something about a slight mistake, and everyone chased him out, we knew that was *it*. And to this day, forty years later, mention "Body and Soul" to any Boston musician and they talk about Serge. I can remember in Detroit, the summer of 1955 shortly after making that album, we were playing the Rouge Lounge or someplace, and during that cadenza ending of "Body and Soul" Serge was playing with such intensity that the neck of the saxophone snapped off clean. It was a coincidence because Serge had bought that baritone from a man in Detroit. Anyway he had to have it fixed the next day, but Boots and I had to finish that night as just the two of us. I remember Pepper Adams, one of the greatest modern baritone players, sitting in the front row every night that gig, absorbing what Serge was doing.

The warmth on his ballads! The intensity that he would rehearse us with! I learned so much. He rehearsed us in Storyville in the Copley Square Hotel two or three mornings a week all that fall and winter, leading up to that record date. You know, Red Garland was the first pianist with that group. Ray Santisi didn't read that well but Ray soaked up what Red was doing and when Red bowed out after a few weeks Ray stepped in. I don't think we gigged with Red at all. I remember Serge would coach us on exaggerating the dynamics so the nuances would come out. He demanded a lot, but especially of himself.

Ironically, just as Serge was gaining visibility once again in the jazz world, Gerry Mulligan began winning the baritone sax honors in the jazz magazine polls, a position Serge had held from 1949 through 1953 despite being less prominent in the jazz world than previously. In *Metronome*'s "Jazz 1956" yearbook, Bill Coss wrote an essay on Serge's comeback and noted a curious resistance, primarily among musicians, toward Serge's reemergence. He attributed this phenomenon to Serge's past excesses. As quoted by Alun Morgan (1957):

> The most subtle, yet the most telling indication of these problems was the reaction of other musicians to him. In the caste system which jazz musicians seem to automatically form, Serge had every right to expect consideration and respect. But it should have been evident in the last years to even the most casual viewer, that he received little of either.

Presumably, the chaotic vacillations in Serge's personality during what he himself called the "nine years of living hell" of his heroin habit, and his role in dealing drugs and rumors of his role in trumpeter Sonny Berman's death at age twenty-two in 1947 from a drug overdose, all contributed to this reserve on the part of his peers. Nevertheless, he received a measure of respect from his supporters on the Boston scene, as in his participation in the Boston Arts Festival's Jazz Night, again held in the Public Gardens on June 13, 1955. Following a panel discussion on "The Anatomy of Jazz," the Serge Chaloff Sextet was featured along with an older styled group:

> Serge Chaloff's group began the musical half of the evening. With Boots Mussulli, Herb Pomeroy, Dick Twardzik (piano), bassist Everett Evans, and drummer Ray Santisi [*sic*], Serge played an impressive set, marred by his own lack of dynamics, but just as considerably aided by the fresher tone and lighter feeling that is now his. "Sharp Six" was an up-tempo romp. Boots' "Kip," named after his boy, had, reasonably enough, fine Mussulli; "Four Brothers" demonstrated the group's precision and swing. Twardzik's "Fable of Mabel" was a considerable improvement over the recorded version, Serge in complete control even when a low-flying plane drowned out the piano and left him up the baritone without a paddle. "Round Robin," dedicated to Boston disc jockey Bob Martin, gave everyone a chance to show off a bit. It's a fine group with Twardzik and Chaloff the most glowing lights in the night.
>
> Older jazz was represented by Ruby Braff. . . . Then there was a free-for-all with both groups jamming. . . . The most interesting thing about all that is that when Ruby played one old standard, Serge played "The Goof and I" line; not the height of musical cooperation but a fascinating exposition of thinking according to eras. (B. Coss 1955)

A review of this night in the *Boston Herald* of June 14, 1955, added details:

> The ingenuity of Chaloff as a soloist is enormous and his use of dissonance always conveys a strength of purpose and of form. In "Body and Soul" he exhibited his capabilities vigorously, taking a deliberate tempo and treating the music from a lyric, delicate, tonal standpoint. Pomeroy, the trumpeter, is in every way his match rhythmically, in the articulation of difficult registers and in tonal nuance, while Mussulli in "Kip" and "No. 6" disclosed a rapport with the rest that proved to be the very heart of the ensemble. As a whole the harmonies of the group are tense and the melodies resourceful and they play with a kind of controlled abandon.

In his "Eulogy for Twardzik" article in *Metronome* that winter, following Twardzik's death in Europe from a drug overdose while on tour with Chet Baker, Serge wrote of this event:

> His performance at the Arts Festival in Boston last summer was probably the greatest and most inspired he ever played. The concert included the playing of his own composition called "The Fable of Mabel" that he had previously recorded with me, for George Wein on Storyville records. . . . He believed in the "Boy Up Stairs" and his many admirers and myself

only wish he could have stayed with us longer and contribute the many wonderful things he had in his mind to do. I'll always miss Dick and music has lost one of its most ardent and inspired crusaders. (Chaloff 1956)

Again, photos found in Madame Chaloff's effects show only the front line hornmen of Serge's group at the mike, this time without mentioning any tunes being played. Unfortunately, no recordings of the event are believed to exist.

A few weeks after this festival, Serge played a dance gig with a pick-up group at Westbrook Junior College in Portland, Maine, sometime that July. The band on this occasion included Dick Cornwall (tenor sax), Jerry Cohen (piano), Gene Whiting (guitar), Bob Lippe (bass), and Charlie Pine (drums). According to Richard Chaloff, over 100 minutes of this group's music were recorded there on 16″ acetates. This material came into the posession of Richard Chaloff in the winter of 1993–94, but was promptly turned over to Bob Sunnenblick, who released several previously unissued broadcast and private recordings of Serge on the 1994 Uptown Records CD (see discography). It is apparently possible that this session could also eventually be issued, at least in part. Unfortunately, to date, details of what was performed could not be ascertained, although Richard Chaloff mentioned "Now's the Time," "Perdido," "Body and Soul," and "Tangerine" being among the numbers he recalled.

Serge again took his regular group on the road for a two-month tour beginning in Baltimore near the end of July 1955. Herb Pomeroy (1995) remarked on this tour in the 1995 interview:

The sextet had a character of its own. Bob Martin managed it and we toured that summer. Serge and Boots would room together and I'd room with Dick Twardzik. The first club we played was in Baltimore, I think the Club Giovanni. Then we went to this Rouge Lounge in Detroit. Then someplace in Washington. Two weeks at a time in clubs all that summer.

You know, the sextet that toured wasn't the same rhythm section as the album. We had Dick Twardzik on piano, and Gus Johnson on drums. Serge had gotten to know Gus when he was with Basie in 1950 and they became really good friends. So when Ray Santisi and Jimmy Zitano decided to stay in Boston and work at the Jazz Workshop, Serge got Dick and Gus. It really made a difference in the feel of the group because Gus was out of that Kansas City style, not the bop style of drumming at all, but it worked.

Are you aware of a child in Detroit whose name was Serge? When we worked at the Rouge Lounge in Detroit in the summer of 1955, every morning when we came downstairs in the hotel where we stayed, there'd be this woman sitting in the lobby with this young boy, looked just like Serge. We all accepted that this was Serge's son. He never introduced us, and I don't know what was going on; maybe she was getting money? The boy was about five years old. We assumed she was somebody he met on the road with Woody at the end of the 1940s, you know how it is. It's interesting because one of the things I remember is his always calling Washington, the state, that is, while we were on the road that season. He was calling Susie out there. But they weren't married yet.

By the end of September, Serge was again back in Boston. Bill Marlowe, who was a popular radio jazz disc jockey in the early 1950s at station WCOP in Boston, had hung out with Serge during 1954–55 "nearly every night" whenever Serge was in town. He reminisced about their association in a brief telephone interview in 1995:

> Serge was the most dedicated musician I ever met. I'd tried to talk him out of using the "hard stuff" [heroin] and was greatly relieved when he finally did stop. I'd tear down to wherever he was playing after my radio show and we'd go to Slade's for barbecued chicken after his gig. There were other musicians' hangouts we would go to: the Pioneer Club with great jazz stars was a "biggie" for musicians. Barbara's on St. Vital Street, was another musicians' hangout.
>
> Serge was an enigma, a paradox. Unique.
>
> Three of us, "Buck" Buckhalter, Serge and I founded a new jazz club called Jazzorama, and even helped pick the waitresses. It was the only real competition to Storyville at the time. Serge would lead the house band there from the opening on, when he wasn't on the road.

The club's opening was mentioned in *Metronome* by reviewer Paul Coss:

> Late in September, a new room called Jazzorama opened in what was formerly The Five O'Clock . . . the best feature of all was the superb sound of the Serge Chaloff Sextet. Serge, fresh from a long road trip, is welcome back in Boston, and his fine album has gained him many more new friends. (P. Coss 1955b)

Although Richard Chaloff took beautiful color photographs of Serge and his band on the stand on opening night, Serge's sidemen (although seen clearly) could not be identified by those who have examined the photos to date. By then, Dick Twardzik had left to tour Europe with Chet Baker, where he died of an overdose, and Herb Pomeroy had left the Sextet to take a teaching job at the Berkelee School of Music. Pomeroy (1995) recalled:

> We were in Washington with the sextet in September when Larry Burke called me to come teach at Berkelee, which was just getting going. When I told Serge I had to leave the sextet to take the position at Berkelee, he was shocked, incredulous. "You're quitting the group to go *teach*??" he asked in amazement. The trumpet player who took my place was Joe Blovello [sp?].

Pomeroy, highly respected as a jazz educator and arranger, went on to a forty-year career teaching at Berkelee while continuing to perform regularly, including being an active and vital participant in the Third Stream Movement of the later 1950s.

During October 1–19, Serge had a group at the Jazzorama in Boston. Serge again played the Celebrity Lounge in Providence, Rhode Island, from October 28 to November 12, in a quintet format along with Boots Mussulli (alto sax), Bob Freedman (piano), Everett Evans (bass), and Paul Drummond (drums). Following this gig, the group went on to a series of one-nighters around western Massachusetts. They were then again at the Jazzorama in Boston from November 21 to December 5.

Later that year Serge was a member of a big band organized by his former sextet trumpet man, Herb Pomeroy. This big band also drew favorable reviews and generated excitement and enthusiasm on the Boston scene at the time. Pomeroy (1995) recalled:

> When Serge was in my big band he played with such authority, so strong, he was playing lead from the baritone chair. Usually the lead player in each section is the first chair, but Serge just pulled everybody along. We started the band in November 1955. We played around New England, two nights a week at the Jazz Workshop, went to New York and played Bird-land, the Apollo, but after a couple of months Serge left and went on the road with pickup groups.

In December 1955, Bob Martin arranged for a television appearance for Serge on the popular Steve Allen Show. A private audiotape of "Stompin' at the Savoy" from this broadcast circulates among collectors and was finally issued on CD in 1994. This performance included Doc Severinsen, then still in his twenties, on trumpet; Boots Mussulli on alto sax; fellow Bostonian Sonny Stitt, with whom Serge had also performed at the Christmas 1949 concert, this time playing tenor sax; and Steve Allen on piano. Viewers who recalled this event could not remember who was on bass or drums (presumably the studio men regularly on Allen's show at the time), and there has been some debate over whether or not this was the only piece played. Only the horns soloed. Stitt and Chaloff followed the opening ensemble with a chorus apiece. Another chorus was split between Mussulli and Severinsen before the ensemble took it out. The entire performance timed at only 2:36, but despite its brevity it would be of great interest if the video survived, as so few videos featuring Serge otherwise exist and all soloists were in good form.

Ironically, it was around this time that Bob Martin and Serge parted company. When asked about his relationship with Serge in a 1995 telephone discussion, Martin did not want to discuss any problems or difficulties in detail. However, he was extremely enthusiastic about Serge's music. He mentioned being "heartbroken" when the Serge Chaloff Sextet dissolved as a steady group, and stressed that, musically, Serge was "the greatest."

Serge began 1956 working at the Storyville in Boston with Jay Migliori's group, from January 2 through 16. Following this engagement, Serge went on tour again, being booked into the Cotton Club in Cleveland during late January and early February.

The February 22, 1956, *Down Beat* noted Serge and Lou Donaldson had opened at the Stage Lounge in Chicago on February 15 for two weeks. They were with a rhythm section consisting of Norman Simmons (piano), Victor Sproles (bass), and Vernel Fournier (drums). A private tape was anonymously made there sometime during this two-week engagement. A dub of this low-fidelity set was broadcast by disc jockey Phil Schaap over station WKCR-FM in New York in 1991, with the date of recording unaccountably being given as March 18, 1957. Copies now circulate among private collectors. Sharing the front line with only an alto saxophonist recalled the quintet Serge had with Boots Mussulli that had recorded for Storyville in 1954, but this group performed with more energy. Donaldson was also very potent in interacting with Chaloff's lines in their simultaneous improvising. This feature was prevalent among the titles preserved, which total more than forty-five minutes of music. (Another title featuring Donaldson, on which Serge did not play, was from the same set.) Despite the high quality of some of Lou Donaldson's earlier work, he was surprisingly strong on this date, as if he was particularly inspired by Serge, casting an even deeper shadow over his own later, rather commercially oriented output. The rhythm section was appropriately supportive and, despite the poor fidelity of circulating dubs, can be heard with reasonable balance. If the original tape could be found, cleaned up with contemporary recording technology, and released, it would provide a major statement concerning Serge's music (see discography).

Serge's next recording session produced his masterpiece, and one of the great jazz albums of all time, the Capitol LP titled "Blue Serge." Serge was still on tour and recorded the album with a pickup group in Los Angeles on March 14 and 16, 1956, immediately after closing two weeks at Hollywood's Jazz City with a group that had consisted of Serge with Sonny Stitt (mostly on alto sax, according to reports), Sonny Clark (piano), Leroy Vinnegar (bass), and Lawrence Marable (drums). There were apparently no rehearsals for the record date. "We just started blowing," Serge was quoted as stating in the liner notes. The quartet consisted of Serge backed by the underrated and undeservedly obscure Sonny Clark on piano, another victim of an early death. The well-known and widely respected Leroy Vinnegar was the bassist; and Philly Joe

Jones, in town with the Miles Davis Quintet which included John Coltrane at the time, was the drummer. Seven titles were released on LP, with another title, "How About You," filling out a later Japanese CD reissue. The rapport of the group was as moving as the music, and the net effect was of every note being in place, flawlessly executed, as if even the slightest nuance was carefully chosen for maximum aesthetic impact. This is a level of achievement beyond the aspirations of all but the masters, and from an ensemble that was not even a working group, it takes on an aura of the miraculous. Such achievements are rare in any medium.

Aside from "The Goof and I" and Serge's own "Susie's Blues," the repertoire consisted of standards. The former was taken very fast and in addition to fleet, precisely articulated solo work, included a superb series of four-bar exchanges between Chaloff and Jones. The blues was also taken up-tempo, and included a section of unaccompanied four-bar exchanges among all four members of the group before Serge and Philly Joe cooked through some more conventional exchanges.

"Thanks for the Memory" was another in the series of moving ballads that featured Serge throughout. "Stairway to the Stars" also opened and closed as a ballad performance, but the rhythm section double-timed in between, and there was also a piano solo. "A Handful of Stars" had a bouncy, happy medium tempo feel. "All the Things You Are" was a bit faster and swung nicely. "I've Got the World on a String" had some particularly intriguing variety, as Jones was on brushes and there were shifting rhythmic patterns. Serge also played along during Vinnegar's otherwise unaccompanied bass solo with sub-tone lines, creating a very effective counterpoint. "How About You" had a happy, swinging feel featuring good solos from Chaloff, Clark, and Jones.

Throughout, all solos were effective and the group was very closely attuned, with sensitive, intelligent accompaniment for the solos. Timings ranged from just under four minutes for "Thanks for the Memory" to just under seven for "I've Got the World on a String." In effect, this quartet session provided more variety than earlier efforts despite the reduction of tonal possibilities, and offered full exposure for Serge's brilliance, undiluted by the presence of other hornmen.

Serge may have been inspired by the presence of the "Susie" of "Susie's Blues" from this session. She was Susan Black, no relation to Linda Black, Serge's first wife. Richard Chaloff referred to her as "a society girl from California who met him in Boston." Richard thought Serge and Susan were married in Mexico shortly after this record date, while Serge was still working on the West Coast, but details could not be confirmed. He went on to describe her:

> This was a great big lanky lady, a very pretty blonde, very, very tall. She was a decorator, designer, and she worked in one of the stores here in

Brookline, on Harvard Avenue, something like "Contemporary Interiors." This young lady came from California, through New York, to Boston. She met him and married him and she was with him right to the very end, to the day he died. She was a lovely girl, devoted. (Chaloff 1985)

Nancy Chaloff also compared Serge's second wife to a film actress: "If Linda resembled Mitzi Gaynor a little, Susie would be more a Gene Tierney type, with a very refined personality, very elegant." (Personal communication 1995)

According to the liner notes to the original "Blue Serge" Capitol LP issue of these performances, Susan had come to Los Angeles from Seattle (her home town) to be present for these recording sessions. In fact, testimony from Bob Martin and others indicated Susan had begun to act in the capacity of Serge's personal manager and that Serge began to defer any decisions and commitments on his musical activities to her, well before the 1956 tour began.

This was clearly a peak period in Serge's life. Healthy and free of drugs at last, in love with a new wife and their relationship blossoming, he was playing better than ever.

Serge was continuing to work on the West Coast, performing at the Starlite in Hollywood during May, when he was suddenly incapacitated one day while playing golf when recurring severe back and abdominal pains escalated to beginning to paralyze his legs. He was flown back to Boston for diagnosis and underwent surgery twice in late May to relieve a depressed nerve on the spine. This condition was due to a tumor, and "After an exploratory operation, he and his doctors and his friends knew it was just a matter of time" (Final Bar 1957).

Richard Chaloff (1985) discussed Serge's final illness:

He was shocked. He did not know what it was, and all of a sudden the feeling came back into his legs, but I told him, "Look, that's not right, there is only one place to come." And he flew in and we took him down there [Massachusetts General Hospital], my mother and I, and they found he had lesions on his spine. They finally operated on his spine, too. They felt a growth. So they operated and took most of the lesions away, and then he went on a series of X-ray treatments. Oh, they were terrible. He must have had twenty or twenty-five in a row. And in those days they really gave you heavy doses of it. Then occasionally he got spots on the lungs.

Amazingly, he was again in the recording studios for another Metronome All-Stars session on June 18, 1956, despite the short time since his surgery. As with the earlier Metronome All-Stars record sessions Serge played for in 1950 and 1951, there were solos by all concerned, but this time for an extended performance with a looser arrangement of only one title, the blues "Billie's Bounce." Since so much time was allotted for the performance, there was generous space for all soloists to stretch out, as opposed to the usual cameo spots in such sessions. There were three takes. The third was chosen for release and timed in at about twenty-one minutes. According to Bill Coss's liner notes for the eventual LP release, Serge had played even better on take #2, but Thad Jones had been late for the session and only made the last take (Coss 1956). The group consisted of Thad Jones (trumpet), Eddie Bert (trombone), Tony Scott (clarinet), Lee Konitz (alto sax), Al Cohn and Zoot Sims (tenor sax), Serge Chaloff (baritone sax), Teddy Charles (vibes), Billy Taylor (piano), Tal Farlow (guitar), Charles Mingus (bass), and Art Blakey (drums). Serge was variously reported playing the date from a wheelchair or on crutches, but there seemed to be no loss of power or imagination in his solos on that date.

Concerning the last year of Serge's life, Richard Chaloff (1993–95) has said:

> Serge had a lot of support during his illness from Mother and his wife, Susie. Mother bought him a kinkajou monkey to keep him company when he was bedridden, and kept encouraging him to fight the disease. I think they kept him going for awhile there, with their encouragement. It even got to be a rivalry thing between his mother and his wife, trying to outdo each other helping him.

Serge continued to work, playing from crutches or a wheelchair. For a while he was leading a group at The Stable in Boston, and he also continued to play in Herb Pomeroy's big band.

His last record date was for the *Four Brothers Together Again!* album, a reunion session recorded for Vik on February 11, 1957. For this session, Serge was reunited with three of the tenor saxophonists with whom he had been in the Second Herd sax section at different times during 1947–49: Al Cohn, Zoot Sims, and Herb Steward. They were backed by a rhythm section consisting of Elliott Lawrence (piano), Buddy Jones (bass), and Serge's old comrade Don Lamond (drums). Serge was in such poor health by then that another baritone saxophonist, Charlie O'Kane, was brought in to play ensemble parts when Serge began to weaken towards the end of the recording session, but all baritone sax solos were by Serge, who was in good form throughout. Unfortunately the rhythm section was poorly recorded on this date, but all four saxophonists played well if not at their most inspired. Serge was the only soloist on "Aged in Wood" for an effective feature, but did not solo on "So Blue" or "The Pretty One." All performances were relatively short. The longest, "Four and One More," timed in at only 4:02. Richard Chaloff (1985) recalled Serge's last record date:

He took a wheelchair down to make that recording, you know. They didn't think he was going to make it. I heard stories from people there. But when he stood up and played, you never knew he was a sick fellow. He played dynamic. If you listen to the record, he sounds like the old Serge. He pulled himself together. I don't know how he did it. But he had tremendous drive, tremendous stamina. He was bombastic. When he was going to do something, he did it.

As late as May 2–15, 1957, despite the debilitating effects of his illness, Serge was performing at The Stable, in Boston, with a local rhythm section. Charlie "The Whale" Johnson (who later was manager for Dizzy Gillespie, among others) was just getting into the business in that era, and remembered Serge's gig there very well. In a 1993 personal interview, he recalled:

I remember pushing Serge's wheelchair into The Stable for his last appearances there. He was in bad shape but could still really play, standing leaning against a pillar. However, he didn't have much stamina. He couldn't actually finish the gig. I also had to go get pot and booze for him. He was imbibing these steadily, even in the hospital at the end.

Of course, it is now widely known that marijuana will ease or eliminate some of the side effects of chemotherapy, which can be appalling. Nevertheless, it has been widely reported that Serge continued his habit of chemical dependency by using these forms of getting high from the time of his recovery from his heroin addiction until his death.

This gig at The Stable was apparently Serge's last public appearance. Two months later, on July 15, 1957, Serge made his final trip to Massachusetts General Hospital. Richard Chaloff (1993–95) described those final days:

He still had the kinkajou monkey Mother got him to keep him company. And he had his horn. I was told they wheeled him into a vacant operating room so he could practice, and that was his last gig, his last public performance, solo baritone sax alone in an operating theater. Nurses, doctors, and even patients were standing outside and listening.

He fought it to the end. Mother would visit him and urge him on, saying, "You can beat it" and things. But that last day, they brought a priest to visit him, and the priest saw Serge in bed asleep looking so wasted, the priest thought he was supposed to perform last rites. Serge woke up in the middle of it and really panicked, sliding away from him and yelling, "No! No! Get out!" But after that, he seemed to give up. I think that's when he realized it was all over.

Serge Chaloff died the next day, four months short of his thirty-fourth birthday.

The Legacy

Because Serge's autobiography, *DA 693*, has not become available, the record of his life consists largely of the performances scattered through the extensive discography on which he was featured as a soloist. Of course, every title on which Serge had performed was an aspect of his legacy, even those in which he was buried in the sections of all of the many big bands in which he worked. However, there his work was basically anonymous, and could have been performed by any good baritone section man. In the big bands with which he performed, he was almost never featured except with the Second Herd, so the focus of interest obviously is: those titles with the Second Herd on which he was featured; the sessions he made with smaller groups, where he was usually featured to advantage; and, most significantly, his recording sessions as leader, whether in formal studio sessions for records or from live broadcasts or private recordings. It is in these contexts that one can hear the evolution of his work and what it was he had to offer musically, in context and presumably representing what he wanted to do.

It should also be apparent that his later recordings, following the 1951–54 hiatus, showed considerable advances in his approach and featured him more extensively and in his most sympathetic contexts. His earlier, pre-hiatus recordings certainly cannot be dismissed, however, since it brought him to prominence and contained outstanding work by all concerned. In fact, these recording sessions stand as landmarks in the history of jazz and helped define the style of the era. In any case, Serge's status as the first baritone saxophonist to be featured extensively and to present an individual style in the new idiom at that time ensure his place in jazz history. His relevant records (and broadcasts) are of interest not only to anyone concerned with the jazz of that era but also to anyone seeking the classic sessions of jazz performance.

Preceding the discography, a list of titles of the pieces on which Serge soloed is provided. In this solo index, the leader of the group with whom the piece was recorded follows the tune title in parentheses, unless it was Serge, in which case it says "(LEADER)." The date of recording follows (except in the case of Serge's recordings with Woody Herman, since those dates appear in the Second Herd tune index in detail). Following the discography, an alphabetical list of tunes known to exist by the Second Herd with their recording dates is provided. The pieces in that section on which Serge soloed can be identified from the alphabetical list of all titles on which Serge was featured as a soloist.

The following list of sources and additional readings not used as references in the text excludes record reviews and entries in standard encyclopedias. Additional information may also appear in liner notes to the various issues of recordings.

List of Sources

Adamson, Steve. 1991. Interview by Rick Paulosky. Boston, October.

Auld Sets New Band. 1947. *Down Beat,* August, 13.

Band Listings. Various Years. *Down Beat.*

Chaloff, Nancy. 1995. Interview by author. Boston, June.

Chaloff, Richard. 1985. Interview by Lewis Porter and Norman Saks. Boston, May, 25.

————. 1993–96. Interviews by author. Boston (many conversations, visiting with him for a week at a time, or by telephone).

Chaloff, Serge. 1956. Eulogy for Twardzik. *Metronome,* January, 25.

Chaloff, Serge (file). Questionnaire for *Jazz Encyclopedia,* Institute of Jazz Studies, Rutgers University.

Cooper, Pat. 1995. Interview by author. Long Island, New York, June.

Coss, Bill. 1955. In Person: Serge Chaloff. *Metronome*, August, 11.

————. *1951. Jazz in Boston. Metronome*, December, 15, 33.

————. 1956. Liner notes to *Metronome All-Stars 1956.* Verve MGV8030.

Coss, Paul D. 1955a. Dateline USA—Boston: Back Bay Shuffle. *Metronome*, June, 9–10.

————. 1955b. Dateline USA—Boston. *Metronome*, November, 14–15.

Feather, Leonard. 1950. Chaloff's Challenge. *The Melody Maker*, 15 July, 5.

————. 1944. I. R. Hutton: From China to Georgia. *Metronome*, March, 31–32.

Final Bar. 1957. *Down Beat*, 22 August, 9.

Gardner, Mark. 1971. *Jazz Journal International*, April, 2–5.

————. 1976. Liner notes to *The Brothers and Other Mothers.* Savoy SJL2210.

Goodspeed, Mert. 1991. Interview by Rick Paulosky. Boston, October.

Hanley, Wayne. 1955. Musician Who Took Dope Cure Wants to Tell Addicts His Story. *Boston Sunday Herald*, 1 May, 1, 16.

Hentoff, Nat. 1951. Serge Seeks Action Again After Two Years in Boston. *Down Beat*, 14 December, 3, 5.

Herman, Woody, and Stuart Troup. 1990. *The Woodchopper's Ball.* New York: E. P. Dutton.

Kuhn, Steve. 1993. Interview. *Cadence*, January, 6–7.

Morgan, Alun. 1957. Serge Chaloff. *Jazz Monthly*, October, 24–26.

Pomeroy, Herb. 1995. Interview by Richard Chaloff and Vladimir Simosko. Boston, June.

Schuller, Gunther. 1990. *The Swing Era*. New York: Oxford University Press.

Shep Fields Switches to Ten Reeds and No Brass. 1941. *Metronome*, May, 19.

Simon, George T. 1967. *The Big Bands*. New York: Macmillan.

———. 1971. *Simon Says*. New York: Galahad Books.

Tommy Reynolds Build-up Like Artie Shaw's. 1939. *Metronome*, December, 10.

Treichel, James A. 1978. *Keeper of the Flame: Woody Herman and the Second Herd*. Spottswood, New Jersey: Joyce Music Publications.

Ulanov, Barry. 1950. In Person: Serge Chaloff. *Metronome*, March, 22.

Verspoor, Dolf. 1972. Liner Notes to *Blue Serge*, Capitol M-11032.

Will Osborne Give Up Band for Hollywood? 1941. *Metronome*, February, 9.

Wilson, John S. Serge, Pres, Erroll Head Birdland Bill. *Down Beat*, 24 February, 3.

Additional Readings

Ansell, Derek. "Serge Chaloff." *Jazz Journal* 48, no. 11 (November 1995):12–13.

Burns, Jim. "Serge Chaloff." *Jazz Journal* 21, no. 3 (March 1968):14–16.

Dumas-Delage, Jean. "Un mort sans importance." *Jazz Magazine*, no. 111 (October 1964):40–42.

Groves, Alan. "Blue Serge Blues." *Jazz Journal* 22, no. 6 (June 1979):8–9.

Harrison, Max. "Backlog 14: Serge Chaloff." *Jazz Monthly,* May 1963, 10–12.

Kopelowicz, Guy. "Mort de Serge Chaloff." *Jazz Hot,* September 1957, 24.

Simosko, Vladimir. "Serge Chaloff." *Montreal Vintage Music Society Bulletin,* no. 200 (November 1988):4–8. (NOTE: This was a brief article and tentative discography).

Simosko, Vladimir. *The Complete Serge Chaloff Sessions.* Booklet in Mosaic Records MD4-147(CD)/MQ5-147(LP), 1993, 16pp.

Williams, Martin. "Blues for Serge Chaloff." *Down Beat,* 16 May 1968, 10.

Serge Chaloff at the Jazzorama, Boston, September 1955.

Serge at The Flame in Minneapolis, 1953, with singer Dell Scott.

Serge and Charlie Mariano at the Boston Arts Festival, June 9, 1954.

Serge soloing at the Boston Arts Festival, June 9, 1954.

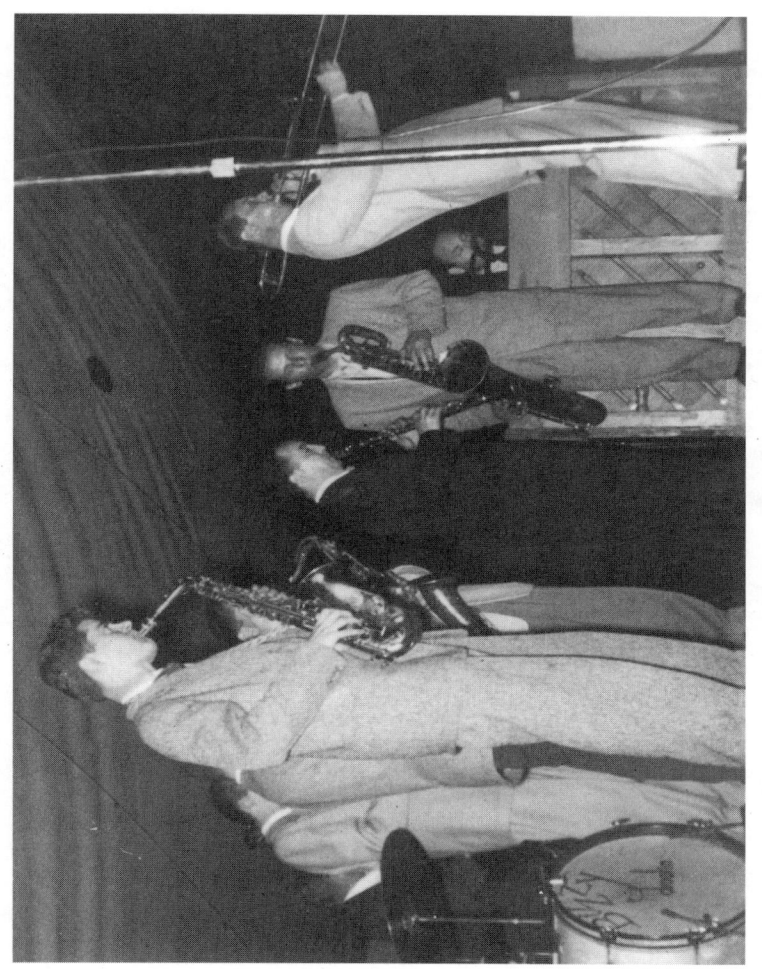

Jam session at the Boston Arts Festival, June 9, 1954.

Serge at Blinstrub's, August 29, 1954, sitting in on tenor sax with Paul Bordeleau's band at Richard and Nancy's wedding reception.

The Boston Arts Festival, June 13, 1955: (left to right) Boots Mussulli, Herb Pomeroy, and Serge.

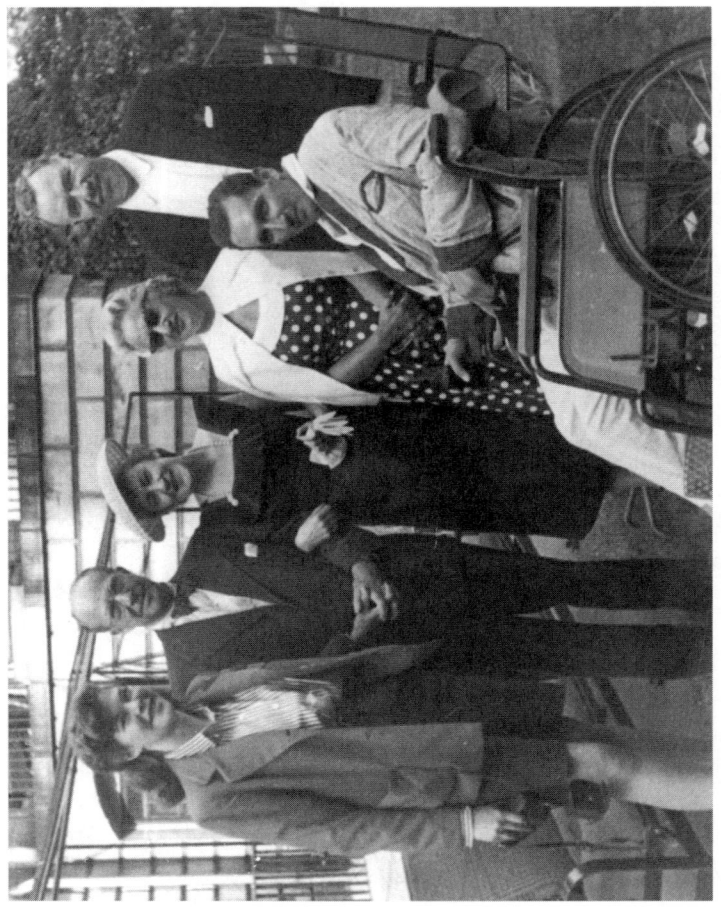

Serge in his wheelchair, about 1957. Left to right: Susan Black Chaloff, unknown, Margaret Chaloff, and Steve Kuhn's parents.

Introduction to the Discography

The primary sources for this discography were *60 Years of Recorded Jazz* by Walter Bruyninckx (Belgium: The Author, various datings) and, as a basis for the section on the Second Herd, *Keeper of the Flame: Woody Herman and the Second Herd* by J. A. Treichel (Spottswood, N.J.: Joyce Music Publications, 1978). Corrections and additions to data from these sources were the result of comparison with the recordings, to original research by Richard Paulosky, and input from other researchers such as Erik Raben for the Jimmy Dorsey segments. Other relevant discographical work was also taken into consideration, and the results shown here often represent a reinterpretation of conflicting information from various sources, refined by additional data. The discography follows standard discographical format. The abbreviations for musical instruments in this listing are as follows:

(as)	=	alto saxophone	(g)	=	guitar
(b)	=	bass	(p)	=	piano
(bar)	=	baritone sax	(ss)	=	soprano sax
(bcl)	=	bass clarinet	(tb)	=	trombone
(btb)	=	bass trombone	(tp)	=	trumpet
(cga)	=	congas	(ts)	=	tenor sax
(cl)	=	clarinet	(v)	=	vocal
(d)	=	drums	(vbs)	=	vibes

Record labels are usually spelled out or with obvious abbreviations apparent in context. Exceptions might include:

AFRS ONS	=	Armed Forces Radio Service One Night Stand
BLCD	=	Black Lion Compact Disc
C&B	=	Cool & Blue Compact Disc
FTR	=	First Time Records
GE	=	Golden Era
IAJRC	=	International Association of Jazz Record Collectors
SoS	=	Sounds of Swing
QD	=	Queen Disc

It is assumed that in most band situations in this era the saxophone section members were all involved in doubling. Many arrangements called for clarinet section work. The baritone saxophonist would double on bass clarinet. Photos of Chaloff in the Second Herd show a bass clarinet on a stand beside him. However soloists were generally featured on their primary saxophone, and discographies usually note only the players' role in the section in that way. In situations such as the Shep Fields band where all members doubled on several woodwinds, instrumentation is listed as simply "(reeds)" for all members of the section. Boyd Raeburn was a multi-reed player, and his reed sections were also often called upon for various doubling roles. Vocalists are identified after each track in parentheses with their initials following "v" for vocal; e.g., (vWH) = Woody Herman vocal.

In 1993, Mosaic Records issued a boxed set with illustrated booklet written by Vladimir Simosko titled *The Complete Serge Chaloff Sessions* on four CDs (MD4–147) or five LPs (MQ5–147). This set contains everything Chaloff recorded in the studios as a leader (with the exception of a few unissued alternate takes from March 5, 1947) as shown in the discography.

As Chaloff spent much of his early career as a sideman in big bands without opportunity to solo on surviving recordings, an index to tunes on which he was featured as soloist is provided for convenience.

Solo Index to the Discography

A Bar a Second (LEADER) 5 March 1947
A Handful of Stars (LEADER) 14 March 1956
A New Kind of Love (LEADER) c. late March 1954
A Quick One (4 Bros.) 11 February 1957
A Salute to Tiny (LEADER) 3 September 1954
Aged in Wood (4 Bros.) 11 February 1957
All God's Chillun Got Rhythm (Rodney) 29 January 1947
All I Do is Dream of You (LEADER) c. late March 1954
All the Things You Are (LEADER) 16 March 1956
All the Things You Are (LEADER) c. late February 1956
Apple Honey (Herman)
Berled in Erl (Herman)
Billie's Bounce (Duo) 17 November 1947
Billie's Bounce (All-Stars) 18 June 1956
Billie's Bounce (LEADER) c. late February 1956
Blue Serge (= Cherokee) (Burns) 21 September 1946
Blue Serge (Duo) 17 November 1947
BMT Face (= The Slumbering Giant) (Berman) 24 January 1946
Bob the Robin (LEADER) 5 April 1955
Body and Soul (solo tenor & piano) c.1939–40/1943
Body and Soul (Duo) 17 November 1947
Body and Soul (LEADER) 4 April 1955
Boomsie (Herman)
Bopscotch (LEADER) 10 March 1949
Cherokee (Burns) 21 September 1946
Cherokee (jam session) late 1949
Chickasaw (LEADER) 10 March 1949
Ciretose (= Sonny's Blues) (Berman) 24 January 1946
Curbstone Scuffle (Berman) 21 September 1946
Dial-ogue (= Cherokee) (Burns) 21 September 1946
Double Date (All-Stars) 10 January 1950
Down With Up (= Woodchopper's Holiday) (Berman) 24 January 1946
Early Spring (All-Stars) 23 January 1951
Easy Street (LEADER) c. late March 1954
Eenie Meenie Minor Mode (LEADER) 3 September 1954
Elevation (Rodney) 29 January 1947
Everything Happens to Me (LEADER) 3 September 1950
Fan It (Herman)
Fine and Dandy (Rodney) 29 January 1947

Fine and Dandy (jam session) late 1949
Flippin' the Wig (= Woodchopper's Holiday) (Berman) 21 September
  1946
Four & One Moore (4 Bros.) 11 February 1957
Four Brothers (Herman)
Four Brothers (LEADER) 3 September 1950
Four Brothers (4 Bros.) 11 February 1957
Four in Hand (4 Bros.) 11 February 1957
Gabardine & Serge (LEADER) 5 March 1947
Gabardine & Serge (LEADER) 22 February 1950
Gabardine & Serge (Theme) (LEADER) 3 September 1950
Gabardine & Serge (LEADER) c. late September–early October 1950
Godchild (Herman)
Gone With the Wind (LEADER) c. late February 1956
Half Past Jumping Time (Herman)
Here We Go Again (4 Bros.) 11 February 1957
Hoggimous Higgamous (= Sonny Speaks Out) (Berman) 24 January
  1946
Honeysuckle Rose (private recording on "4-hands" piano) 1943
Hot House (All-Stars) 24 December 1949
How About You (LEADER) 16 March 1956
I Got Rhythm (jam session) spring 1950
I Told Ya I Love Ya (Herman)
I've Got the World on a String (LEADER) 14 March 1956
Junior (LEADER) 5 April 1955
Keen & Peachy (Herman)
Keen & Peachy (LEADER) c. late September–early October 1950
Keeper of the Flame (Herman)
King Edward the Flatted Fifth (LEADER) 16 April 1949
Kip (LEADER) 4 April 1955
Lemon Drop (Herman)
Let's Jump (LEADER) 3 September 1954
Local 802 Blues (All-Stars) 23 January 1951
Lollypop (Herman)
Love Is Just Around the Corner (LEADER) c. late March 1954
Lover Man (LEADER) c. late February 1956
Lullaby in Rhythm (Herman)
Man Don't Be Ridiculous (Herman)
Mar-dros (LEADER) 4 April 1955
Moon Burns (= Nocturne) (Berman) 21 September 1946
Move (All-Stars) 24 December 1949
My Fair Lady (Herman)
My Pal Gonzales (Herman)
Neal's Deal (Basie) 16 May 1950

No Figs (All-Stars) 10 January 1950
Nocturne (= Moon Burns) (Berman) 21 September 1946
Non-Alcoholic (Herman)
Northwest Passage (Herman)
Now's the Time (LEADER) c. July 1955
Oh Baby (LEADER) c. late March 1954
Ornithology (All-Stars) 24 December 1949
Pat (LEADER) 16 April 1949
Pennies From Heaven (LEADER) 22 February 1950
Pennies From Heaven (LEADER) 3 September 1950
Pennies From Heaven (LEADER) c. late September–early October 1950
Perdido (Dorsey) 25 September 1946
Pumpernickel (LEADER) 5 March 1947
Red Cross (Duo) 17 November 1947
Serge's Urge (LEADER) 5 March 1947
Sergical (LEADER) 5 April 1955
Slam (LEADER) 3 September 1954
Sonny Speaks Out (= Hoggimous Higgamous) (Berman) 24 January
    1946
Sonny's Blues (= Ciretose) (Berman) 24 January 1946
Stairway to the Stars (LEADER) 16 March 1956
Stompin' at the Savoy (LEADER) c. December 1955
Summer Sequence (Herman)
Susie's Blues (LEADER) 14 March 1956
Tempus Fugit (Herman)
Ten Years Later (4 Bros.) 11 February 1957
Thanks for the Memory (LEADER) 14 March 1956
That's Right (Herman)
The Fable of Mabel (LEADER) 3 September 1954
The Golden Bullet (Basie) 16 May 1950
The Goof and I (Rodney) 29 January 1947
The Goof and I (Herman)
The Goof and I (LEADER) 3 September 1950
The Goof and I (LEADER) 14 March 1956
The Goof and I (LEADER) c. late February 1956
The Happy Song (Herman)
The Mad Monk (= Cherokee) (Burns) 21 September 1946
The Most (LEADER) 10 March 1949
The Slumbering Giant (= BMT Face) (Berman) 24 January 1946
The Swinging Door (4 Bros.) 11 February 1957
These Foolish Things (LEADER) c. late September–early October 1950
Unison (LEADER) 4 April 1955
We the People Bop (Herman)
What's New (LEADER) 5 April 1955

Wild Root (Herman)
Woodchopper's Holiday (Berman) 24 January 1946
Woodchopper's Holiday (Berman) 21 September 1946
Yesterday's Gardenias (LEADER) 5 April 1955
You Rascal You (Herman)
Zdot (LEADER) c. late March 1954

The Discography

SERGE CHALOFF

Newton, Massachusetts, c. 1939–40

Serge Chaloff(ts)

    Body and Soul   (private recording)

NOTE: This acetate of Chaloff performing an imitatively Coleman Hawkins-like unaccompanied tenor sax version of "Body and Soul" was recorded by Richard Chaloff in Serge's bedroom.

TOMMY REYNOLDS AND HIS ORCHESTRA

New York, 21 December 1939

Tommy Reynolds(cl), Marshall Hutchins, Peter Abramo, Chuck Hill(tp), Don Cavanaugh, Dick Hathaway(tb), Louis Colombo, Joe Fandel(as), Tino Isgro, Harold Raymond, or Serge Chaloff(ts), George Kohler(p), Parker Lee(g), Wilfred Dufresne(b), Kenny Unwin(d), Marion Page(v)

25606	Marcheta	Vocalion 5339
25607	Night After Night With You (vMP)	Vocalion 5317
25608	Deep Night	Vocalion 5339
25609	It's a Blue World (vMP)	Vocalion 5317
25610	Promenade Strut	(rejected)

NOTE: All issued titles also on Swing Era LP1005.

Penny Porter(v) for Page

New York, 24 January 1940

25872	Now You Know (vPP)	OK5418
25873	Pipe Dreams	—
25874	Wouldst Could I But Kiss Thy Hand	
	(vPP)	OK5373
25875	Make Love With a Guitar (vPP)	—

NOTE: First two titles also on Swing Era LP1005.

Sally Richards(v) for Porter

New York, 28 February 1940

| 26568 | Whispering Grass (vSR) | OK5463 |
| 26569 | If It Weren't for You (vSR) | Vocalion 5431 |

| 26570 | Just a Memory | OK5468 |
| 26571 | Moments in the Moonlight (vSR) | Vocalion 5431 |

NOTE: 26568 & 26570 also on Swing Era LP1005.

Same or similar
New York, 17 April 1940

26745	Sierra Sue (vSR)	OK5521
26746	Dolly Doolittle (vSR)	OK5554
26747	Two Guitars	—
26748	I Can't Love You Any More (vSR)	OK5521

NOTE: 26747 also on Swing Era LP1005.

Same or similar
New York, 14 May 1940

27277	Missouri Scrambler	OK5594
27278	I'll Wait for You Forever (vSR)	—
27279	On a Simmery Summery Day (vSR)	OK5569
27280	I Love to Watch the Moonlight (vSR)	—

Add Gene Saunders(v)
New York, 10 June 1940

26904	Please Take a Letter Miss Brown (vGS)	OK5645
26905	Once Over Lightly	—
26906	The Sailor With the Navy Blue Eyes (vGS,SR)	OK5604
26907	I Bought a Wooden Whistle (vSR)	—

NOTE: 26905 also on Swing Era LP1005.

Same or similar
New York, 25 July 1940

27693	Jungle Jive	OK5791
27694	I Don't Want to Cry Any More	OK5718
27695	Stop Pretending (vSR)	—
27696	I'll Tell It to the Breeze (vSR)	OK5791

NOTE: First 3 titles also on Swing Era LP1005. Various personnel changes occurred during the above interval. Sidemen who came and went in Reynolds' band that year included Peanuts Hucko(ts), Joe Neil(tb), and Whitey Orton(d), according to announcements in *Down Beat*. The band worked regularly at the Playland Casino in Rye, New York, that spring and summer. Although Chaloff stated he had joined

Reynolds shortly after he turned 16 in 1939 and recorded with the band (confirmed by Richard Chaloff), standard discographies (often inaccurate) have failed to list him in the personnel. Consequently it is not known which, if any, of the indicated sessions may have included Serge. Since he was never given solo space on records, the question is academic, and the above listing is of interest primarily in documenting the band's repertoire. The personnel for the following date, from Bruyninckx, also did not mention Chaloff.

TOMMY REYNOLDS AND HIS ORCHESTRA
New York, 21 September 1940

Tommy Reynolds(cl), Hank Maddalena, Julio Tancredi, Cy Siok(tp), Tom Bell, Nick DiMaio(tb), Al Anthony, Lanny Ross, Floyd Smith, Nick Peters, and/or Serge Chaloff(reeds), Joe Cribari(p), George Robinson(g), Eddie Spear(b), Joe Kurtz(d), Mary Ann McCall, Ralph Young(v)

28605	If You See Margie (vRY)	OK5807
28606	Halfway Down the Street (vMAM)	—
28607	Something to Live For (vRY)	OK5902
28608	Nickle's Worth of Rhythm (vMAM)	—

Same or similar
Lang-Worth Transcriptions, New York, c. 1941

Aloha	Golden Era GE 15006
Lone Prairie	—
In Old Havana	—
Taboo	—
Photo Finish	—
Swanee River	—
Frenesi	—
Beautiful Dreamer	—
Two Guitars	(unissued)
There'll Be Some Changes Made	Swing Era LP 1005
Sweet and Low	—
Home on the Range	—

NOTE: Exact dates and personnel uncertain; Chaloff probably present.

TOMMY REYNOLDS AND HIS ORCHESTRA
New York, 3/4 February 1942

Tommy Reynolds(cl,v), Andy Szule, Walter Shark, unk.(tp), Walt Szule, Gus Dixon(tb), Fred Guerra, unk.(as), Jerry Morin(ts), Serge Chaloff (ts,bar), Guy Borielli(p), unk.(b), unk.(d), Mary Ann McCall(v)

Smiles (vTR&B)	Soundie #5902
Farewell Blues	Soundie #6107
I'm Coming Virginia (vMAM)	Soundie #6403

NOTE: Chaloff can be seen in the sax section playing tenor, with a baritone on the stand next to him, on "Smiles." On Soundie #6403, the band played the soundtrack, but "Aileen Shirley and Her Minoco Maids of Melody" were seen on the screen.

SERGE CHALOFF–MARGARET CHALOFF DUO
Newton, Massachusetts, 28 January 1943

Serge Chaloff(p), Margaret Chaloff(p)

"4-hands" boogie woogie	(private recording)
Honeysuckle Rose	—

Serge Chaloff(p); same session

Body and Soul	—
Body and Soul	—

NOTE: The above is a homemade acetate made by Richard Chaloff.

SHEP FIELDS AND HIS ALL-REED ORCHESTRA
Broadcasts, c. 1941–1944

Collective personnel include: Sol Schlinger, Mike Cuozzo, Al Ouiellet, Dave Kurtzer, Lew Weinstein, John Gentile, Tom Lucas, Joe Soldo, Serge Chaloff, Nick Santucci, Ray Eckstrand, Bob Ploland, Birge Vaughan, Babe Fresk, Ben Glassman, George Ford, Romeo Penque, Al Freistat(reeds), Henry Lapidus, Sid Schwartz, Bill Clifton(p), Al Casamenti, Tommy Kaye(g), William Bendy, Al Benson(b), Sid Greenfield, Fred Noble(d)

Gloworm	GE 15012	
Lover's Lament	—	, Hindsight HSR 160
1600 on the Clock	—	—
Harlem Nocturne	—	
105 Groove Street	—	
Jump Fever	—	
Copa-ca-boogie	—	
Brahms' Hungarian		
Dance #5	—	
Shakey	—	—
Nightfall	—	
Powder Puff	—	—

Dinner at the Brown's	—
Major 6th	—
Dance of the Clowns	—
Mellow Moods	—
Skeleton Dance	—
The Fire Dance	—
Sophisticated Lady	—
American Patrol	—
Heavenly Isn't It	—
Autumn Nocturne	—
If I Had You	—
Stormy Weather	—
Things Ain't What They Used To Be	—
Little Pink Elephants	—
Sheik of Araby	—
The Moon Is Low	—

NOTE: Exact dating for the above airchecks and/or transcriptions is not certain. Therefore it is uncertain which, if any, titles Chaloff may have participated in. Nevertheless, as he did not solo, the question is academic, but the above material certainly represents the band's book at the time Chaloff was with them, and is therefore typical of the repertoire he would have performed.

By mid-1943 Chaloff was certainly with Ina Ray Hutton's band (see text) and can be seen in their feature film *Ever Since Venus* playing bass clarinet and baritone sax at different points, but does not solo. His participation on the following AFRS programs is therefore certain.

INA RAY HUTTON AND HER ORCHESTRA
AFRS Spotlite Bands #312, Batavia, New York, c. August 1943

Stan Fishelson, Roger Ellick, unk.(tp), Ollie Wilson, unk.(tb), Joe Megro, Serge Chaloff, unk.(reeds), Hal Schaefer(p), Jack Purcell(g), unk.(b),(d), Ina Ray Hutton, Stuart Foster, Kim Loo Sisters (Pat, Alice, Margaret), Morton Downey(v)

> No Two Ways About Love (vIRH)
> Put Your Arms Around Me Honey (vMD)
> In My Arms (vKLS)
> Star Eyes (vSF)
> Goodbye Sue (vMD)
> King Porter Stomp

Post Picture Corp. film *Ever Since Venus*
Hollywood, c. early 1944

Similar personnel; add unidentified string section

> The Wedding of the Boogie and the Samba (vIRH)
> Glamour for Sale (vSF)
> Beauty Through the Ages (vIRH,SF)
> Miss 1944 (vIRH)
> (unidentified incidental instrumental music)

Omit strings
AFRS Spotlite Bands #463, Naval Air Station,
Quonsett Point, Rhode Island, 13 March 1944

Blue Skies	Joyce LP 4009
That Old Black Magic (vSF)	—
Georgia	—

Same
Army Air Base, Spence Field, Georgia, 5 June 1944

King Porter Stomp	Sunbeam SB 223
All of Me (vIRH)	—
Blue Moon	—
Milkman Keep Those Bottles Quiet (vIRH)	—
Take It Easy (vIRH,KLS)	—

NOTE: This material was also taken from an AFRS Spotlite Bands broadcast but the number of this show is unknown.

Same
AFRS Spotlite Bands #551, Miami, Florida, 23 June 1944

All of Me (vIRH)
Honeysuckle Rose
Theme

NOTE: Shortly after the above broadcast, Ina Ray Hutton disbanded her orchestra for medical reasons. Several band members promptly joined Boyd Raeburn.

BOYD RAEBURN AND HIS ORCHESTRA
AFRS ONS #316, Roosevelt Hotel, Washington, D.C., 9 July 1944

Roy Eldridge, Tommy Allison, Stan Fishelson, Benny Harris(tp), Jack Carmen, Ollie Wilson, Trummy Young(tb), Walter Robertson(tp,tb),

Johnny Bothwell, Hal McCusick(as), Al Cohn, Joe Megro(ts), Serge Chaloff(bar,bcl), Boyd Raeburn(reeds), Ike Carpenter(p), Steve Jordan(g), Oscar Pettiford(b), Shelley Manne(d), Don Darcy, Margie Wood(v)

> Sweet Lorraine (vDD)
> March of the Boyds
> I'll Remember April
> Milkman Keep Those Bottles Quiet (vMW)
> Night in Tunisia
> It Could Happen to You (vDD)
> Sequence
> I Don't Want to Love You (vDD)
> Little Boyd Blue (inc)

Same

> AFRS ONS #342, West End Casino, Long Branch, New Jersey, 16 July 1944

> An Hour Never Passes (vDD)
> Come Out Come Out Wherever You Are (vMW)
> Street of Dreams
> Sweet Lorraine (vDD)
> Two Spoos in an Igloo
> Milkman Keep Those Bottles Quiet (vMW)
> I'll Remember April
> Medley (vDD,MW)
> Sequence (inc)

NOTE: Personnel from Bruyninckx, *60 Years of Recorded Jazz*. Conflicting data have been published concerning these sessions and listing different personnel.

BOYD RAEBURN AND HIS ORCHESTRA
> AFRS ONS #445, Dayton, Ohio, 19 August 1944

Lou Cless, Pinky Savitt, Stan Fishelson, Benny Harris(tp), Earl Swope, Bob Swift, Trummy Young(tb), Johnny Bothwell, Hal McCusick(as), Joe Megro, Angelo Tompros(ts), Serge Chaloff(bar,bcl), Boyd Raeburn (reeds), George Handy(p), John Payuo(g), Mert Oliver(b), Don Lamond(d), Don Darcy, Margie Wood(v)

> (unknown titles)

Same

> Lang-Worth Transcriptions, New York, 21 August 1944

3456	Bernie's Tune (Bobby Socks)	LW1070, FTR1515
	Duck Waddle	—

	Magic is the Moonlight	— , SoS115
	Theme	— , FTR1515
3457	Come Out Come Out Wherever You Are (vMW)	LW100
	I'll Walk Alone (vMW)	—
	Is You Is Or Is You Ain't My Baby? (vTY)	—
	Too Much In Love (vDD)	—
	An Hour Never Passes (vDD)	—

OSCAR PETTIFORD AND HIS ORCHESTRA
New York, 9 January 1945

Dizzy Gillespie, Bill Coleman, Benny Harris(tp), Vic Dickenson, Trummy Young(tb), Johnny Bothwell(as), Don Byas(ts), Serge Chaloff (bar), Clyde Hart(p), Al Casey(g), Oscar Pettiford(b), Shelly Manne(d), Rubberlegs Williams(v), others unknown

W1218	Something for You	Manor 1034, Xanadu 124
W1219	Worried Life Blues (vRW)	Manor 1002, —
W1220	Empty Bed Blues, pt. 1 (vRW)	— —
W1221	Empty Bed Blues, pt. 2 (vRW)	Manor 1034, —

BOYD RAEBURN AND HIS ORCHESTRA
Lang-Worth Transcriptions, New York, 17 January 1945

Dizzy Gillespie, Stan Fishelson, Tommy Allison, Benny Harris(tp), Walter Robertson(tp,tb), Jack Carman, Ollie Wilson(tb), Johnny Bothwell, Hal McKusick(as), Al Cohn, Joe Megro(ts), Serge Chaloff(bar), Boyd Raeburn(reeds), Ike Carpenter(p), Steve Jordan(g), Oscar Pettiford(b), Shelly Manne(d), Margie Wood, Don Darcy(v)

3995	Barefoot Boyd With Cheek	LW1097, FTR1515
	Lonely Serenade	— , GE 15014
	Sequence	— , FTR1515
	Who's to Answer? (vDD)	—
3996	Blue Moon	LW134, FTR1515
	I'll Always Be in Love With You	— , GE 15014
	Summertime	—
	Solitude (vDD)	—

Same
WEAF Broadcast, Apollo Theatre, New York City, 19 January 1945

The Hep Boyds
Swingin' for Josie

Same

New York, 26 January 1945

542	Night in Tunisia	Guild 107, Musicraft MVS505

Joe Berisco(b) for Pettiford

New York, 27 January 1945

543	March of the Boyds	Guild 111
544	Prisoner of Love (vDD)	Guild 104
545	I Wanna Get Married (vMW)	—
546	I Didn't Know About You (vDD)	Guild 107
547	I Promised You (vDD)	Guild 103
548	This Heart of Mine (vMW)	—
549	Summertime	Guild 111

NOTE: All titles also on Musicraft LP MVS505. Above substitution not always listed and remains uncertain. These Guild masters have been reissued many times on such labels as Musicraft, Allegro, Savoy, etc. All titles appeared in chronological order on Musicraft MVS505.

JOHNNY BOTHWELL AND HIS ORCHESTRA

New York, 12 February 1945

Same personnel except omit Gillespie

110	I'll Remember April	Signature 15003, BBM1-0641
111	Street of Dreams	Signature 15012, —
112	Our Delight	(unissued)

GEORGIE AULD AND HIS ORCHESTRA

New York, 24 May 1945

Al Aaron, Danny Blue, Art House, Al Porcino(tp), Rudy DeLuca, Al Esposito, Mike Datz(tb), Georgie Auld(as,ss,ts,v), Musky Ruffo, Gene Zanoni(as), Hy Rubenstein, Jack Schwartz(ts), Serge Chaloff(bar), Joe Albany(p), Turk Van Lake(g), Iggy Shevak(b), Stan Levy(d)

573	Honey (vGA)	Guild 135, Musicraft MVS501
574	Stompin' at the Savoy	— —
575	Jump Georgie Jump	Mus.377, —
576	Daily Double	Mus.15059, —

NOTE: As with the Raeburn Guild recordings, Auld's recordings for this label have appeared on many reissue labels, e.g., Allegro, Halo, Evon, Sutton, Viking, and others. They have been issued in chronological order on Musicraft MVS501 and MVS509 as indicated.

Add Patti Powers(v)

Trianon Ballroom, California, c. July–August 1945

Theme	Hep-27
Sentimental Journey (vPP)	—
Jump Georgie Jump	—
I'm Always Chasing Rainbows	—
Stompin' at the Savoy	—

GEORGIE AULD AND HIS ORCHESTRA

New York, 16 October 1945

Al Aaron, Danny Blue, Art House, Al Porcino(tp), Rudy DeLuca, Tracy Allen, Mike Datz(tb), Georgie Auld(ss,as,ts), Lou Prisby, Gene Zanoni (as), Al Cohn, Joe Megro(ts), Serge Chaloff(bar), Harry Biss(p), Barry Galbraith(g), Ed Cunningham(b), Buddy Christian(d), Lynn Stevens(v)

5310	Here Comes Heaven Again (vLS)	Mus.15043, MVS501
5311	It Had to Be You	Mus.375, —
5312	Air Mail Special	Mus.373, —
5313	Just A-Sittin' and A-Rockin'	Mus.15044, —

Same

New York, 23 October 1945

5314	Time on My Hands (vLS)	Mus.15046, MVS501
5315	Blue Moon	Musicraft MVS509
5316	Come To Baby Do (vLS)	Mus.15044
5317	Let's Jump	Mus.15046, —

NOTE: 5315 usually cited as "You Can Depend on Me" (unissued), but Musicraft MVS509 has a previously unissued "Blue Moon" instead. (Note also the 16 January 1946 session.)

Irv Roth(ts) for Megro

New York, 15 January 1946

5365	Chicken Lickin'	Musicraft MVS509
5366	I've Got a Right to Know (vLS)	(unissued)
5367	Stormy Weather (vLS)	Mus.374
5368	You Haven't Changed at All (vLS)	Mus.15059
5369	Blue Moon	Mus.373, —
5370	Seems Like Old Times (vLS)	Mus.15060, —

Same

New York, 16 January 1946

5383	Daily Double	Mus. 15059
5384	You Can Depend on Me	(unissued)

NOTE: While most copies of Musicraft 15059 have mx.#'s 576/5368, some have been reported that show "Daily Double" as mx.#5371 and others as mx.#5383.

SONNY BERMAN

New York, 24 January 1946

Sonny Berman, Marky Markowitz(tp), Earl Swope(tb), Al Cohn(ts), Serge Chaloff(bar), Ralph Burns(p), Eddie Safranski(b), Don Lamond(d)

Down With Up	
(Woodchopper's Holiday)	Esoteric ES532
Ciretose (Sonny's Blues)	—
The Slumbering Giant (BMT Face)	—
Hoggimous, Higgamous	
(Sonny Speaks Out)	—

NOTE: All titles also on Onyx LP 211 and Cool & Blue CD 111. Session privately recorded by Jerry Newman in his apartment, beginning at 2 a.m. on the above date; all titles are extended performances. Scheduled bassist Chubby Jackson failed to show, and Lamond brought only his snare drum. Safranski and Lamond (with full kit) were overdubbed later. Original titles, as listed by Esoteric, are followed above by the titles reassigned on reissues, in parentheses. This is the earliest known issued recording featuring Chaloff solos.

JIMMY DORSEY AND HIS ORCHESTRA

New York, 6 February 1946

Irving Goodman, Bob Alexy, Red Solomon, Cy Baker(tp), Don Matteson, Sonny Lee, Bob Alexander, Fred Mancusi(tb), Jimmy Dorsey (cl,as), Nick Stern, Cliff Jackson(as), Gil Koerner, Chuck Travis(ts), Serge Chaloff(bar,bcl), Lou Carter(p), Herb Ellis(g), Norman Bates(b), Karl Kiffe(d), Dee Parker(v)

73346	Ain't Misbehavin' (vDP)	Decca 18799
73347	I'll Always Be in Love With You (vDP)	Decca 24363
73348	I'm Glad There Is You (vDP)	Decca 18799
73349	Perdido	Decca 18812

NOTE: All titles from the above session also on LP on Ajaz 296. Although Chaloff solos on "Perdido" on the broadcast version of September 25, 1946, the abbreviated arrangement on mx#73349 does not feature Chaloff.

Same

World Transcriptions, c. March–April 1946

S250   Come To Baby Do (vDP)
S251   Autumn Serenade
S252   Outer Drive
S253   I'm Glad There Is You (vDP)
S254   Star Dust
S255   Jumpin' Jehosophat
S256   Begin the Beguine
S257   Oh What a Beautiful Morning

JIMMY DORSEY AND HIS ORCHESTRA
AFRS ONS #971, New York, 10 April 1946

Irv Goodman, Cy Baker, Red Solomon, Tony Faso(tp), Don Matteson, Fred Mancusi, Bob Alexander, Chauncey Welsch(tb), Jimmy Dorsey (as,cl), Nick Stern, Cliff Jackson(as), George Koerner, Vinnie Francis(ts), Serge Chaloff(bar), Lou Carter(p), Herb Ellis(g), Johnny Frigo(b), Karl Kiffe(d), Dee Parker, Bob Carroll(v)

(unknown titles)

Same

Broadcast, Terrace Room, Newark, New Jersey, 13 April 1946

Super Chief	Golden Era GE 15011
I Can't Begin to Tell You (vBC)	Magic (E) AWE27
Outer Drive	Golden Era GE 15011
Coax Me a Little (vDP)	Magic (E) AWE27

Same

Broadcasts, Terrace Room, Newark, New Jersey, c. April 1946

King Porter Stomp	
This Can't Be Love	
Perdido	
Tea for Two	
Ee-Bop-a-Lee-Bop (vDP,BC)	
I May Be Wrong (vDP)	
Royal Garden Blues	Golden Era GE 15082
Just One of Those Things	Golden Era GE 15011

NOTE: As the above version of "Perdido" could not be reviewed it is uncertain whether the abbreviated arrangement used on the Decca recording, or the extended arrangement broadcast on September 25, 1946, was used.

Same

New York, 15 April 1946

73504	Doin' What Comes Naturally (vDP)	Decca 18872
73505	All That Glitters Is Not Gold (vDP)	—
73506	The Way That the Wind Blows (vBC)	Decca 18900
73507	A Rose Was a Rose (vBC)	World 7941
73508	Apache Serenade (vDP)	Decca 18917
73509	The Same Little Chapel (vBC)	Decca 24363

NOTE: All titles on LP on Ajaz 296.

GEORGIE AULD AND HIS ORCHESTRA

New York, 30 April 1946

Al Aaron, Danny Blue, Art House, Al Porcino(tp), Tracy Allen, Rudy DeLuca, Mike Datz(tb), Georgie Auld(as,ss,ts,v), Lou Prisby, Gene Zanoni(as), Al Cohn, Irv Roth(ts), Serge Chaloff(bar), Roy Kral(p), Barry Galbraith(g), Ed Cunningham(b), Art Mardigan(d), Sarah Vaughan(v)

5457	Just You Just Me	Mus.15078
5458	A Hundred Years From Today (vSV)	Mus.15072
5450	Don't Know Why (vGA)	Mus.15078
5451	Route 66 (vGA)	Mus.15072

NOTE: All titles on LP on Musicraft MVS509. During spring 1946, Auld was not leading a regular working band, but was reconvening occasionally for recording sessions, according to the musical press.

GEORGIE AULD AND HIS ORCHESTRA

New York, 14 June 1946

Neal Hefti, Al Porcino, Sonny Rich, George Schwartz(tp), Johnny Mandel, Mike Datz, Gus Dixon(tb), Georgie Auld(ss,as,ts), Gene Zanoni, Sam Zittman(as), Al Cohn, Irv Roth(ts), Serge Chaloff(bar), Harvey Leonard(p), Joe Pellicane(b), Art Mardigan(d), Sarah Vaughan(v)

5560	Canyon Passage	Musicraft MVS509
5561	You're Blase (vSV)	Mus.394
5562	Handicap	—
5563	Mo-Mo (Georgie Porgie)	— —

JIMMY DORSEY AND HIS ORCHESTRA

AFRS ONS #1179, Edgewater Beach, San Francisco, 5 July 1946

Irv Goodman, Cy Baker, Red Solomon, Tony Faso(tp), Don Matteson, Fred Mancusi, Bob Alexander, Chauncey Welsch(tb), Jimmy Dorsey (as,cl), Cliff Jackson, Nick Stern(as), George Koerner, Vinnie Francis(ts), Serge Chaloff(bar), Lou Carter(p), Herb Ellis(g), Johnny Frigo(b), Karl Kiffe(d), Dee Parker, Bob Carroll(v)

(unknown titles)

Same

Hollywood, 25 July 1946

4249	The Whole World Is Singing My Song	
	(vBC)	Decca 18917
4250	One More Kiss (vDP)	Decca 18905

NOTE: Both titles on LP on Ajaz 296.

Same

AFRS ONS #1157, Casino Gardens Ballroom, Ocean Park, California, 12 August 1946

(unknown titles)

Add Bing Crosby(v)

Hollywood, 21 August 1946

4254	Make Me Know It (vDP)	Decca 18923, Ajaz 296
4255	The Language of Love (vBC)	— —
4256	If I'm Lucky (vBC)	Decca 18905, Ajaz 305
4257	The Things We Did Last Summer	
	(vBC)	Decca 23655, —

Same

AFRS ONS #1164, Casino Gardens, 22 August 1946

(unknown titles)

Same

AFRS ONS #1171, Casino Gardens, 23 August 1946

(unknown titles)

Same

Casino Gardens, c. August 1946

Apache Serenade (vDP)	AFRS Teen Timers #30
Perdido	AFRS Teen Timers #33

NOTE: It has not been possible to verify which arrangemnt of "Perdido" was used.

United Artists film *The Fabulous Dorseys*
Hollywood, c. September 1946

Add Helen O'Connell, Bob Eberly(v) for film only

Green Eyes (vBE,HOC)	FRE-5622
Contrasts (Theme)	—

NOTE: This entire film has been issued in VHS format by several companies, such as on Front Row Entertainment 5622; the film featured the then-current Jimmy Dorsey Orchestra for the above numbers. Chaloff can be briefly glimpsed at the extreme left edge of the screen during the few long shots of the whole band in this segment.

Same
Casino Gardens, 19 September 1946

Ain't Misbehavin' (vDP)	Sunbeam SB210
Oh What a Beautiful Morning	—
If I'm Lucky (vBC)	(unissued)

Add Tommy Dorsey and His Orchestra

Brotherly Jump	Sunbeam SB223

NOTE: Remaining titles from this broadcast are by Tommy Dorsey's Orchestra; bands were combined to close each show on "Brotherly Jump" (see September 25, 1946).

SONNY BERMAN/BILL HARRIS BIG 8
Hollywood, 21 September 1946

Sonny Berman(tp), Bill Harris(tb), Flip Phillips(ts), Serge Chaloff(bar), Ralph Burns(p), Chuck Wayne(g), Artie Bernstein(b), Don Lamond(d)

1031-F	Curbstone Scuffle	Dial 210	
1031-G	Curbstone Scuffle	Dial 1006,	C&B CD 102
1032-D	Nocturne (Moon Burns)	Dial 1020, Dial 210,	—
1033-C	Woodchopper's Holiday	Dial 1009	
1033-D	Woodchopper's Holiday	—	—

NOTE: All titles issued in order on Spotlite LP132. 1031-F mistitled "Woodchopper's Holiday" and 1033-D titled "Flippin' the Wig" on the 10″ LP Dial 210. All titles have been reissued often, on many labels under various titles, without indicating which take was used. Mx#1034 featured Bill Harris with the rhythm section only; mx#1035 featured Chaloff with the rhythm section as the SERGE CHALOFF–RALPH BURNS QUINTET as follows.

1035-A	Blue Serge (The Mad Monk)	Dial 211
1035-B	Blue Serge (pt. 1)	Dial 210
1035-C	Blue Serge (pt. 2) (Dial-ogue)	— , Dial 1008

NOTE: 1035-B/C issued as a continuous performance on LP & CD; 1035-C was issued on the 78 rpm Dial 1008 as "Dial-ogue" beginning with Burns' piano solo (see text). Both versions on Spotlite LP 132, Cool & Blue CD 102, and Mosaic MD4-147(CD) and MQ5-147(LP).

JIMMY DORSEY AND HIS ORCHESTRA
Casino Gardens, 25 September 1946

As previous

With the Language of Love (vBC)	Sunbeam SB210
South America Take It Away	Joyce LP 1101
Perdido	Sunbeam SB210, FHR-4

Add Tommy Dorsey and His Orchestra

| Brotherly Jump | Sunbeam SB210 |

NOTE: "Perdido" opens with a long Chaloff solo. Although First Heard Records FHR-4 has a skip in Chaloff's solo attributed to a "flaw in the master" the Sunbeam SB210 issue has no skip.

SERGE CHALOFF–ROLLINS GRIFFITH DUO
Boston, 17 November 1946

Serge Chaloff(bar), Rollins Griffith(p)

Billie's Bounce	Uptown UPCD 27.38
Body and Soul	—
Blue Serge	—
Red Cross	—

NOTE: This private session was recorded at the Chaloff home by Serge's brother, Richard (see text).

HERBIE FIELDS AND HIS ORCHESTRA
New York, 11/12 December 1946

Vince Badale, Jimmy Maxwell, Carl Poole, Bunny Snyder(tp), Bert Prager, George Arus, Sy Zelden(tb), Herbie Fields(cl,ss,as,ts), Art Baker, Paul Ricci(as), Al Klink, Stan Webb(ts), Serge Chaloff(bar), Marty Napoleon(p), Rudy Cafro(g), Martin Marino(b), Tiny Kahn(d)

| 3384 | Years and Years Ago | Victor 20-2104 |
| 3385 | Connecticut | — |

3405	Baby Made a Change in Me	Victor 20-2138
3406	Misirlou	—
3407	Cherokee	Victor 20-2054

RED RODNEY'S BEBOPPERS

New York, 29 January 1947

Red Rodney(tp), Allen Eager(ts), Serge Chaloff(bar), Al Haig(p), Chubby Jackson(b), Tiny Kahn(d)

196-2	All God's Chillun Got Rhythm	Keynote Col.	LP-20
196-5	All God's Chillun Got Rhythm	EmArcy MG36016,	—
197-1	Elevation	Keynote K670,	—
198-2	Fine and Dandy		—
198-3	Fine and Dandy	—	—
199-2	The Goof and I		—
199-4	The Goof and I	EmArcy MG36016,	—

NOTE: The master takes from this session as issued on Keynote K670 & EmArcy MG36016 also on Cool & Blue CD 102. *The Complete Keynote Sessions* set of LPs were issued in Japan.

SERGE CHALOFF SEXTET

New York, 5 March 1947

Red Rodney(tp), Earl Swope(tb), Serge Chaloff(bar), George Wallington(p), Curley Russell(b), Tiny Kahn(d)

3412-1	Pumpernickel	(unissued)
3412-2	Pumpernickel	—
3412-3	Pumpernickel (false start)	—
3412-4	Pumpernickel	Savoy SJL2210
3412-5	Pumpernickel	Savoy 956, —
3413-1	Gabardine and Serge	—
3413-2	Gabardine and Serge (incomplete)	(unissued)
3413-3	Gabardine and Serge	Savoy 978, —
3414-1	Serge's Urge	(unissued)
3414-2	Serge's Urge	—
3414-3	Serge's Urge	Savoy 956, —
3415-1	A Bar a Second	(unissued)
3415-2	A Bar a Second	—
3415-3	A Bar a Second	—
3415-4	A Bar a Second	Savoy 906, —

NOTE: All titles on Savoy SJL2210 from this session also on Mosaic MD4-147/MQ5-147. Despite Mosaic Records being assured by those holding the Savoy masters that additional takes did not exist, the above additional unissued takes began to circulate among collectors late in 1993 following a radio broadcast by Phil Schaap in New York. The first two takes of "Pumpernickel" included ensemble riffing behind the second chorus of Serge's solo. The second take of "Gabardine and Serge" broke down and was incomplete. The acetate for the first take of "Serge's Urge" was lost. The first take of "A Bar a Second" has a clipped beginning in circulating copies, starting midway through Serge's solo. The second take is complete and comparable in quality to the issued takes.

WOODY HERMAN AND HIS ORCHESTRA
Los Angeles, 19 October 1947

Stan Fishelson, Bernie Glow, Marky Markowitz, Shorty Rogers, Ernie Royal(tp), Bob Swift, Earl Swope, Ollie Wilson(tb), Woody Herman (cl,as,v), Sam Marowitz(as), Herbie Steward(as,ts), Stan Getz, Zoot Sims (ts), Serge Chaloff(bar), Fred Otis(p), Gene Sargent(g), Walt Yoder(b), Don Lamond(d)

| 2705 | If Anybody Can Steal My Baby (vWH) | Columbia 38047 |
| 2706 | I Told Ya I Love Ya (vWH) | —   , C3L-25 |

Same

Los Angeles, 22 December 1947

3043	Sabre Dance	Columbia 38102
3044	Cherokee Canyon (vWH)	Columbia CL2509
3045	I've Got News for You (vWH)	Columbia 38213, C3L-25
3046	Keen and Peachy	— —

Same

Los Angeles, 24 December 1947

| 3055 | The Goof and I | Columbia 38369, C3L-25 |
| 3056 | Lazy Lullaby (vWH) | —   — |

Same

Los Angeles, 27 December 1947

| 3061 | Four Brothers | Columbia 38304, C3L-25 |

Ralph Burns(p) for Otis, same session

| 3062 | Summer Sequence Pt.4 | Columbia 38367, — |

Fred Otis(p) for Burns; add Mary Ann McCall(v)
Los Angeles, 30 December 1947

| 3079 | Swing Low Sweet Clarinet (vMAM) Columbia 38102 |
| 3080 | My Pal Gonzales (vWH) | Columbia 38289 |

3081 P.S. I Love You (vMAM)   — , C3L-25
3082 Baby I Need You (vWH,MAM)   (unissued)

Same

Los Angeles, 31 December 1947

3088 Take a Little Time to Smile   (unissued)

NOTE: Other titles attributed to this session are spurious.

Universal Movie Short: *Woody Herman and His Orchestra*
Los Angeles, 2 February 1948

Jimmy Raney(g) for Sargent; Al Cohn(ts) for Steward. Add Modern-aires(v); Don & Beverly Dance Duo (for movie short only)

Blue Flame (Theme)
Sabre Dance
I Can't Get Offa My Horse (vM)
Caledonia (vWH)   MCA-V.2
Jingle Bell Polka (vM)
Cake Walk
Northwest Passage   —

NOTE: MCA-V.2 = MCA Home Video *Swing: The Big Band Era Vol. 2*. Chaloff, seen in the section, was featured only for a four-bar break on "Northwest Passage." "Cake Walk" (usually listed as "Cane Walk") shows dancers obviously doing the cakewalk to a medley of "Camptown Races" and "Oh Dem Golden Slippers." Ernie Royal, the Negro trumpet star of the band, is not shown on-screen but performed the music.

The band opened at the Hollywood Palladium February 3 (without the Modernaires) and broadcast regularly for the Armed Forces Radio Service "One Night Stand" programs. Treichel notes that the Armed Forces Radio Service "One Night Stand" broadcasts often shuffled tunes among broadcasts; therefore, some of the following may be repeated performances.

Same

AFRS ONS #1590, Hollywood Palladium, 3 February 1948

The Good Earth
P.S. I Love You (vMAM)
I Told Ya I Love Ya (vWH)
Wildroot   First Heard FH-21, Hep-18
Star Dust

I Got It Bad (vMAM)
Sabre Dance
Let's Fall in Love
Non-Alcoholic (inc)

Same

AFRS ONS #1579, Hollywood Palladium, 5 February 1948

Blue Flame (Theme)	
Four Brothers	First Heard FH-21
I've Got the World on a String (vWH)	
Golden Earrings (vMAM)	—
The Goof and I	—
Baby I Need You (vWH,MAM)	
Cherokee Canyon (vWH)	
P.S. I Love You (vMAM)	—
Non-Alcoholic	—
Four Brothers (inc)	

Same

AFRS ONS #1596, Hollywood Palladium, 6 February 1948

Blue Flame (Theme)
Sidewalks of Cuba
Golden Earrings (vMAM)
If Anybody Can Steal My Baby (vWH)
Non-Alcoholic
Sabre Dance
Swing Low Sweet Clarinet (vMAM)
Star Dust
I Told Ya I Love Ya (vWH)
The Goof and I (inc)

Same

AFRS ONS #1584, Hollywood Palladium, 7 February 1948

Blue Flame (Theme)	
The Goof and I	
How Soon? (vMAM)	
Cherokee Canyon (vWH)	
Keen and Peachy	First Heard FH-21
P.S. I Love You (vMAM)	
Am I Blue? (vWH)	
There'll Be Some Changes Made (vMAM)	—

Baby I Need You (vWH,MAM)
Northwest Passage (inc)

Same

AFRS ONS #1608, Hollywood Palladium, 8 February 1948

Blue Flame (Theme)
Sidewalks of Cuba
I Got It Bad (vMAM)
If Anybody Can Steal My Baby (vWH)   First Heard FH-21
It's Been So Long (vMAM)
Dance Ballerina Dance (vMAM)
Laura (vWH)
Baby I Need You (vWH,MAM)
Northwest Passage   Swing Treasury ST-108
Apple Honey (inc)

Same

AFRS ONS #1620, Hollywood Palladium, 12 February 1948

Blue Flame (Theme)	Hep-7
The Goof and I	—
There'll Be Some Changes Made (vMAM)	—
Let's Fall In Love (vWH)	
Baby I Need You (vWH,MAM)	—
The Good Earth	— , FH-21
Swing Low Sweet Clarinet (vMAM)	—
I Told Ya I Love Ya (vWH)	—
Apple Honey	—
Blue Flame (Theme)	—

Same

AFRS ONS #1602, Hollywood Palladium, 14 February 1948

Blue Flame (Theme)	
The Good Earth	
There'll Be Some Changes Made (vMAM)	
The Best Things in Life Are Free	
Sabre Dance	
Star Dust	FH-21
If Anybody Can Steal My Baby (vWH)	
Happiness Is a Thing Called Joe	
(vMM)	Hep-18
Apple Honey (inc)	

Same

AFRS ONS #1614, Hollywood Palladium, 29 February 1948

Blue Flame (Theme)
Half Past Jumping Time
I've Got It Bad (vMAM)
If Anybody Can Steal My Baby (vWH)
Star Dust
The Best Things in Life Are Free
Lazy Lullaby (vWH)
Toolie Oolie Doolie (vWH,MAM)
Apple Honey

Same

AFRS ONS #1626, Hollywood Palladium, 3 March 1948

Lullaby in Rhythm
Swing Low Sweet Clarinet (vMAM)
My Pal Gonzales (vWH)
I Cover the Waterfront
The Good Earth
Dance Ballerina Dance (vMAM)
P.S. I Love You (vMAM)
Laura (vWH)

Same

AFRS ONS #1632, Hollywood Palladium, 4 March 1948

Four Brothers
P.S. I Love You (vMAM)
If Anybody Can Steal My Baby (vWH)
I Cover the Waterfront
You Go To My Head (vMAM)
Sabre Dance
Let's Fall In Love (vWH)
Apple Honey

Same

AFRS ONS #1668, Hollywood Palladium, 5 March 1948

Blue Flame (Theme)			
Half Past Jumping Time	Hep-7, ST-113, QD-37		
I Got It Bad (vMAM)	—		
My Pal Gonzales (vWH)	—	—	—
Star Dust	—	—	—
Swing Low Sweet Clarinet (vMAM)	—		

Sabre Dance
Am I Blue? (vWH)
Keen and Peachy   —
Half Past Jumping Time

Same

AFRS ONS #1662, Hollywood Palladium, 6 March 1948

Blue Flame (Theme)
Lullaby in Rhythm   Hep-18, ST-113, QD-37
I've Got the World on a String
   (vWH)   —   —
You Turned the Tables on Me
   (vMAM)   —   —   —
Sabre Dance
I Cover the Waterfront   —   —
Just for Laughs (vMAM)
Baby I Need You (vWH,MAM)   —
Star Dust
Lullaby in Rhythm

NOTE: This entire broadcast issued on Raretone 5001-FC except for
the Theme and last title.

Same

AFRS ONS #1638, Hollywood Palladium, 7 March 1948

Blue Flame (Theme)
The Goof and I   QD-37, ST-113
Just for Laughs (vMAM)
I Cover the Waterfront
My Pal Gonzales (vWH)   —
Four Brothers   —   —
We'll Be Together Again (vMAM)   —
Lazy Lullaby (vWH)
Keen and Peachy (inc)   —   —

NOTE: Entire broadcast except Theme on Raretone 5001-FC.

Same

AFRS ONS #1644, Hollywood Palladium, 11 March 1948

The Goof and I
Bill (vMAM)
I Told Ya I Love Ya (vWH)

Just for Laughs (vMAM)
Dance Ballerina Dance (vMAM)
Sabre Dance
Lazy Lullaby (vWH)
Let's Fall In Love (vWH)

Same

AFRS ONS #1650, Hollywood Palladium, 12 March 1948

Blue Flame (Theme)	
Half Past Jumping Time	ST-108
I Got It Bad (vMAM)	
I've Got News for You (vWH)	—
What'll I Do?	QD-37
Bill (vMAM)	
Sabre Dance	
Am I Blue? (vWH)	
Non-Alcoholic	ST-108
Apple Honey	

NOTE: Entire broadcast except Theme on Raretone 5002-FC.

Same

AFRS ONS #1674, Hollywood Palladium, 13 March 1948

The Goof and I
How Soon? (vMAM)
Cherokee Canyon (vWH)
Keen and Peachy
The Best Things In Life Are Free
Just for Laughs (vMAM)
The Good Earth
Northwest Passage

Same

AFRS ONS #1656, Hollywood Palladium, c. March 1948

The Goof and I
Bill (vMAM)
I Told Ya I Love Ya (vWH)
Just for Laughs (vMAM)
Dance Ballerina Dance (vMAM)
Sabre Dance
Let's Fall In Love (vWH)

Toolie Oolie Doolie (vWH,MAM)
Northwest Passage

NOTE: Band closed at the Palladium March 15, 1948, to tour and opened at the Century Room, Hotel Commodore, New York City, on April 20, 1948, continuing their AFRS show series.

Harry Babasin(b) for Yoder
AFRS ONS #1793, Commodore Hotel, 28 April 1948

Blue Flame (Theme)	
Tiny's Blues	ST-108, Hep-18
My Fair Lady (vWH)	
The Happy Song (Fire Island)	
When You're Smiling (vMAM)	—
This Is New	— —
Dance Ballerina Dance (vMAM)	—
Nature Boy (vWH)	
Elevation (inc)	—

NOTE: Entire broadcast except Theme on Raretone 5002-FC. The Hep-18 LP notes dated these numbers as May 12.

Same
AFRS ONS #1782, Commodore Hotel, c. April–May 1948

The Goof and I
Swing Low Sweet Clarinet (vMAM)
But Beautiful (vWH)
Sabre Dance
Bill (vMAM)
I Cover the Waterfront
Let's Fall In Love (vWH)
Keen and Peachy

Same
AFRS ONS #1801, Commodore Hotel, 5 May 1948

Tiny's Blues
Blue Prelude (vWH)
I May Be Wrong (vMAM)
Sabre Dance
Trouble is a Man (vMAM)
The Happy Song (Fire Island)
My Fair Lady (vWH)
Keen and Peachy

Same

AFRS ONS #1745, Commodore Hotel, 12 May 1948

Blue Flame (Theme)	
The Goof and I	Swing Treasury ST-108
Nature Boy (vWH)	
The Happy Song (Fire Island)	Hep-18
Dream Peddler (vMAM)	—
Four Brothers	— —
Swing Low Sweet Clarinet (vMAM)	
I've Got News for You (vWH)	—
Keen and Peachy	— —

NOTE: Hep-18 dated the items indicated on April 28 as from May 12.

Band left the Century Room of the Commodore Hotel on May 17, 1948, to play the Capitol Theatre in New York May 20–June 17, then the Click Club in Philadelphia, Pennsylvania, June 28–July 4, 1948.

Ralph Burns(p) for Otis

AFRS ONS #1715, The Click Club, Philadelphia, 2 July 1948

Blue Flame (Theme)
Sidewalks of Cuba
But Beautiful (vWH)
You Turned the Tables on Me (vMAM)
P.S. I Love You (vMAM)
Berled in Erl
I've Got News for You (vWH)
Dream Peddler (vMAM)
Four Brothers
Sidewalks of Cuba (inc)

NOTE: Treichel indicated "Dream Peddler" and "Four Brothers" were dubbed from the May 12 broadcast.

Chubby Jackson(b) for Babison; add Bill Harris(tb)

AFRS ONS #1769, Steel Pier, Atlantic City, 8 August 1948

Blue Flame (Theme)	
Berled in Erl	ST-108, Hep-7
Trouble Is a Man (vMAM)	
My Fair Lady (vWH)	
Fan It (vWH)	— —
P.S. I Love You (vMAM)	
Sidewalks of Cuba	—
No Time (vWH)	

Northwest Passage   —
Berled in Erl

Same

Broadcast, Hershey, Pennsylvania, 26 August 1948

Blue Flame (Theme)
Elevation
(unk. vocal) (vMAM)
Keeper of the Flame
We the People Bop (vWH,Ens)
Sidewalks of Cuba
Keen & Peachy
Blue Flame (Theme)

Band opened at the Royal Roost, New York City, October 24.

WOODY HERMAN AND HIS ORCHESTRA
Royal Roost, New York City, 30 October 1948

Stan Fishelson, Bernie Glow, Marky Markowitz, Shorty Rogers, Ernie
Royal(tp), Bill Harris, Earl Swope, Ollie Wilson(tb), Bob Swift(btb),
Woody Herman(cl,as,v) Sam Marowitz(as), Al Cohn, Stan Getz, Zoot
Sims(ts), Serge Chaloff(bar), Terry Gibbs(vibes), Lou Levy(p), Chubby
Jackson(b), Don Lamond(d), Mary Ann McCall(v)

Keeper of the Flame	Cicala 8027, Alto 705	
Happiness Is a Thing Called Joe		
(vMAM)	—	
Yucca	—	—
I Can't Get Started		—
I've Got News for You (vWH)	—	—
Four Brothers	—	—
Bijou	—	—
Keen and Peachy		

Red Rodney(tp) for Markowitz
Royal Roost, 6 November 1948

Tiny's Blues		
Four Brothers		
Romance in the Dark (vMAM)	Alto 705, Cicala 8027	
John Had the Number	—	
Flamingo	—	
We the People Bop (vWH,ens)		
I've Got News for You (vWH)		

Boomsie   —   —
Blue Flame (Theme)

Same

Royal Roost, 8 November 1948

Tiny's Blues
I Can't Get Started
Bijou
My Last Affair (vMAM)
Four Brothers
I've Got News for You (vWH)
We the People Bop (vWH,ens)
Boomsie

Same

Royal Roost, 11 November 1948

Blue Flame (Theme)
Yucca
Keen and Peachy
I Can't Get Started
Romance in the Dark (vMAM)
Keeper of the Flame
Blue Flame (Theme)

Same

Royal Roost, 16 November 1948

Blue Flame (Theme)
Four Brothers
Oh Henry   Swing Treasury ST-108
I Got It Bad (vMAM)
Tiny's Blues
Flamingo   —
Keeper of the Flame   Swing Treasury ST-113
Out of Nowhere
I've Got a Way With Women (vWH)
Boomsie
Blue Flame (Theme)

Same

Royal Roost, 20 November 1948

Blue Flame (Theme)   Queen Disc QD 005
Oh Henry   —

I Got It Bad (vMAM)
We the People Bop
  (vWH,ens)   —   , C&B CD102
Flamingo
Tiny's Blues   —
Out of Nowhere   —
I've Got a Way With Women
  (vWH)   —
Boomsie   —
Blue Flame (Theme)   —

Same

                          Royal Roost, 22 November 1948

Four Brothers
My Last Affair (vMAM)
Oh Henry
I've Got News for You (vWH)
I Can't Get Started
We the People Bop (vWH,ens)
Keeper of the Flame

Same

                 Empire Room, Hollywood, 11 December 1948

Boomsie
My Last Affair (vMAM)
Yucca
I've Got a Way With Women (vWH)
Four Brothers
Keen and Peachy

Same

             AFRS Just Jazz #33, Empire Room, c. December 1948

Boomsie
Bill (vMAM)
I Only Have Eyes for You
Four Brothers
Let's Fall In Love (vWH)
Keen and Peachy

Same

        AFRS Just Jazz #37 & 54, Empire Room, c. December 1948

Blue Flame (Theme)   First Heard FH-29
Tiny's Blues   —

I Got It Bad (vMAM)
Four Brothers
Early Autumn
Keeper of the Flame

Same

AFRS Just Jazz #38 & 52, Empire Room, c. December 1948

Tempus Fugit	
Bill (vMAM)	
I've Got the World on a String	
(vWH)	First Heard FH-29
Tiny's Blues	—
Let's Fall In Love (vWH)	
Boomsie	—

Same

AFRS Just Jazz #41 & 59, Empire Room, c. December 1948

Blue Flame (Theme)
Lemon Drop (vEns)
I Only Have Eyes for You
My Last Affair (vMAM)
Someone to Watch Over Me (vWH)
Godchild
Out of Nowhere (inc)

Same

Los Angeles, 29 December 1948

3827-1	That's Right	Capitol 15427
3828-5	Lemon Drop (vWH,ens)	Capitol 15365

Same

Los Angeles, 30 December 1948

3829-1	I Got It Bad (vMAM)	Capitol 15427
3830-2	I Ain't Gettin' Any Younger (vWH)	Capitol 15365
3831-2	Early Autumn	Capitol 57-616
3832	More Than You Know	
3833-2	Keeper of the Flame	—

NOTE: All titles the Second Herd recorded for Capitol have been issued on CD on *Woody Herman: Keeper of the Flame* (Capitol Jazz CDP 7 98453 2). Mx#3832 has been listed in earlier discographies as an unissued version of "You Can Depend On Me" (vMAM) but the above instrumental appears on the CD issue.

Same

CBS Broadcast (1st show), Empire Room, 1 January 1949

The Goof and I	Artistry 109
You Go To My Head (vMAM)	
Four Brothers	
Early Autumn	
I've Got News for You (vWH)	
Keen and Peachy	
Lemon Drop (vWH,ens)	First Heard FH-29

Same (2nd show)

I Only Have Eyes for You	—
My Last Affair (vMAM)	—
Godchild	Artistry 109, —
Let's Fall In Love (vWH)	
Out of Nowhere	
Tiny's Blues	
Blue Flame (Theme)	

NOTE: There were two shows broadcast as above. Band closed at the Empire Room on January 3, 1949, and went on tour.

WOODY HERMAN AND HIS ORCHESTRA
Eddie Condon TV Show, New York, 26 February 1949

Ed Badgley, Bernie Glow, Red Rodney, Shorty Rogers, Ernie Royal(tp), Bill Harris, Earl Swope, Ollie Wilson(tb), Bart Varselona(btb), Woody Herman(cl,as,v), Sam Marowitz(as), Al Cohn, Stan Getz, Jimmy Giuffre(ts), Serge Chaloff(bar), Terry Gibbs(vibes), Lou Levy(p), Oscar Pettiford(b), Don Lamond(d), Mary Ann McCall(v)

Keen and Peachy
I Ain't Gettin' Any Younger (vWH)
Four Brothers
I Got It Bad (vMAM)
Bijou
Lemon Drop (vWH,ens)
Concerto for Cootie [add Cootie Williams(tp)](inc)

NOTE: Video portion of the show could not be reviewed. Tap dancer Teddy Hale was featured on "Keen and Peachy" and "Four Brothers." Chaloff soloed on his usual features.

Al Porcino, Charlie Walp(tp) for Glow & Rodney
Probably: Blue Note, Chicago, 4 March 1949

John Had the Number
Four Brothers
Out of Nowhere
Don Delves In
Man Don't Be Ridiculous
Everywhere
Bijou
Summer Sequence
More Than You Know (vMAM)
I Got It Bad (vMAM)
Lemon Drop (vWH,ens)

NOTE: The above broadcast has been dated both February 3 and March 4, 1949, from the Blue Note; however, the band was only reported at the Blue Note January 10–23, 1949. The band was in Chicago at the Music Bowl, January 31–February 5, but was reported in Baltimore at the Hippodrome March 3–9. Treichel noted this was drummer Don Lamond's last night with the band, being replaced first by Shadow Wilson, then shortly after by Shelly Manne; therefore March 4th seems most likely.

SERGE CHALOFF AND THE HERDSMEN
New York, 10 March 1949

Red Rodney(tp), Earl Swope(tb), Al Cohn(ts), Serge Chaloff(bar), Terry Gibbs(vbs), Barbara Carroll(p), Oscar Pettiford(b), Denzil Best(d)

704	Chickasaw	Futurama 3003
705	Bopscotch	—
706	The Most	Futurama 3004
707	Chasin' the Bass	—

NOTE: All titles on LP on Mercer 103, Prestige 7813, and Mosaic MQ5-147, and on CD on Cool & Blue CD 102 and Mosaic MD4-147. Chaloff does not solo on mx#707.

As noted, the confusion concerning the exact touring schedule of the Second Herd during the late winter and early spring of 1949 creates some doubts about locations and personnel changes.

WOODY HERMAN AND HIS ORCHESTRA
NBC broadcast, The Click Club, Philadelphia, 14 March 1949

Probably: Ed Badgley, Al Porcino, Charlie Walp, Shorty Rogers, Ernie Royal(tp), Bill Harris, Earl Swope, Ollie Wilson(tb), Bart Varselona (btb), Woody Herman(cl,as,v), Sam Marowitz(as), Al Cohn, Stan Getz, Jimmy Giuffre(ts), Serge Chaloff(bar), Terry Gibbs(vibes), Lou Levy(p), Oscar Pettiford(b), Don Lamond(d), Mary Ann McCall(v)

> I Ain't Gettin' Any Younger (vWH)
> More Than You Know (vMAM)

NOTE: Band was at the Click Club March 10–16, 1949.

SERGE CHALOFF–RALPH BURNS SEPTET
Boston, 16 April 1949

Gait Preddy(tp), Mert Goodspeed(tb), Charlie Mariano(as), Serge Chaloff(bar), Ralph Burns(p), Frank Vaccaro(b), Pete DeRosa(d)

Pat	Motif M-002, Hep-13
King Edward the Flatted Fifth	— —

NOTE: Arrangements by Ralph Burns. Treichel noted the band played the Capitol Theatre in Washington, D.C., April 15–21 and the Apollo Theatre in New York City April 23–27, and that it was probably at the Apollo that Shelly Manne replaced Shadow Wilson on drums. Both titles also Mosaic MQ5-147 and MD4-147, and Cool & Blue C&B CD102.

BUDDY DEFRANCO AND HIS ORCHESTRA
New York, 23 April 1949

Bernie Glow, Jimmy Pupa, Paul Cohen, Jack Eagle(tp), Earl Swope, Ollie Wilson, Bart Varsalona(tb), Buddy DeFranco(cl), Lee Konitz, Frank Socolow(as), Jerry Sanfino, Al Cohn(ts), Serge Chaloff(bar), Gene Di Novi(p), Oscar Pettiford(b), Irv Kluger(d)

3769	A Bird in Igor's Yard	Capitol M11060
3770	The Boy Next Door	(unissued)
3771	This Time the Dream's On Me	Capitol M11060
3772	(untitled original)	(unissued)

WOODY HERMAN AND HIS ORCHESTRA
New York, 26 May 1949

Ernie Royal, Al Porcino, Shorty Rogers, Stan Fishelson, Charlie Walp(tp), Bill Harris, Earl Swope, Ollie Wilson(tb), Bart Varsalona (btb), Woody Herman(cl,as,v), Sam Marowitz(as), Gene Ammons, Jimmy Giuffre, Buddy Savitt(ts), Serge Chaloff(bar), Lou Levy(p), Oscar Pettiford(b), Shelley Manne(d), Mary Ann McCall(v)

3794-4   The Crickets (vWH,MAM)   Capitol 57-682
3795-2   More Moon   —

NOTE: Both titles on CD on Capitol Jazz CDP 7 98453 2.

Add Terry Gibbs(vbs)

Rendezvous Ballroom, Balboa Beach, Los Angeles, 2 July 1949

Blue Flame (Theme)
Lemon Drop (vWH,ens)
Laura (vWH)
I Got It Bad (vMAM)   Artistry 109
More Moon   —
Four Brothers
The Crickets (vWH,MAM)
Terry and the Pirates
The Man I Love (vMAM)
I Ain't Gettin' Any Younger (vWH)   —
Everywhere   —
That's Right   —
Blue Flame (Theme)   —

Universal Movie Short: *Herman's Herd*

Los Angeles, 6 July 1949

Add Mello-Larks(v), Patricia Lynn, Margaret Brown, Peggy Castle (for film only)

Jamaica Rhumba (vMAM)
Tap Dance
I've Got News for You (vWH)
It's a Great Day for the Irish (v?)
Lollypop (vWH,ens)
Skip to My Lou (vM-L)
Keen and Peachy

NOTE: Chaloff can be seen in the section but solos only on "Lollypop" in the above film short.

Same

Rendezvous Ballroom, 9 July 1949

Not Really the Blues
Bijou
Medley (of Herman Hits) (vWH,ens)
Pennies From Heaven
Apple Honey (inc)

What's New
Jamaica Rhumba (vMAM)
Keen and Peachy

Same

Los Angeles, 14 July 1949

4666-2	Detour Ahead (vMAM)	Capitol 57-837
4667-3	Jamaica Rhumba (vMAM)	Capitol 57-720
4668-2	Not Really the Blues	Capitol 57-837

NOTE: All three titles on CD on Capitol Jazz CDP 7 98453 2.

Same

Rendezvous Ballroom, 16 July 1949

The Goof and I
P.S. I Love You (vMAM)
I Only Have Eyes for You
Lollypop (vWH,ens)
You've Got a Date With the Blues (vWH)
Jamaica Rhumba (vMAM)
Tiny's Blues
Man Don't Be Ridiculous (inc)
Early Autumn   Artistry 109
Apple Honey
Blue Flame (Theme)

Joe Mondragon(b) for Pettiford

Los Angeles, 20 July 1949

4673-3	Tenderly	Capitol 57-720
4674-1	Lollypop (vWH,ens)	Capitol EAP3-324
4675-5	You Rascal You (vWH)	Capitol 57-772

Same

Los Angeles, 21 July 1949

4678	You've Got a Date With the Blues (vWH)	
4679-3	Rhapsody in Wood	Capitol 57-772
4680-1	The Great Lie	Capitol M11034
4681	In the Beginning (vWH)	

NOTE: All titles from the above Capitol sessions on CD on Capitol Jazz CDP 7 98453 2; mx#s 4678 and 4681 were previously unissued.

Same

Rendezvous Ballroom, 23 July 1949

Not Really the Blues
Detour Ahead (vMAM)
Rhapsody in Wood
Tenderly
That's Right
You Rascal You (vWH)
I've Got News for You (vWH)
Out of Nowhere
More Moon
Blue Flame (Theme)

Mert Oliver(b) for Mondragon

AFRS Just Jazz #76, Shrine Auditorium,
Los Angeles, 29 July 1949

I've Got News for You (vWH)
I Ain't Gettin' Any Younger
   (vWH)   First Heard FH-29
Everywhere
Four Brothers   —
Keen and Peachy (inc)

Same

Rendezvous Ballroom, 30 July 1949

Lollypop (vWH,ens)   Joyce LP-1012
Four Brothers   —
That's Right   —
I Got It Bad (vMAM)   —
Early Autumn   —

Add Charlie Barnet and his Orchestra: Rolf Ericson, Doc Severinsen, Ray Wetzel, John Howell, Maynard Ferguson(tp), Obie Massingill, Dick Kenney, Herbie Harper, Ken Matlock(tb), Charlie Barnet(as,ts), Vinnie Dean, Reuben Leon(as), Dick Hafer, Kurt Bloom(ts), Manny Albam(bar), Nat Cole(p), Eddie Safranski(b), Shelley Manne(d), Carlos Vidal(cga)

Ornithology   Joyce LP-1012

NOTE: Combined bands play "Ornithology" (announced by M.C. Tom Reddy as "How High the Moon" and often listed as "More Moon").

Same

AFRS Just Jazz #75, Shrine Auditorium, c. August 1949

Early Autumn	Redwood Jazz RWJ1001
Keen and Peachy	—
Pennies From Heaven	Artistry 109, —
Rhapsody in Wood	First Heard FH-29
What's New (inc)	

Same

AFRS Just Jazz #77, Shrine Auditorium, c. August 1949

Terry and the Pirates	Queen Disc 005, Artistry 109
Man Don't Be Ridiculous	Cicala 8027, — —
Summer Sequence	—
Jamaica Rhumba (vMAM)	
The Man I Love (vMAM)	
Detour Ahead (vMAM)	
Apple Honey (inc)	

Same

AFRS Just Jazz #79, Shrine Auditorium, c. August 1949

Lemon Drop (vWH,ens)	Artistry 109
Keen and Peachy	—
More Moon	

NOTE: The band went on tour on August 7, 1949. The Second Herd was disbanded on December 4, 1949.

SERGE CHALOFF–ALAN EAGER

New York, c. late 1949

Alan Eager(ts), Serge Chaloff(bar), unk(d)

Fine and Dandy (inc)	(unissued)

NOTE: This private jam session was recorded by Milton Green at his home studio. The drummer is possibly Don Lamond. Other details unknown (see text).

Add Terry Gibbs(vibes), unk(p), (b)

New York, c. late 1949

Cherokee	(unissued)

NOTE: Recorded by Milton Green but from a different session than the above (see text).

ALL-STARS
                        Carnegie Hall, New York City, 25 December 1949

Miles Davis(tp), Benny Green(tb), Sonny Stitt(as), Serge Chaloff(bar),
Bud Powell(p), Curley Russell(b), Max Roach(d)

Move	IAJRC-20, Jass JCD16	
Hot House	—	—
Ornithology (inc)	—	—

NOTE: The issued version of "Ornithology" faded out during Stitt's
solo, but Chaloff's solo was intact. The above titles also on "Serge Chaloff Memorial" (Cool & Blue CD102). All three titles were extended
concert performances.

The Serge Chaloff Quintet with Earl Swope(tb), Bud Powell(p), Joe
Shulman(b), and Don Lamond(d) performed at Birdland during January
1950, but broadcasts (if any) have not surfaced.

METRONOME ALL-STARS
                                           New York, 10 January 1950

Dizzy Gillespie(tp), Kai Winding(tb), Buddy DeFranco(cl), Lee Konitz
(as), Stan Getz(ts), Serge Chaloff(bar), Lennie Tristano(p), Billy Bauer(g),
Eddie Safranski(b), Max Roach(d)

42629	Double Date	Columbia 38734, Harmony HL7044	
42630	No Figs	—	—

NOTE: Original 78 rpm issue of "No Figs" edited out solos by Stan
Getz and Dizzy Gillespie; complete version is restored on the Harmony
LP.

SERGE CHALOFF QUARTET
                                     Hi Hat Club, Boston, 22 February 1950

Serge Chaloff(bar), Nat Pierce(p), Joe Shulman(b), Joe MacDonald(d)

Pennies From Heaven	Uptown UPCD 27.38	
Gabardine and Serge (inc)	—	

NOTE: This private recording from a broadcast was made by Serge's
brother Dick Chaloff. The first title cuts off due to the acetate having to
be turned over, but the ending was preserved. The second side of the
acetate ran out during Chaloff's solo on the latter title. Editing on the
issued CD attempted to "clean up" these flaws.

During the spring of 1950, Chaloff disbanded his own group and became a member of the Count Basie Octet. They performed at the Hi Hat

starting Monday, April 10, 1950, for 2 weeks, and made the following record date, which is all that is known to have been recorded by this ensemble.

COUNT BASIE OCTET

New York, 16 May 1950

Clark Terry(tp), Buddy DeFranco(cl), Charlie Rouse(ts), Serge Chaloff (bar), Count Basie(p), Freddie Green(g), Jimmy Lewis(b), Buddy Rich(d)

43261-1	Neal's Deal	Columbia 39075, CBS66102	
43261-2	Neal's Deal		—
43261-3	Neal's Deal		—
43261-4	Neal's Deal		—
43262-1	Bluebeard's Blues	Columbia 38888,	—
43262-2	Bluebeard's Blues		—
43263-1	The Golden Bullet		—
43263-2	The Golden Bullet		—
43263-3	The Golden Bullet		—
43264-1	You're My Baby, You		—
43264-2	You're My Baby, You (vCT)		—

NOTE: Information from Chris Sheridan's Basie discography. CBS66102 is a 10 LP set of Basie recordings containing considerable unissued material and alternate takes. Although Chaloff reportedly may have performed with Basie in Boston again in October 1950, and has often been listed as being on the later Basie Octet recordings of November 2/3, 1950, Rudy Rutherford performed on baritone sax and bass clarinet on those recordings.

JAM SESSION

Christy's Restaurant, Framingham, Massachusetts, spring 1950

Howard McGhee, Dick Wetmore(tp), Wardell Gray(ts), Serge Chaloff (bar), Nat Pierce(p), Eli Whitney Cronin(b), Joe MacDonald(d)

I Got Rhythm   (unissued)

NOTE: The dating of this session is very uncertain.

SERGE CHALOFF QUINTET

Celebrity Club, Providence, Rhode Island, 3 September 1950

Serge Chaloff(bar), Sonny Truitt(tb), Nat Pierce(p), George Jones(b), Joe MacDonald(d)

Theme (Gabardine and Serge)   Uptown UPCD 27.38
The Goof and I   —

Everything Happens to Me	—
Pennies from Heaven	—
Four Brothers	—
Gabardine and Serge (closing)	—

NOTE: Chaloff was also interviewed briefly on this broadcast by announcer Carl Henry.

SERGE CHALOFF QUINTET
Hi Hat Club, Boston, late September–early October 1950

Serge Chaloff(bar), Milt Gold(tb), Al Vega(p), Jack Lawlor(b), Sonny Taclof(d)

Gabardine and Serge	Uptown UPCD 27.38
Pennies From Heaven	—
These Foolish Things	—
Keen and Peachy	—

NOTE: Session privately recorded on acetates by Freddie Taylor from a front table in the club. The Uptown CD noted this was from a Sunday afternoon session during the time Serge is known to have worked there in late September–early October 1950; possible dates are September 24 or October 1, 8, or 15.

METRONOME ALL-STARS
New York, 23 January 1951

Miles Davis(tp), Kai Winding(tb), John LaPorta(cl), Lee Konitz(as), Stan Getz(ts), Serge Chaloff(bar), Terry Gibbs(vibes), George Shearing(p), Billy Bauer(g), Eddie Safranski(b), Max Roach(d)

6252	Early Spring	Capitol 1550, M11031
6253	Local 802 Blues	— —

NOTE: This was Chaloff's last known studio session until 1954.

SERGE CHALOFF–BOOTS MUSSULLI QUINTET
Boston, c. late March 1954

Serge Chaloff(bar), Boots Mussulli(as), Russ Freeman(p), Jimmy Woode(b), Buzzy Drootin(d)

A New Kind of Love	Storyville LP310, BLCD-760923
Zdot	— —
Oh Baby	— —
Love Is Just Around the Corner	— —

	All I Do Is Dream		
	of You	—	—
	Easy Street	—	—

NOTE: Session usually dated as June 9, 1954 (see text). All titles also on Mosaic MD4-147 & MQ5-147.

SERGE CHALOFF SEXTET/NONET

Boston, 3 September 1954

Herb Pomeroy(tp), Charlie Mariano(as), Serge Chaloff(bar), Dick Twardzik(p), Ray Olivieri(b), Jimmy Zitano(d)

	Slam	Storyville LP317, BLCD-760923	
	Let's Jump	—	—
	Let's Jump	Trio TD-7,	—

Omit (p), (b), (d)

| | Sherry | Storyville LP317, BLCD-760923 |

Herb Pomeroy, Nick Capazutto(tp), Gene DiStachio(tb), Charlie Mariano(as), Varty Haritounian(ts), Serge Chaloff(bar), Dick Twardzik(p), Ray Olivieri(b), Jimmy Zitano(d)

	The Fable of Mabel	Storyville LP317, BLCD-760923	
	The Fable of Mabel	—	
	The Fable of Mabel	—	
	A Salute to Tiny	—	—
	A Salute to Tiny	—	
	Eenie Meenie Minor Mode	—	—
	Eenie Meenie Minor Mode	—	

NOTE: All titles also on Mosaic MD4-147 & MQ5-147.

SERGE CHALOFF SEXTET

Boston, 4 April 1955

Herb Pomeroy(tp), Boots Mussulli(as), Serge Chaloff(bar), Ray Santisi(p), Everett Evans(b), Jimmy Zitano(d)

20628	Mar-Dros	Capitol T6510, Affinity 63	
20629	Kip	—	—
20630	Unison	—	—
20631	Body and Soul	—	—

Same

Boston, 5 April 1955

| 20632 | Yesterday's Gardenias | Capitol T6510, Affinity 63 | |
| 20633 | Bob the Robin | — | — |

20634	What's New?	—	—
20635	Boomaree Maroja		
20636	Diana's Melody [omit p,b]	—	—
20637-1	Herbs		
20637-2	Herbs		
20638	Sergical	—	—
20639	Junior	—	—

NOTE: All titles on Mosaic MD4-147 & MQ5-147; mx3s 20635 & 20637 were previously unissued.

SERGE CHALOFF SEXTET
Westbrook Junior College, Portland, Maine, c. July 1955

Serge Chaloff(bar), Dick Cornwall(ts), Jerry Cohen(p), Gene Whiting(g), Bob Lippe(b), Charlie Pine(d)

Now's the Time	(unissued)
Body and Soul	—
Tangerine	—
Perdido	—
(other titles)	—

NOTE: According to Richard Chaloff, six 12″ discs with 108 minutes of music were recorded at 33 1/3 rpm on a "Presto" acetate recorder at a dance, and the above numbers were among those played. The discs were given to Bob Sunnenblick for possible issue on his Uptown CD label, but no other data have been forthcoming.

SERGE CHALOFF SEPTET
Steve Allen TV Show, Boston, c. December 1955

Doc Severinsen(tp), Boots Mussulli(as), Sonny Stitt(ts), Serge Chaloff (bar), Steve Allen(p), unknown(b),(d)

Stompin' at the Savoy	Philology CD W43-2

NOTE: It is not known if the video portion of this show still exists. The above issue is a Sonny Stitt CD titled *Loose Walk* which lists the rhythm section as for 4–5 April 1955 as above, but this is obviously not likely (see text).

SERGE CHALOFF QUINTET
Stage Lounge, Chicago, c. 15–28 February 1956

Serge Chaloff(bar), Lou Donaldson(as), Norman Simmons(p), Victor Sproles(b), Vernel Fournier(d)

The Goof and I	(unissued)
Gone With the Wind	—

All the Things You Are	—
Lover Man	—
Billie's Bounce	—

NOTE: The above private recording was broadcast over WKCR-FM in New York City by disc jockey Phil Schaap in 1991 (unaccountably dated as March 18, 1957). The above group was at the Stage Lounge during 15–28 February 1956 but the exact night of recording is unknown. An additional title omitting Chaloff also exists from this session.

SERGE CHALOFF QUARTET

Los Angeles, 14 March 1956

Serge Chaloff(bar), Sonny Clark(p), Leroy Vinnegar(b), Philly Joe Jones(d)

15153	I've Got the World on a String	Capitol T742, M11032	
15154	Thanks for the Memory	—	—
15155	The Goof and I	—	—
15156	Susie's Blues	—	—
15157	A Handful of Stars	—	—

Same

Los Angeles, 16 March 1956

15249	All the Things You Are	Capitol T742, M11032	
15250	Stairway to the Stars	—	—
15251	How About You		

NOTE: The above two sessions are usually dated March 4, 1956. All titles also on ToCP32-5185, Mosaic MD4-147 & MQ5-147; mx#15251 not previously issued.

METRONOME ALL-STARS

New York, 18 June 1956

Eddie Bert(tb), Tony Scott(cl), Lee Konitz(as), Al Cohn, Zoot Sims(ts), Serge Chaloff(bar), Teddy Charles(vibes), Billy Taylor(p), Tal Farlow(g), Charles Mingus(b), Art Blakey(d)

| Billie's Bounce | Verve (unissued) |
| Billie's Bounce | — |

Add Thad Jones(tp); same session

| Billie's Bounce | Clef MGC743, Verve MGV8030 |

THE FOUR BROTHERS
New York, 11 February 1957

Al Cohn, Zoot Sims, Herbie Steward(ts), Charlie O'Kane, Serge Chaloff
(bar), Elliot Lawrence(p), Buddy Jones(b), Don Lamond(d)

Ten Years Later	Vik LX1096,	RCA(J)RA-5408
Here We Go Again	—	—
Four Brothers	—	—
Four In Hand	—	—
The Swinging Door	—	—
Aged in Wood	—	—
So Blue	—	—
The Pretty One	—	—
Four and One Moore	—	—
A Quick One	—	—

NOTE: Charlie O'Kane replaced Chaloff for section passages only, on
some of the above titles.

Second Herd Tune Index

by Vladimir Simosko

Am I Blue? (1948/Feb. 7)
Am I Blue? (1948/Mar. 5)
Am I Blue? (1948/Mar. 12)

Apple Honey (1948/Feb. 8)(inc)
Apple Honey (1948/Feb. 12)
Apple Honey (1948/Feb. 14)(inc)
Apple Honey (1948/Feb. 29)
Apple Honey (1948/Mar. 4)
Apple Honey (1948/Mar. 12)
Apple Honey (1949/Jul. 9)(inc)
Apple Honey (1949/Jul. 16)
Apple Honey (1949/Aug. ?)(inc)

Baby I Need You (1947/Dec. 30)
Baby I Need You (1948/Feb. 5)
Baby I Need You (1948/Feb. 7)
Baby I Need You (1948/Feb. 8)
Baby I Need You (1948/Feb. 12)
Baby I Need You (1948/Mar. 6)

Berled in Erl (1948/Jul. 2)
Berled in Erl (1948/Aug. 8)

Bijou (1948/Oct. 30)
Bijou (1948/Nov. 8)
Bijou (1949/Mar. 4)
Bijou (1949/Feb. 26)
Bijou (1949/Jul. 9)

Bill (1948/Mar. 11)
Bill (1948/Mar. 12)
Bill (1948/c. March)
Bill (1948/c. April–May)
Bill (1948/Dec. ?)

Blue Flame (Theme) (not listed)

Blue Prelude (1948/May 5)

Boomsie (1948/Nov. 6)
Boomsie (1948/Nov. 8)
Boomsie (1948/Nov. 16)
Boomsie (1948/Nov. 20)
Boomsie (1948/Dec. ?)
Boomsie (1948/Dec. 11)

But Beautiful (1948/c. April–May)
But Beautiful (1948/Jul. 2)

Caldonia (1948/Feb. 2)

Cake Walk (1948/Feb. 2)

Cherokee Canyon (1947/Dec. 22)
Cherokee Canyon (1948/Feb. 5)
Cherokee Canyon (1948/Feb. 7)
Cherokee Canyon (1948/Mar. 13)

Concerto for Cootie (1949/Feb. 26)

Dance Ballerina Dance (1948/Feb. 8)
Dance Ballerina Dance (1948/Mar. 3)
Dance Ballerina Dance (1948/Mar. 11)
Dance Ballerina Dance (1948/c. March)
Dance Ballerina Dance (1948/Apr. 28)

Detour Ahead (1949/Jul. 14)
Detour Ahead (1949/Jul. 23)
Detour Ahead (1949/Aug. ?)

Don Delves In (1949/Mar. 4)

Dream Peddler (1948/May 12)
Dream Peddler (1948/Jul. 2)

Early Autumn (1948/Dec. ?)
Early Autumn (1948/Dec. 30)
Early Autumn (1949/Jan. 1)
Early Autumn (1949/Jul. 16)
Early Autumn (1949/Jul. 30)
Early Autumn (1949/Aug. ?)

Elevation (1948/Apr. 28)
Elevation (1948/Aug. 26)

Everywhere (1949/Mar. 4)
Everywhere (1949/Jul. 2)
Everywhere (1949/Jul. 29)

Fan It (1948/Aug. 8)

Flamingo (1948/Nov. 6)
Flamingo (1948/Nov. 16)
Flamingo (1948/Nov. 20)

Four Brothers (1947/Dec. 27)
Four Brothers (1948/Feb. 5)
Four Brothers (1948/Mar. 4)
Four Brothers (1948/Mar. 7)
Four Brothers (1948/May 12)
Four Brothers (1948/Jul. 2)
Four Brothers (1948/Oct. 30)
Four Brothers (1948/Nov. 6)
Four Brothers (1948/Nov. 8)
Four Brothers (1948/Nov. 16)
Four Brothers (1948/Nov. 22)
Four Brothers (1948/Dec. ?)
Four Brothers (1948/Dec. 11)
Four Brothers (1949/Jan. 1)
Four Brothers (1949/Mar. 4)
Four Brothers (1949/Feb. 26)
Four Brothers (1949/Jul. 2)
Four Brothers (1949/Jul. 29)
Four Brothers (1949/Jul. 30)

Godchild (1948/Dec. ?)
Godchild (1949/Jan. 1)

Golden Earrings (1948/Feb. 5)
Golden Earrings (1948/Feb. 6)

Half Past Jumping Time (1948/Feb. 29)
Half Past Jumping Time (1948/Mar. 5)
Half Past Jumping Time (1948/Mar. 12)

Happiness Is a Thing Called Joe (1948/Feb. 14)
Happiness Is a Thing Called Joe (1948/Oct. 30)

How Soon? (1948/Feb. 7)
How Soon? (1948/Mar. 13)

I Ain't Gettin' Any Younger (1948/Dec. 30)
I Ain't Gettin' Any Younger (1949/Feb. 26)
I Ain't Gettin' Any Younger (1949/Mar. 14)
I Ain't Gettin' Any Younger (1949/Jul. 2)
I Ain't Gettin' Any Younger (1949/Jul. 29)

I Can't Get Offa My Horse (1948/Feb. 2)

I Can't Get Started (1948/Oct. 30)
I Can't Get Started (1948/Nov. 8)
I Can't Get Started (1948/Nov. 11)
I Can't Get Started (1948/Nov. 22)

I Cover the Waterfront (1948/Mar. 3)
I Cover the Waterfront (1948/Mar. 4)
I Cover the Waterfront (1948/Mar. 6)
I Cover the Waterfront (1948/Mar. 7)
I Cover the Waterfront (1948/c. April–May)

I Got It Bad (1948/Feb. 3)
I Got It Bad (1948/Feb. 8)
I Got It Bad (1948/Feb. 29)
I Got It Bad (1948/Mar. 5)
I Got It Bad (1948/Mar. 12)
I Got It Bad (1948/Nov. 16)
I Got It Bad (1948/Nov. 20)
I Got It Bad (1948/Dec. ?)
I Got It Bad (1948/Dec. 30)
I Got It Bad (1949/Mar. 4)
I Got It Bad (1949/Feb. 26)
I Got It Bad (1949/Jul. 2)
I Got It Bad (1949/Jul. 30)

I May Be Wrong (1948/May 5)

I Only Have Eyes for You (1948/Dec. ?)
I Only Have Eyes for You (1949/Jan. 1)
I Only Have Eyes for You (1949/Jul. 16)

I Told Ya I Love Ya (1947/Oct. 19)
I Told Ya I Love Ya (1948/Feb. 3)

I Told Ya I Love Ya (1948/Feb. 6)
I Told Ya I Love Ya (1948/Feb. 12)
I Told Ya I Love Ya (1948/c. March)
I Told Ya I Love Ya (1948/Mar. 11)

I've Got a Way With Women (1948/Nov. 16)
I've Got a Way With Women (1948/Nov. 20)
I've Got a Way With Women (1948/Dec. 11)

I've Got News for You (1947/Dec. 22)
I've Got News for You (1948/Mar. 12)
I've Got News for You (1948/May 12)
I've Got News for You (1948/Jul. 2)
I've Got News for You (1948/Oct. 30)
I've Got News for You (1948/Nov. 6)
I've Got News for You (1948/Nov. 8)
I've Got News for You (1948/Nov. 22)
I've Got News for You (1949/Jan. 1)
I've Got News for You (1949/Jul. 6)
I've Got News for You (1949/Jul. 23)
I've Got News for You (1949/Jul. 29)

I've Got the World on a String (1948/Feb. 5)
I've Got the World on a String (1948/Mar. 6)
I've Got the World on a String (1948/Dec. ?)

If Anybody Can Steal My Baby (1947/Oct. 19)
If Anybody Can Steal My Baby (1948/Feb. 6)
If Anybody Can Steal My Baby (1948/Feb. 8)
If Anybody Can Steal My Baby (1948/Feb. 14)
If Anybody Can Steal My Baby (1948/Feb. 29)
If Anybody Can Steal My Baby (1948/Mar. 4)

In the Beginning (1949/Jul. 21)

It's a Great Day for the Irish (1949/Jul. 6)

It's Been So Long (1948/Feb. 8)

Jamaica Rhumba (1949/Jul. 6)
Jamaica Rhumba (1949/Jul. 9)
Jamaica Rhumba (1949/Jul. 14)
Jamaica Rhumba (1949/Jul. 16)
Jamaica Rhumba (1949/Aug. ?)

Jingle Bell Polka (1948/Feb. 2)

John Had the Number (1948/Nov. 6)
John Had the Number (1949/Mar. 4)

Just for Laughs (1948/Mar. 6)
Just for Laughs (1948/Mar. 7)
Just for Laughs (1948/Mar. 11)
Just for Laughs (1948/Mar. 13)
Just for Laughs (1948/c. March)

Keen and Peachy (1947/Dec. 22)
Keen and Peachy (1948/Feb. 7)
Keen and Peachy (1948/Mar. 5)
Keen and Peachy (1948/Mar. 7)(inc)
Keen and Peachy (1948/Mar. 13)
Keen and Peachy (1948/c. April–May)
Keen and Peachy (1948/May 5)
Keen and Peachy (1948/May 12)
Keen and Peachy (1948/Aug. 26)
Keen and Peachy (1948/Oct. 30)
Keen and Peachy (1948/Nov. 11)
Keen and Peachy (1948/Dec. 11)
Keen and Peachy (1948/Dec. ?)
Keen and Peachy (1949/Jan. 1)
Keen and Peachy (1949/Feb. 26)
Keen and Peachy (1949/Jul. 6)
Keen and Peachy (1949/Jul. 9)
Keen and Peachy (1949/Jul. 29)(inc)
Keen and Peachy (1949/Aug. ?)

Keeper of the Flame (1948/Aug. 26)
Keeper of the Flame (1948/Oct. 30)
Keeper of the Flame (1948/Nov. 11)
Keeper of the Flame (1948/Nov. 16)
Keeper of the Flame (1948/Nov. 22)
Keeper of the Flame (1948/Dec. ?)
Keeper of the Flame (1948/Dec. 30)

Laura (1948/Feb. 8)
Laura (1948/Mar. 3)
Laura (1949/Jul. 2)

Lazy Lullaby (1947/Dec. 24)
Lazy Lullaby (1948/Feb. 29)

Lazy Lullaby (1948/Mar. 7)
Lazy Lullaby (1948/Mar. 11)

Lemon Drop (1948/Dec. ?)
Lemon Drop (1948/Dec. 29)
Lemon Drop (1949/Jan. 1)
Lemon Drop (1949/Mar. 4)
Lemon Drop (1949/Feb. 26)
Lemon Drop (1949/Jul. 2)
Lemon Drop (1949/Aug. ?)

Let's Fall in Love (1948/Feb. 3)
Let's Fall in Love (1948/Feb. 12)
Let's Fall in Love (1948/Mar. 4)
Let's Fall in Love (1948/Mar. 11)
Let's Fall in Love (1948/c. March)
Let's Fall in Love (1948/c. April–May)
Let's Fall in Love (1948/Dec. ?)
Let's Fall in Love (1949/Jan. 1)

Lollypop (1949/Jul. 6)
Lollypop (1949/Jul. 16)
Lollypop (1949/Jul. 20)
Lollypop (1949/Jul. 30)

Lullaby in Rhythm (1948/Mar. 3)
Lullaby in Rhythm (1948/Mar. 6)

Man Don't Be Ridiculous (1949/Mar. 4)
Man Don't Be Ridiculous (1949/Jul. 16)(inc)
Man Don't Be Ridiculous (1949/Aug. ?)

Medley (of Herman Hits) (1949/Jul. 9)

More Moon (1949/May 26)
More Moon (1949/Jul. 2)
More Moon (1949/Jul. 23)
More Moon (1949/Jul. 30)
More Moon (1949/Aug. ?)

More Than You Know (1948/Dec. 30)
More Than You Know (1949/Mar. 4)
More Than You Know (1949/Mar. 14)

My Fair Lady (1948/Apr. 28)
My Fair Lady (1948/May 5)
My Fair Lady (1948/Aug. 8)

My Last Affair (1948/Nov. 8)
My Last Affair (1948/Nov. 22)
My Last Affair (1948/Dec. 11)
My Last Affair (1948/Dec. ?)
My Last Affair (1949/Jan. 1)

My Pal Gonzales (1947/Dec. 30)
My Pal Gonzales (1948/Mar. 3)
My Pal Gonzales (1948/Mar. 5)
My Pal Gonzales (1948/Mar. 7)

Nature Boy (1948/Apr. 28)
Nature Boy (1948/May 12)

No Time (1948/Aug. 8)

Non-Alcoholic (1948/Feb. 3)(inc)
Non-Alcoholic (1948/Feb. 5)
Non-Alcoholic (1948/Feb. 6)
Non-Alcoholic (1948/Mar. 12)

Northwest Passage (1948/Feb. 2)
Northwest Passage (1948/Feb. 7)(inc)
Northwest Passage (1948/Feb. 8)
Northwest Passage (1948/Mar. 13)
Northwest Passage (1948/c. March)
Northwest Passage (1948/Aug. 8)

Not Really the Blues (1949/Jul. 9)
Not Really the Blues (1949/Jul. 14)
Not Really the Blues (1949/Jul. 23)

Oh Henry (1948/Nov. 16)
Oh Henry (1948/Nov. 20)
Oh Henry (1948/Nov. 22)

Out of Nowhere (1948/Nov. 16)
Out of Nowhere (1948/Nov. 20)
Out of Nowhere (1948/Dec. ?)(inc)
Out of Nowhere (1949/Jan. 1)

Out of Nowhere (1949/Mar. 4)
Out of Nowhere (1949/Jul. 23)

P. S. I Love You (1947/Dec. 30)
P. S. I Love You (1948/Feb. 3)
P. S. I Love You (1948/Feb. 5)
P. S. I Love You (1948/Feb. 7)
P. S. I Love You (1948/Mar. 3)
P. S. I Love You (1948/Mar. 4)
P. S. I Love You (1948/Jul. 2)
P. S. I Love You (1948/Aug. 8)
P. S. I Love You (1949/Jul. 16)

Pennies from Heaven (1949/Jul. 9)
Pennies from Heaven (1949/Aug. ?)

Rhapsody in Wood (1949/Jul. 21)
Rhapsody in Wood (1949/Jul. 23)
Rhapsody in Wood (1949/Aug. ?)

Romance in the Dark (1948/Nov. 6)
Romance in the Dark (1948/Nov. 11)

Sabre Dance (1947/Dec. 22)
Sabre Dance (1948/Feb. 2)
Sabre Dance (1948/Feb. 3)
Sabre Dance (1948/Feb. 6)
Sabre Dance (1948/Feb. 14)
Sabre Dance (1948/Mar. 4)
Sabre Dance (1948/Mar. 5)
Sabre Dance (1948/Mar. 6)
Sabre Dance (1948/Mar. 11)
Sabre Dance (1948/Mar. 12)
Sabre Dance (1948/c. March)
Sabre Dance (1948/c. April–May)
Sabre Dance (1948/May 5)

Sidewalks of Cuba (1948/Feb. 6)
Sidewalks of Cuba (1948/Feb. 8)
Sidewalks of Cuba (1948/Jul. 2)
Sidewalks of Cuba (1948/Aug. 8)
Sidewalks of Cuba (1948/Aug. 26)

Skip to My Lou (1949/Jul. 6)

Someone to Watch Over Me (1948/Dec. ?)

Star Dust (1948/Feb. 3)
Star Dust (1948/Feb. 6)
Star Dust (1948/Feb. 14)
Star Dust (1948/Feb. 29)
Star Dust (1948/Mar. 5)
Star Dust (1948/Mar. 6)

Summer Sequence, Pt. 4 (1947/Dec. 27)
Summer Sequence, Pts. 1–3 (1949/Mar. 4)
Summer Sequence (1949/Aug. ?)

Swing Low Sweet Clarinet (1947/Dec. 30)
Swing Low Sweet Clarinet (1948/Feb. 6)
Swing Low Sweet Clarinet (1948/Feb. 12)
Swing Low Sweet Clarinet (1948/Mar. 3)
Swing Low Sweet Clarinet (1948/Mar. 5)
Swing Low Sweet Clarinet (1948/c. April–May)
Swing Low Sweet Clarinet (1948/May 12)

Take A Little Time to Smile (1947/Dec. 31)

Tap Dance (1949/Jul. 6)

Tempus Fugit (1948/Dec. ?)

Tenderly (1949/Jul. 20)
Tenderly (1949/Jul. 23)

Terry & the Pirates (1949/Jul. 2)
Terry & the Pirates (1949/Aug. ?)

That's Right (1948/Dec. 29)
That's Right (1949/Jul. 2)
That's Right (1949/Jul. 23)
That's Right (1949/Jul. 30)

The Best Things in Life are Free (1948/Feb. 14)
The Best Things in Life are Free (1948/Feb. 29)
The Best Things in Life are Free (1948/Mar. 13)

The Crickets (1949/May 26)
The Crickets (1949/Jul. 2)

The Good Earth (1948/Feb. 3)
The Good Earth (1948/Feb. 12)
The Good Earth (1948/Feb. 14)
The Good Earth (1948/Mar. 3)
The Good Earth (1948/Mar. 13)

The Goof & I (1947/Dec. 24)
The Goof & I (1948/Feb. 5)
The Goof & I (1948/Feb. 6)(inc)
The Goof & I (1948/Feb. 7)
The Goof & I (1948/Feb. 12)
The Goof & I (1948/Mar. 7)
The Goof & I (1948/Mar. 11)
The Goof & I (1948/Mar. 13)
The Goof & I (1948/c. March)
The Goof & I (1948/c. April–May)
The Goof & I (1948/May 12)
The Goof & I (1949/Jan. 1)
The Goof & I (1949/Jul. 16)

The Great Lie (1949/Jul. 21)

The Happy Song (1948/Apr. 28)
The Happy Song (1948/May 5)
The Happy Song (1948/May 12)

The Man I Love (1949/Jul. 2)
The Man I Love (1949/Aug. ?)

There'll Be Some Changes Made (1948/Feb. 7)
There'll Be Some Changes Made (1948/Feb. 12)
There'll Be Some Changes Made (1948/Feb. 14)

This Is New (1948/Apr. 28)

Tiny's Blues (1948/Apr. 28)
Tiny's Blues (1948/May 5)
Tiny's Blues (1948/Nov. 6)
Tiny's Blues (1948/Nov. 8)
Tiny's Blues (1948/Nov. 16)
Tiny's Blues (1948/Nov. 20)
Tiny's Blues (1948/Dec. ?)
Tiny's Blues (1949/Jan. 1)
Tiny's Blues (1949/Jul. 16)

Toolie Oolie Doolie (1948/Feb. 29)
Toolie Oolie Doolie (1948/c. March)

Trouble is a Man (1948/May 5)
Trouble is a Man (1948/Aug. 8)

We the People Bop (1948/Aug. 26)
We the People Bop (1948/Nov. 6)
We the People Bop (1948/Nov. 8)
We the People Bop (1948/Nov. 20)
We the People Bop (1948/Nov. 22)

We'll Be Together Again (1948/Mar. 7)

What'll I Do? (1948/Mar. 12)

What's New (1949/Jul. 9)
What's New (1949/Aug. ?)(inc)

When You're Smiling (1948/Apr. 28)

Wild Root (1948/Feb. 3)

You Go To My Head (1948/Mar. 4)
You Go To My Head (1949/Jan. 1)

You Rascal You (1949/Jul. 20)
You Rascal You (1949/Jul. 23)

You Turned the Tables on Me (1948/Mar. 6)
You Turned the Tables on Me (1948/Jul. 2)

You've Got a Date With the Blues (1949/Jul. 16)
You've Got a Date With the Blues (1949/Jul. 21)

Yucca (1948/Oct. 30)
Yucca (1948/Nov. 11)
Yucca (1948/Dec. 11)

Appendix

Leo Parker Discography

Leo Parker (April 18, 1925–February 11, 1962) was the only serious challenger to the claim that Chaloff was the first prominent bop soloist to emerge on baritone sax. Ironically, his career pattern and lifestyle paralleled Chaloff's to a degree: heroin addiction; first recording as a sideman in some of the best big bands of the day without soloing; making many excellent small group records as a sideman and as a leader in the late 1940s and working with one of the most popular bands of that era; ceasing to record for some years in the 1950s; then making a brief comeback before dying in their mid-thirties.

Leo's first recording was on alto sax with Coleman Hawkins in 1944 (no solos). He switched to baritone to work with Billy Eckstine's bop big band from 1944 into 1946. He then worked briefly with Dizzy Gillespie in a combo on 52nd Street and in Dizzy's big band, but there were still no solos on records. He recorded his first solo on Sarah Vaughan's "My Kinda Love" on May 7, 1946 (see discography).

By early 1947 he had joined Illinois Jacquet's jump-styled "Black Velvet" band, with which he worked and recorded intermittently into the 1950s. This edition of Jacquet's band achieved several hit records and considerable renown, even appearing on television on the *Ed Sullivan Show* in 1948; video clips may eventually surface. Leo's recordings as a sideman during 1947 with Jacquet, Gene Ammons, Fats Navarro, J. J. Johnson, Dexter Gordon, and Sir Charles Thompson, and under his own name also beginning in 1947, often exposed his solo work to good effect, attracting attention and respect. "Settin' the Pace" (with Dexter Gordon) was a double-length performance (two sides of a 78) in the style of the "tenor battles" popular in the era, but with Leo of course on baritone. One of his features with Sir Charles Thompson, "Mad Lad" (Leo's nickname), became something of a jazz hit; in fact all titles made under Thompson's name in that period were superb and are among Leo Parker's best recordings. "El Sino" was another hit, recorded under his own name in 1947 for Savoy. Leo was modeling his playing on Charlie Parker, with large doses of Lester Young. He was often fleet and fluent, but tended to be very reliant on bop cliches and rhythm-and-blues, crowd-rousing techniques. His ballad style was notably insipid on several quartet records made for Prestige in 1950.

Leo made a few more records for some relatively obscure labels, and then ceased recording by the end of 1954. He made a comeback with a slightly more developed style on two LP records for Blue Note that were recorded in September and October 1961, still basically in the approach of the late 1940s jump bands such as Jacquet's. He was on an Illinois Jacquet record date at the beginning of February 1962 (no solos), but died suddenly a few days later of a heart attack.

The other most prominent modern baritone figures to emerge from the 1940s were Cecil Payne, who replaced Leo Parker in Gillespie's big band, but did not make any records under his own name until 1949, and thus is slightly later on both counts; and Gerry Mulligan, who became the most widely known of modern baritone saxophonists and one of the most famous jazzmen of the era, but whose first session under his own name was not until 1951. Both men continued working and recording for decades longer than either Chaloff or Parker.

The following Leo Parker discography makes no claim for completeness, but is included for convenience.

COLEMAN HAWKINS AND HIS ORCHESTRA
New York, 16 February 1944

Dizzy Gillespie, Vic Coulson, Ed VanDervere(tp), Leo Parker, Leonard Lowry(as), Coleman Hawkins, Don Byas, Ray Abrams(ts), Budd Johnson(bar), Clyde Hart(p), Oscar Pettiford(b), Max Roach(d)

R1000	Woody'n You	Apollo 751, Grand Award 33-316
R1001	Bu-Dee-Daht	Apollo 752, —
R1002	Yesterdays	— —

Same
New York, 22 February 1944

R1003	Disorder at the Border	Apollo 753, GA 33-316
R1004	Feeling Zero	—
R1005	Rainbow Mist	Apollo 751

NOTE: "Rainbow Mist" = "Body and Soul." All titles also on Apollo LP101, Vogue LP56, and Mode LP9863.

BILLY ECKSTINE AND HIS ORCHESTRA
New York, 5 December 1944

Dizzy Gillespie, Shorty McConnell, Gail Brockman, Boonie Hazel(tp), Howard Scott, Gerald Valentine, Taswell Baird, Chips Outcalt(tb), John Jackson, Bill Frazier(as), Dexter Gordon, Gene Ammons(ts), Leo Parker(bar), John Malachai(p), Connie Wainwright(g), Tommy Potter(b), Art Blakey(d), Billy Eckstine, Sarah Vaughan(v)

118	If That's the Way You Feel (vBE)	DeLuxe 2001

119	I Want To Talk About You (vBE)	DeLuxe 2003
120	Blowing the Blues Away (vBE)	DeLuxe 2001
121	Opus X	DeLuxe 2002
122	I'll Wait and Pray (vSV)	DeLuxe 2003
123	The Real Thing Happened To Me (vBE)	DeLuxe 2002

NOTE: First 4 titles also on King LP265-12.

Fats Navarro(tp) for Gillespie; Budd Johnson, Sonny Stitt(as) for Jackson & Frazier

New York, 2 May 1945

NSC53-1	Lonesome Lover Blues (vBE)	National 9015
NSC54-3	A Cottage for Sale (vBE)	National 9014
NSC55-2	I Love the Rhythm in a Riff (vBE)	—
NSC56	Last Night (vBE)	National 9015

NOTE: All titles on LP on Regent MG6058 and Savoy SJL2214.

BILLY ECKSTINE AND HIS ORCHESTRA
New York, c. February 1946

Fats Navarro, Shorty McConnell, Boonie Hazel, Raymond Orr(tp), Chippy Outcault, Gerald Valentine, Robert Scott(tb), Norris Turney, Bob Williams(as), Gene Ammons, Josh Jackson(ts), Leo Parker(bar), Jimmy Golden(p), Bill McMahon(b), Art Blakey(d), Billy Eckstine(v)

NSC114	Blue (vBE)	National 9018
NSC115	Second Balcony Jump	—
NSC116	Gloomy Sunday (vBE)	National 9037
NSC117	Tell Me Pretty Baby (vBE)	National 9019

NOTE: All titles except NSC116 on LP on Savoy SJL2214.

Same
New York, c. March 1946

NSC122	Love is the Thing (vBE)	National 9125
NSC123	Without a Song (vBE)	National 9061
NSC124	Cool Breeze (vBE)	National 9052
NSC125	Don't Take Your Love From Me (vBE)	National 9023

NOTE: All titles on LP on Savoy SJL2214.

SARAH VAUGHAN
New York, 7 May 1946

Freddie Webster(tp), Leroy Harris(as), Hank Ross(bcl), Leo Parker(bar),

Bud Powell(p), Ted Sturgis(b), Kenny Clarke(d), 9 unk.strings, Sarah
Vaughan(v)

5485	If You Could See Me Now (vSV)	Musicraft 380
5486	I Can Make You Love Me (vSV)	Musicraft 398
5487	You're Not the Kind (vSV)	Musicraft 380
5488	My Kinda Love (vSV)	Musicraft 398

NOTE: All titles on Lion L70052. Despite some earlier discographies
listing Cecil Payne on baritone sax for this session, Leo Parker's first
recorded solo is on mx#5488; two takes reportedly exist.

DIZZY GILLESPIE AND HIS ORCHESTRA
Broadcasts, Spotlite Club, New York, c. May–June 1946

Dizzy Gillespie, Dave Burns, Talib Daawud, Kenny Dorham, John
Lynch, Elmon Wright(tp), Leon Comegeys, Charles Greenlea, Alton
Moore(tb), Howard Johnson, Sonny Stitt(as), Ray Abrams, Warren
Luckey(ts), Leo Parker(bar), Milt Jackson(vbs), Thelonious Monk(p),
Ray Brown(b), Kenny Clarke(d), Band(v)

Our Delight	Hi-Fly H01
Things To Come	—
Groovin' High	—
Ray's Idea	—
The Man I Love	—
Cool Breeze	—
Oop-Bop-Sh'bam (vB)	—
'Round Midnight	—
Second Balcony Jump	—
One Bass Hit	—
(Unknown title)	—
I Waited for You	(unissued)
How High the Moon	—
Algo Bueno	—
Shaw 'Nuff	—
(Unknown titles)	—

NOTE: Leo Parker not featured on issued titles; others not reviewed.

DIZZY GILLESPIE AND HIS ORCHESTRA
New York, 9 July 1946

Dizzy Gillespie, Dave Burns, Talib Daawud, Kenny Dorham, John
Lynch, Elmon Wright(tp), Leon Comegeys, Gordon Thomas, Alton

Moore(tb), Howard Johnson, Sonny Stitt(as), Ray Abrams, Warren Luckey(ts), Leo Parker(bar), Milt Jackson(vbs), John Lewis(p), Ray Brown(b), Kenny Clarke(d), Alice Roberts(v)

5609	One Bass Hit #2	Prestige PR24030
5610	Ray's Idea	—
5611	Things To Come	—
5612	He Beeped When He Should Have Bopped (vAR)	—

NOTE: Originally recorded for Musicraft. Data from Ruppli's *The Prestige Label* and *The Savoy Label* discographies. Leo Parker did not solo on these titles.

LEO PARKER–DIZZY GILLESPIE

unknown location c. 1946

Dizzy Gillespie(tp), Leo Parker(as,bar), others unknown

IM5032	Instrumental	(unknown issues)
IM5033	Cool Me Off	—

NOTE: Data from Ruppli's *The Aladdin/Imperial Labels*; other details unknown.

ILLINOIS JACQUET

New York, 7 January 1947

Joe Newman, Fats Navarro, Marion Hazel, Miles Davis(tp), Gus Chapel, Fred Robinson, Ted Kelly, Dickie Wells(tb), Ray Perry, Jimmy Powell(as), Illinois Jacquet, Big Nick Nicholas(ts), Leo Parker(bar), Bill Doggett(p), Al Lucas(b), Shadow Wilson(d)

NR94-4	For Europeans Only	Aladdin 180
NR95-3	Big Dog	—
NR96-4	You Left Me All Alone	Aladdin 179
NR97-2	Jivin' With Jack the Bellboy	—

NOTE: Leonard Feather(p) for Doggett on mx#NR95. All titles on LP on Aladdin LP708, LP803, Imperial LP9184, and on LP/CD on *The Complete Illinois Jacquet Sessions 1945–1950* (Mosaic MQ6-165/MD4-165). Leo Parker solos only on mx#NR97.

FATS NAVARRO–LEO PARKER

New York, 29 January 1947

Fats Navarro(tp), Leo Parker(as,bar), Tadd Dameron(p), Gene Ramey(b), Denzil Best(d)

3383-2	Fat Girl	Savoy 906
3384-2	Ice Freezes Red	Savoy 976
3385	Eb Pob	Savoy 906
3386	Goin' To Minton's	Savoy 976

NOTE: All titles on LP on Savoy XP8025, MG9005, MG12114, and SJL2216. Savoy MG12114 (an anthology titled *Opus de Bop*) reissued on CD as SV-0118. Leo Parker featured on all titles.

ILLINOIS JACQUET
New York, 1 April 1947

Russell Jacquet, Joe Newman(tp), J. J. Johnson(tb), Ray Perry(as), Illinois Jacquet(ts), Leo Parker(bar), Sir Charles Thompson(p), Freddie Green(g), Al Lucas(b), Shadow Wilson(d)

| 137A | Blow Illinois Blow | Aladdin 3001 |

NOTE: Also on Aladdin LP701, 803, Imperial LP9184, and Mosaic MQ6-165/MD4-165. Leo Parker not featured, and not on mx#138 from this session. Personnel from Mosaic booklet.

ILLINOIS JACQUET
New York, 21 May 1947

Joe Newman(tp), Illinois Jacquet(ts), Leo Parker(bar), Sir Charles Thompson(p), Al Lucas(b), Shadow Wilson(d)

R1214	South Street Special	Apollo 785
R1214	South Street Special	Apollo LP477
R1215	Diggin' the Count	Apollo 785, LP477
R1216	Robbins Nest	Apollo 769, LP104
R1217	Music Hall Beat	Apollo 777
R1218	Jumpin' at the Woodside	—
R1218	Jumpin' at the Woodside	Grand Award LP33-315

NOTE: Mx#s 1215, 1216, and 1218 on Jazztone LP J1250, Grand Award LP33-315. All titles on Mosaic MQ6-165/MD4-165. Leo Parker featured on mx#s 1214, 1215, and 1218.

ILLINOIS JACQUET
New York, 10 September 1947

Russell Jacquet, Joe Newman(tp), J. J. Johnson(tb), Illinois Jacquet(ts), Leo Parker(bar), Sir Charles Thompson(p), John Collins(g), Al Lucas(b), Shadow Wilson(d)

| 260-1 | Goofin' Off | Aladdin 3011, LP701, LP803, LP(F)803 |

261-2	Riffin' With Jacquet		—
262-1	Don't Push Daddy	Aladdin 3260,	—
263-2	Sahara Heat		
263-3	Sahara Heat	—	—

NOTE: All takes except mx#262 on Mosaic MQ6-165/MD4-165. Leo Parker not featured, and not present on mx#264 from this session.

GENE AMMONS QUINTET

Chicago, 23 September 1947

Gene Ammons(ts), Leo Parker(as,bar), Junior Mance(p), Gene Wright(b), Ellis Bartee(d)

301-5	Concentration	Aladdin 3012
302-7	Jack's Town	(unissued)
303-8	Blowin' Red's Top	Aladdin 3012
304-9	Bartee Meets Gene	(unissued)

LEO PARKER'S ALL-STARS

Detroit, 4 October 1947

Howard McGhee(tp), Gene Ammons(ts), Leo Parker(bar), Junior Mance(p), Gene Wright(b), Charles Williams(d)

DET800	El Sino	Savoy 912, XP8081, MG9018
DET801	Ineta	Savoy 954, MG1009
DET802	Wild Leo	Savoy 912, XP8081, —
DET803	Leapin' Leo	Savoy 950, — —

NOTE: All titles on the Gene Ammons LP *Red Top* (Savoy SJL1103).

ILLINOIS JACQUET

Chicago, 28 November 1947

Russell Jacquet(tp,v), Joe Newman(tp), Illinois Jacquet(ts), Leo Parker (bar), Sir Charles Thompson(p), John Collins(g), Al Lucas(b), Shadow Wilson(d).

480-4	Destination Moon	Aladdin 3180, LP(F)803
481-4	For Truly	— —
482-1	I Surrender Dear	
482-3	I Surrender Dear	—

NOTE: First 2 titles also on Aladdin LP703, LP803, and Imperial LP9184. All takes on Mosaic MQ6-165/MD4-165. Leo Parker solos only on mx#481.

DEXTER GORDON QUINTET
New York, 11 December 1947

Dexter Gordon(ts), Leo Parker(bar), Tadd Dameron(p), Curley Russell(b), Art Blakey(d)

3491-3	Settin' the Pace Pt. 1	Savoy 913
3492-3	Settin' the Pace Pt. 2	—
3493	So Easy	
3493	So Easy	Savoy 960
3494	Dexter's Riff	
3494	Dexter's Riff	—

NOTE: All takes on Savoy SJL2211, a two-LP Dexter Gordon set titled *Long Tall Dexter* (see also 19 December 1947). Leo Parker solos on all titles.

ILLINOIS JACQUET
New York, 18 December 1947

Joe Newman(tp), Russell Jacquet(tp,v), J. J. Johnson(tb), Illinois Jacquet(ts), Leo Parker(bar), Sir Charles Thompson(p), Al Lucas(b), Shadow Wilson(d)

2854	Jet Propulsion	Victor 20-2892
2855	King Jacquet	Victor 20-2702
2856	Try Me One More Time (vRJ)	Victor 20-2892
2857	Embryo	Victor 20-3278

NOTE: All titles on Bluebird CD6571-2, Mosaic MQ6-165/MD4-165. Leo Parker solos only on mx#2857.

Add John Collins(g)
New York, 19 December 1947

2889	Riffin' at 24th Street	Victor 20-2702
2890	Mutton Leg	Victor 20-3060
2891	Symphony in Sid	—

NOTE: All titles on Bluebird CD6571-2, Mosaic MQ6-165/MD4-165. Leo Parker solos only on mx#'s 2890 & 2891 and was not present for mx#2892 from this session.

LEO PARKER'S ALL-STARS
New York, 19 December 1947

Joe Newman(tp), J. J. Johnson(tb), Dexter Gordon(as,ts), Leo Parker (bar), Hank Jones(p), Curley Russell(b), Shadow Wilson(d)

3495-1	Wee Dot	Savoy SJL2211
3495-2	Wee Dot	Savoy SJL2225
3495-3	Wee Dot	Savoy 950, SJL2211
3495-4	Wee Dot	Savoy SJL2225
3496	Solitude	Savoy 929, SJL2225
3497-1	The Lion Roars	Savoy SJL2211
3497-2	The Lion Roars	Savoy SJL2225
3497-3	The Lion Roars	Savoy SJL2211
3497-4	The Lion Roars	Savoy SJL2225
3498	Mad Lad Boogie	Savoy 929

NOTE: Savoy SJL2225 is a two-LP anthology titled *The Bebop Boys*.

JAY JAY JOHNSON
New York, 24 December 1947

J. J. Johnson(tb), Leo Parker(bar), Hank Jones(p), Al Lucas(b), Shadow Wilson(d)

3519	Boneology	Savoy 942, MG12106, SJL2232
3520	Down Vernon's Alley	— — —
3521	Yesterdays	— —
3522	Riffette	— —

NOTE: Leo Parker solos on all but mx#S3521. SJL2232 is a two-LP J. J. Johnson set titled *Mad Be Bop*.

SIR CHARLES THOMPSON
New York, c. 1947

Joe Newman, Taft Jordan(tp), R. B. Mitchell(tb), Bob Dorsey(ts), Leo Parker(bar), Sir Charles Thompson(p), Hank Morton(g), John Simmons(b), Shadow Wilson(d)

1305	Benson's Alley	Apollo 796, Vogue LDAP769
1308	Mr. Big Horn	— —

SIR CHARLES THOMPSON
New York, c. 1947

Joe Newman(tp), Bob Dorsey(ts), Leo Parker(bar), Sir Charles Thompson(p), Freddie Green(g), John Simmons(b), Shadow Wilson(d)

1427	Tunis In	Apollo 773, LP103, Vogue LADP769
1428	Strange Hours	Apollo 782, — —
1429	Rhythm	— — —
1430	Mad Lad	Apollo 773, — —

NOTE: Leo Parker was well featured on all titles from the above two Sir Charles Thompson sessions.

LEO PARKER'S ALL-STARS

Detroit, 23 March 1948

Joe Newman(tp), Leo Parker(bar), Sir Charles Thompson(p), Al Lucas(b), Jack "The Bear" Parker(d)

D842	On the House	Savoy 957, SJL2225	
D843	Dinky	—	—
D844	Senor Leo	Savoy 935,	—
D845	Chase 'n Lion	—	—

Add Charlie Rouse(ts)

D846	Leo's Bells	Savoy MG9009,	—
D847	Sweet Talkin' Leo	—	—
D848	Swinging for Love	—	—
D849	The New Look	—	—

NOTE: Savoy SJL2225 is a two-LP anthology titled *The Bebop Boys.*

RUSSELL JACQUET AND HIS ALL-STARS

Detroit, c. May 1948

Russell Jacquet(tp,v), J. J. Johnson(tb), Sonny Stitt(as), Maurice Simon(ts), Leo Parker(bar), Sir Charles Thompson(p), Al Lucas(b), Shadow Wilson(d)

4009	Relaxin' With Randle	Sensation 12, King 4259
4010	Lion's Roar	Sensation 8, King 4242
4011	Suede Jacquet	— —
4011	Suede Jacquet	
4012	Scamparoo	Sensation 12, King 4249

NOTE: All takes on King LP295-30, OJC CD1771-2.

LEO PARKER AND HIS MAD LADS

New York, c. 1949

Roy Eldridge(tp), Ben Webster(ts), Leo Parker(bar), Wild Bill Davis (p,org), Ira Pettiford(b), Jack Parker(d)

| LP1 | Woody | Gotham G262 |
| LP2 | Rollin With Parker | — |

NOTE: Personnel from Jepsen's *Jazz Records.*

LEO PARKER QUARTET

New York, 20 July 1950

Leo Parker(bar), Al Haig(p), Oscar Pettiford(b), Max Roach(d)

JRC95	Mona Lisa (inc)	Misterioso LP1984
JRC95	Mona Lisa	Prestige P-24081
JRC96	Who's Mad	—
JRC97	Darn That Dream (inc)	Misterioso LP1984
JRC97	Darn That Dream	Prestige P-24081
JRC98	I'll Cross My Fingers	Pr.720, —
JRC99	Mad Lad Returns	— , P-24046
JRC99	Mad Lad Returns	Misterioso LP1984
JRC99	Mad Lad Returns	—
JRC99	Mad Lad Returns (inc)	—

NOTE: Jack "The Bear" Parker replaces Roach on drums on JRC96 & JRC99. Data from Ruppli's *The Prestige Label*. Prestige P-24081 is a two-LP anthology titled *First Sessions 1949–1950*.

LEO PARKER QUINTET

Chicago, 7 July 1951

Eddie Johnson(ts), Leo Parker(bar), Claude Jones(p), Johnny Pate(b), Al Williams(d), Leonard Chess(v)(?)

U7353	Candlelight Serenade	Chess 1477, CHV413
U7354	Hornet	—
U7355	Reed Rock	—
U7356	Leo's Blues	—

NOTE: Presence of vocalist uncertain; data from Ruppli's *The Chess Labels*.

LEO PARKER QUINTET

Chicago, c. 1953

Ira Pettiford(tp,b), Leo Parker(bar), unk.(p), unk.(g), Jack Parker(d)

U1159	Leo's Boogie	United 141, Vogue(F)V3279
U1160	Cool Leo	— —

NOTE: Data from Jepsen's *Jazz Records* discography.

LEO PARKER QUARTET

Chicago, 10 August 1953

Leo Parker(bar), unk.(p,b,d)

	Anything Can Happen	Chess CHV413

Blue Sails   —
Smoke Gets In Your Eyes   —
Tippin' Lightly   —

NOTE: Masters from the Parrot label; data from Ruppli's *The Chess Labels*.

BILL JENNINGS–LEO PARKER QUINTET
Cincinnati, 6–8 July 1954

Leo Parker(bar), Andy Johnson(org,p), Bill Jennings(g), Joe Williams(b), George DeHart(d)

K9452	Picadilly Circus	King LP527
K9453	There Will Never Be Another You	—
K9454	What'll I Do	—
K9455	Billy in the Lion's Den	—
K9456	Fine and Dandy	—
K9457	Just You Just Me	—
K9458	Down to Earth	—
K9459	May I?	—
K9460	Get Hot	—
K9461	Stuffy	—
K9462	Solitude	—

ILLINOIS JACQUET
New York, 13 December 1954

Russell Jacquet(tp), Matthew Gee(tb), Illinois Jacquet(ts), Leo Parker (bar), Johnny Acea(p), Al Lucas(b), Osie Johnson(d)

2117-5	Jacquet Dilemma	Clef 89133, MGC680, Verve MGV8065
2118-2	Mambocito Mio	— — —
2119-3	September Song	— — —
2120-1	Saph	— — —

NOTE: Add Chino Pozo on mx#2118. Leo Parker solos only on mx#2120 and reportedly did not play on mx#s2121 & 2122 from this session.

LEO PARKER SEXTET
Englewood Cliffs, New Jersey, 9 September 1961

John Burks(tp), Bill Swindell(ts), Leo Parker(bar), Yusef Salim(p), Stan Conover(b), Purnell Rice(d)

tk.4	Glad Lad	Blue Note BLP(BST8)4087
tk.5	Low Brown (long)	

tk.6	Low Brown (short)	—
tk.9	Parker's Pals	—
tk.1	TCTB	—
tk.1	Jump Blues	—
tk.25	Vi	—
tk.28	Let Me Tell You 'Bout It	—
tk.31	Blue Leo	—

LEO PARKER SEXTET

Englewood Cliffs, New Jersey, 12 October 1961

Dave Burns(tp), Johnny Acea(p) for Burks & Salim

tk.1	Rollin' With Leo	Blue Note BST84095
tk.8	Music Hall Beat	—
	Bad Girl	(rejected)
	Jumpin' Leo	—
	Stuffy	—
	Mad Lad Returns	—

LEO PARKER SEXTET

Englewood Cliffs, New Jersey, 20 October 1961

Al Lucas(b), Wilburt Hogan(d) for Conover & Rice

	Rollin' With Leo	(rejected)
	Music Hall Beat	—
tk.22	Bad Girl	Blue Note BST84095
tk.27	Mad Lad Returns	—
tk.30	Stuffy	—
tk.32	Jumpin' Leo	—
tk.37	Talkin' the Blues	—
tk.38	The Lion's Roar	—

ILLINOIS JACQUET

New York, 5 February 1962

Ernie Royal, Roy Eldridge(tp), Matthew Gee(tb), Illinois Jacquet(ts), Leo Parker(bar), Sir Charles Thompson(p), Kenny Burrell(g), Jimmy Rowser(b), Jimmy Crawford(d)

Co69366	Satin Doll	Epic LA16033, BA17033
Co69367	Pucker Up	— —

NOTE: Both titles on Portrait RK44391(CD). Leo Parker was not featured at this session.

Name Index

Italic page numbers refer to entries in the Discography.

Adams, Pepper, 86
Adamson, Steve, 17–18, 76–79, 80
Akiyoshi, Toshiko, 5
Allen, Steve, 90
Allison, Steve, 56
Ammons, Gene, 165, *171*
Anderson, Stu, 71, 72
Andrews Sisters, 16, 18
Auld, Georgie, 2, 22–23, 25, 26, 29, 30, 31, 32–34, 63, 69, *117–19, 121*

Babasin, Harry, 38, 39
Badgley, Ed, 47
Baker, Chet, 75, 87, 89
Barnet, Charlie, 46, 58
Barringer, George, 80–81
Basie, Count, 4, 9, 57–58, 59, 60, 88, *147*
Bauer, Billy, 56, 65
Beaupre, Billy, 12
Beiderbecke, Bix, 1, 12
Berigan, Bunny, 23
Berman, Sonny, 25, 28, 29–30, 86, *119, 123–24*
Bernstein, Artie, 28
Bernstein, Leonard, 5
Bert, Eddie, 94
Best, Denzil, 42, 43
Bittick, Jerry, 13
Blakey, Art, 33, 94
Blakkestad, Bill, 71, 72
Blovello, Joe, 89
Bordeleau, Paul, 81
Boswell Sisters, 18
Bothwell, Johnny, *117*
Braff, Ruby, 75, 87

Brooks, John Benson, 18
Brooks, Randy, 17
Brown, Clifford, 80
Brown, Les, 37
Bryant, Marie, 31
Burns, Ralph, 7, 25, 28, 37, 39, 40, 43, 44, 65, *141*
Butts, Jimmy, 33
Byard, Jaki, 59, 85
Byas, Don, 22

Caceres, Ernie, 51
Capazutto, Nick, 60, 81
Carney, Harry, 9, 51, 67, 77
Carreno, Larry, 68
Carroll, Barbara, 42, 43
Carruthers, Earl, 77
Carter, Jack, 75
Catton, Roy, 60
Chaloff, Julius L., 5–6, 9–10. *See also* Chaloff, Julius, in Subject Index
Chaloff, Margaret Stedman, as musician, 5–6, 10, 15, 29, 76, 79. *See also* Chaloff, Margaret Stedman, in Subject Index
Chaloff, Serge, *109, 112, 124, 125–26, 140, 141, 145, 146–51. See also* Chaloff, Serge, in Subject Index
Chapman, Dave, 60
Charles, Teddy, 94
Childers, Buddy, 47
Christian, Charlie, 25
Clark, Sonny, 91, 92
Clarke, Kenny, 25, 40
Clayton, Buck, 78
Cohen, Jerry, 88

Cohn, Al, 22, 25, 30, 36, 37, 40, 43, 94
Cole, Cozy, 31
Cole, Nat "King," 33, 46, 47
Coltrane, John, 92
Condoli, Conte, 72
Cooper, Pat, 16–17, 18
Cooper, Sid, 16
Corea, Chick, 5
Cornwall, Dick, 88
Crea, Bob, 71
Cronin, Eli Whitney, 58

Dameron, Tadd, 33, 40, 41, 68
Davis, Bob, 71
Davis, Miles, 33, 40, 55, 57, 65, 92
Dawson, Alan, 59, 67–68
DeFranco, Buddy, 42, 43, 56, 58, *141*
di Carlo, Joe, 81
Di Stachio, Gene, 81
Dickenson, Vic, 22, 75
Dixon, Gus, 63
Dolphy, Eric, 62
Donaldson, Lou, 91
Dorsey, Jimmy, 1, 2, 4, 7, 22, 23, 26–27, 29, 46, *119–23, 124*
Dorsey, Tommy, 1, 15, 16, 17, 27, 46, 58
Drootin, Buzzy, 75, 76
Drummond, Paul, 90

Eager, Allan, 30, 40, 53, *145*
Eardley, John, 72
Eberly, Bob, 27
Eckstine, Billy, 165,*166–67*
Eldridge, Roy, 58
Ellick, Roger, 16, 18
Ellington, Duke, 51, 58
Ellis, Don, 71
Evans, Everett, 84, 87,90

Farlow, Tal, 94
Feather, Leonard, as musician, 43, 55.

See also Feather, Leonard, in Subject Index
Fields, Herbie, 29, *124–25*
Fields, Shep, 2, 13–14, 104, *112–13*
Finkel, Ed, 21
Fishelson, Stan, 17, 21, 35, 40, 47
Foster, Stuart, 15, 16, 17, 18
Fournier, Vernel, 91
Freedman, Bob, 90
Freeman, Russ, 75, 76

Garland, Red, 86
Garner, Erroll, 56
Getz, Stan, 35, 37, 40, 55, 56, 65, 77, 79
Gibbs, Terry, 39, 40, 42, 53, 65
Gillespie, Dizzy, 21, 22, 25, 40, 41, 56, 95, 165, 166,*168–69*
Giuffre, Jimmy, 37, 47
Glow, Bernie, 35, 40
Gold, Milt, 62
Goodman, Benny, 23
Goodspeed, Mert, 23, 44, 60–61, 68
Gordon, Dexter, 165, *172*
Gordon, Joe, 59
Gray, Wardell, 58
Green, Benny, 55
Green, George, 60
Griffith, Rollins, 4, 29, *124*
Gryce, Gigi, 59

Haig, Al, 30
Hampton, Lionel, 58
Hancock, Herbie, 5
Handy, George, 21, 33
Haritounian, Varty, 81
Harris, Benny, 21
Harris, Bill, 28, 30–31, 39, 40, 47, *123–24*
Harris, Lew, 14
Harvell, Robert, 33
Hawkins, Coleman, 11, 15, 25, 165, *166*
Herman, Woody, 1, 2, 3, 17, 25, 27–

28, 34, 35, 36, 37, 38, 39, 45, 47,
49–50,
56, 63, 69, 72, 80, 85, 89, 97, *126–45*
Holiday, Billie, 1
Hooks, Charlie, 60
Hovhaness, Alan, 5
Hutton, Ina Ray, 2, 14, 15–19, 21, 76,
113–14
Hutton, June, 15
Hyman, Dick, 68

Jackson, Chubby, 25, 30, 39, 40, 41
Jacquet, Illinois, 32–33, 165–66, *169,
170–71, 172, 176, 177*
Jacquet, Russell, *174*
James, Harry, 27
Jarrett, Keith, 5
Jennings, Bill, *176*
Johnson, Gus, 58, 88
Johnson, J. J., 165, *173*
Johnston, Jimmy, 33
Jones, Buddy, 94
Jones, George, 62–63
Jones, Jo, 58
Jones, Philly Joe, 91–92
Jones, Thad, 94

Kahn, Tiny, 30, 31, 32, 33, 53, 82
Karr, Dave, 72
Kelly, Paula, 38
Kenton, Stan, 62, 75
Kenyon, Dan, 17
Kersey, Ken, 25
Khachaturian, Aram, 36
Killian, Al, 82
Kim Loo Sisters, 15, 16–17, 18
King Sisters, 18
Konitz, Lee, 55, 56, 65, 94
Kuhn, Steve, 5, 79–80

Lambert, Dave, 31
Lamond, Don, 25, 28, 35, 36, 40, 53,
56, 94
Land, Harold, 80

Lanphere, Dan, 47
LaPorta, John, 65
Lawlor, Jack, 61, 62, 68, 70
Lawrence, Elliot, 69, 94
Leighton, Bernie, 31
Leonard, Harvey, 33
Levy, Lou, 40, 47, 71, 72
Lewis, Sabby, 62–63
Lifeman, Mel, 72
Lippe, Bob, 88
Littman, Peter, 78

MacDonald, Joe, 57, 58, 61, 62, 68
Maisell, Ralph, 69
Manne, Shelly, 47
Marable, Lawrence, 91
Mariano, Charlie, 59, 62, 75, 80, 81,
82
Markowitz, Irv "Marky," 25, 35, 40
Marowitz, Sam, 35, 40, 47
McCaffery, Bob, 70–73, 75, 76
McCall, Mary Ann, 37, 38, 40, 45–46,
47
McElroy, "Chief," 72, 73
McGhee, Howard, 58
Megro, Joe, 16, 18, 21
Mellow-Larks, 46
Migliori, Jay, 91
Miller, Glenn, 12, 57
Miller, Mulgrew, 5
Mills, Dick "Buzzy," 72
Mingus, Charles, 82, 94
Modernaires, 37
Monk, Thelonius, 25, 58
Mulligan, Gerry, 30, 33, 62, 77, 86,
166
Murphy, Lyle, 16
Mussulli, Boots, 75–76, 78, 81, 84,
86, 87, 88, 90, 91, *148–49*

Navarro, Fats, 40, 58, 165, *169–70*
Newman, Jerry, 3, 25
Ney, Jerri, 35
Noble, Freddy, 14

Norman, Fred, 18

O'Connell, Helen, 27
O'Kane, Charlie, 94
Oliver, Mert, 47
Olivieri, Ray, 81
Osborne, Will, 13
Osser, Glenn, 14
Otis, Fred, 35, 37, 39

Parker, Charlie "Bird," 1, 21, 22, 29,
    40, 44, 55, 77, 165
Parker, Dee, 26
Parker, Leo, 32–33, 165–66, *169–70,*
    171, 172–73, 174, 175–77
Pastor, Tony, 71, 72
Paxton, George, 18
Payne, Cecil, 166
Pettiford, Oscar, 21, 22, 41, 43, *116*
Phillips, Flip, 28
Pied Pipers, 15
Pierce, Nat, 57, 58, 59, 60, 61, 62, 68
Pine, Charlie, 88
Pomeroy, Herb, 67, 78, 80, 81, 82, 84,
    85–86, 87, 88, 89–90, 94
Powell, Bud, 41, 55, 56
Powell, Ritchie, 80
Preddy, Gait, 44
Pullman, Steve, 33
Purcell, Jack, 16, 17, 18

Rachmaninoff, Sergei, 6, 49
Raeburn, Boyd, 2, 17, 21–22, 58, 104,
    114–17
Raney, Jimmy, 37
Reese, Hampton, 59
Reynolds, Tommy, 2, 11, 12–13, 63,
    109–12
Rich, Buddy, 39, 58
Richards, Johnny, 33
Rivers, Sam, 58, 59–60
Roach, Max, 55, 56, 65, 80
Rodney, Red, 3, 30–31, 32, 33, 36, 40,
    42–43, 55, *125*

Rogers, Dick "Stinky," 13
Rogers, Shorty, 35, 40, 42, 47, 69
Roland, Gene, 33
Rouse, Charlie, 58
Royal, Ernie, 35, 36, 40
Rugolo, Pete, 62, 65
Russell, Curley, 30, 55
Russell, Pee Wee, 78
Russell, Ross, 27
Rutherford, Rudy, 58

Safranski, Eddie, 25, 56, 65
Santisi, Ray, 75, 80, 84, 86, 87, 88
Sargent, Gene, 35, 37
Savitt, Buddy, 47
Schaefer, Hal, 16, 18
Scott, Dell, 72–73
Scott, Tony, 94
Severinsen, Doc, 90
Shaw, Artie, 3, 12, 13, 23, 58
Shearing, George, 5, 65
Sheldon, Don, 71, 72
Shulman, Joe, 56, 57
Silva, Mario, 16
Simmons, Norman, 91
Sims, Zoot, 35, 37, 40, 94
Singer, Hal, 33
Spivak, Charlie, 70–71
Sproles, Victor, 91
Stafford, Jo, 15
Stratton, Don, 60, 68
Steward, Herb, 35, 37, 94
Stewart, Buddy, 31
Stitt, Sonny, 55, 90, 91
Stutz, Jimmy, 41
Swift, Bob, 35, 40
Swope, Earl, 21, 25, 31, 32, 35, 40,
    42, 47, 56
Swope, Terry, 37

Tacloff, Sonny, 62
Tatum, Art, 15
Taylor, Billy, 94
Taylor, Cecil, 81

Terry, Clark, 58
Thomas, Joe, 31
Thompson, Dick, 71
Thompson, Sir Charles, 165, *173–74*
Thornhill, Claude, 57, 62
Tristano, Lennie, 31, 55, 56, 57
Truitt, Sonny, 59, 60, 61, 62
Twardzik, Dick, 5, 63, 68, 69, 70, 78, 80, 81, 85, 87–88, 89
Tyler, Jimmy, 56

Vaughan, Sarah, 26, 55, *167–68*
Vasta, Sal, 68
Vega, Al, 62
Ventura, Charlie, 31
Vinnegar, Leroy, 91, 92

Wallington, George, 30, 31, 32, 41
Walp, Charlie, 47

Washington, Ernie, 33
Washington, Jack, 9, 77
Wayne, Chuck, 28
Wein, George, 8, 75, 78, 80, 87
Weiner, Jimmy, 69, 70
Wetmore, Dick, 58, 81
Whiting, Gene, 88
Williams, "Rubberlegs," 22
Wilson, Ollie, 17, 21, 35, 40, 47
Winding, Kai, 55, 56, 65
Woode, Jimmy, 76, 78

Yoder, Walt, 35, 38
Young, Al, 33
Young, Lester, 30, 43, 56, 58, 165

Zanoni, Gene, 33
Zitano, Jimmy, 62, 81, 84, 88

Subject Index

Armed Forces Radio Service, 15–16, 18, 21, 38, 39, 41, 46, 58

The Big Bands, 13, 14
Billboard, 35, 39
Black Beauty, White Heat, 33, 69
Black, Joanne Mary "Linda," 61, 62, 63–65, 72, 73–74, 85
Black, Susan, 89, 92–93, 94
Boston Daily Record, 56, 63
Boston Herald, 87
Boston Sunday Herald, 82–84
The Bride Goes Wild, 39
Buckhalter, "Buck," 89
Burke, Larry, 89

Carroll, Jean, 39
Chaloff, Julius L., 7–12, 81. *See also* Chaloff, Julius L., in Name Index
Chaloff, Linda Jeanne, 65, 69, 73–74, 76, 85
Chaloff, Margaret Stedman, 7–12, 15, 25, 29, 58, 64, 69, 70, 73, 76, 78, 79, 80, 81, 83, 88, 93, 94, 95. *See also* Chaloff, Margaret Stedman, in Name Index
Chaloff, Nancy, 64, 81, 93
Chaloff, Richard Stedman, 5–12, 15, 19, 22, 27, 29–30, 49, 57, 59, 63–65, 70, 73, 79–80, 81, 88, 89, 93, 94–95
Chaloff, Serge: appearance of, 6, 12, 27, 77–78; childhood of, 5–8; daughter of. *See* Chaloff, Linda Jeanne; drug problems of, 1, 2, 3, 29–30, 49–50, 61, 70, 71, 73, 77, 78–79, 82–84, 86; final illness of, 93–98; as teacher, 76–79, 80;

wives of. *See* Black, Joanne Mary "Linda"; Black, Susan. *See also* Chaloff, Serge, in Name Index
Condon, Eddie, 51
Copen, Irving S., 83
Coss, Bill, 86, 94
Coss, Paul D., 84, 89
Cowan, Will, 37

DA 693, 84, 97
Davis, Duke, 12
Devine, George, 36
Don & Beverly, 37–38
Down Beat, 23, 31, 33, 35, 36, 39, 41, 44, 49, 56, 68, 76, 83, 91
Downes, Olin, 7
Dreifuss, Arthur, 16

Edwards, Ernie, 46
Encyclopedia of Jazz, 3, 11, 16, 28, 82
Ever Since Venus, 16, 17, 18

The Fabulous Dorseys, 1, 7, 27
Feather, Leonard, 3, 9, 11, 13, 17, 18, 21, 28–29, 34, 42, 55, 76. *See also* Feather, Leonard, in Name Index
Friedman, Ignace, 6

Gardner, Mark, 32
Gleason, Ralph, 35
Green, Milton, 53

Hallock, Ted, 36
Hentoff, Nat, 59, 60, 67, 68–69
Herman's Herd, 45–46

Jackson, Johnny, 32
Jazz Workshop, 75, 80, 90
Jazzorama, 89, 90

185

Johnson, Charlie "The Whale," 95

Kay, Monte, 55
Kramer, Marvin Howard, 74

Lee, Jung Jen, 17
Leroy, Hal, 39
Linn, Harry, 31
Lowney, Fred, 39

Marlowe, Bill, 89
Martin, Bob "The Robin," 80, 83, 84, 86, 88, 90–91, 93
Metronome, 14, 18, 22–23, 26, 56, 63, 68, 83, 84, 86, 87–88, 89
Miner, John W., 69
Miss Bobby Socks, 17
Morgan, Alun, 86
Morros, Borros, 6, 27

Nelson, Sally, 73
New York Times, 43
New Yorker, 43

O'Connor, Norman, 80
One Touch of Venus, 16
Ort, Izzy, 11–12, 60
Osborne, Will, 13

Pauloski, Rick, 26, 43, 59–60
Porter, Lewis, 5

Powers, Robert, 74
Powers, William E., 74
Powers, William E., Jr., 74

Raben, Erik, 26
Rae, Dorothy, 39
Rose, Boris, 32
Russell, Ross, 27

Saks, Norman, 5
Schaap, Phil, 91
Schuller, Gunther, 14
Shribman, Si, 12–13
Simon, George T., 13, 14, 18
Starr, Kay, 64
Steve Allen Show, 90
Sunnenblick, Bob, 88
The Swing Era, 14

Taylor, Freddie, 61–62
Torin, "Symphony Sid," 55
Treichel, James A., 35–36, 37, 38, 39, 40, 41, 43, 45, 47, 51

Ulanov, Barry, 13, 56

Woody Herman and His Orchestra, 37–38

Yates, Charlie, 17

About the Author

Vladimir Simosko was born in Pittsburgh, Pennsylvania, in 1943. He is the music librarian at the University of Manitoba and former curator of the Institute of Jazz Studies at Rutgers University, has taught jazz history courses since 1968, and is also a musician. He has published more than 130 articles and reviews in magazines including *Coda* and *The Journal of Jazz Studies* since 1973. His first book, *Eric Dolphy: A Musical Biography and Discography* (Smithsonian Institution Press, 1974), has been published in several languages and editions. He is also the author of *Artie Shaw: A Musical Biography and Discography*, in the Studies in Jazz Series published by Scarecrow Press.